Literary Criticism
- 16 -

1. Gaetano Cipolla, *Labyrinth*
2. Jane V. Bertolino, *The Many Faces of Pamela*
3. Zina Gimpelevich, *Boris Pasternak: What M is out there?*
4. Natalia Pervukhina, *Anton Chekhov: the Sense and the Nonsense*
5. Francesco Guardiani, ed., *The Sense of Marino*
6. Alice Rathé, *Fragments de théorie dramatique dans sept pièces de Pierre Corneille*
7. Cristina E. Trevisan, *Violenza e immaginazione nella prosa di Luigi Malerba*
8. Northrop Frye (Branko Gorjup, ed.), *Mythologizing Canada: Essays on the Canadian Literary Imagination*
9. Antonio Scuderi, *Dario Fo and Popular Performance*
10. Rosanna Marsico, *Il romanesco del Belli "extravagante" ed il continuum linguistico della Roma primo-ottocentesca*
11. Sergio Villani, Paul Perron et Pascal Michelucci, codir., *Lectures de Guillevic. Approches critiques*
12. Sergio Villani e Paul Perron, codir., *Lectures de Pierre Torreilles. Approches critiques*
13. Marie-Laure Girou Swiderski, dir., *Terrrae incognitae de l'écriture féminine*
14. Karin Schwerdtner, *La femme errante*
15. Sergio Villani, dir., *Paul Claudel 2005: perspectives critiques*
16. Veronika Ambros, Roland Le Huenen, Adil D'Souza and Andrés Pérez-Simón, eds. *Structuralism(s) Today. Paris, Prague, Tartu*

Structuralism(s) Today
Paris, Prague, Tartu

Veronika Amdros, Roland Le Huenen,
Adil D'Sousa and Andrés Pérez-Simón

Editors

New York   Ottawa   Toronto

© 2009 LEGAS No part of this book may be reproduced in any form, by print, photoprint, microfilm, microfiche, or any other means, without written permission from the publisher.

Library and Archives Canada Cataloguing in Publication

Structuralism(s) today : Paris, Prague, Tartu / Veronika Ambros ... [et al.] editors.

Includes bibliographical references.
ISBN 978-1-897493-06-9

1. Structuralism (Literary analysis). I. Ambros, Veronika, 1947-

PN98.S7S76 2009   801'.959   C2008-908152-8

http://www.legaspublishing.com

LEGAS
P. O. Box 040328   3 Wood Aster Bay   2908 Dufferin Street
Brooklyn, New York Ottawa, Ontario   Toronto, Ontario
USA 11204   K2R 1B3   M6B 3S8

Printed and bound in Canada
by Imprimerie Gauvin

Contents

Laudatio Lubomír Doložel
ROLAND LE HUENEN   7

Foreword
ADIL D'SOUSA   17

General Aesthetics

Futures of the past: Steps and Mis(sed)steps in Structuralism(s), Semiotics, and Aesthetics from a Metacritical Perspective
EMIL VOLEK   21

Avatars of a Research Tradition: From Slavic Structuralism to Anglo-American Poetics and Aesthetics
URI MARGOLIN   39

The Semantic Gesture: An Invitation to a Journey from the Poetics to the Aesthetics of a Literary Work
TOMÁŠ KUBÍČEK   49

Felix Vodička's Legacy for Literary History
TETIANA SOVIAK   61

Subjectivity and Language Revisited: Benveniste, Agamben, and Recent Theories of Testimony
BARBARA HAVERCROFT   69

The Theory of Opposition Revisited
MARCEL DANESI   89

Applied Aesthetics

Narratology, Eventfulness and Context
WOLF SCHMID   101

Reading Functionally Polyvalent Events
EMMA KAFALENOS   111

*Plot Structures and Semantic Resonances in Ancient Greek
'Almost Incest' Narratives*
NANCY FELSON   121

*Narratology: Between Dream and Scientific Intention.
Or Why the Marquise no Longer Goes Out at Five*
WLADIMIR KRYSINSKI   137

Performance: Film & Theatre

*How Kitano's Fireworks are Made: A Structuralist Approach to Space
and Time in Takeshi Kitano's* Fireworks (1997)
ADAM GRUNZKE   145

Between Theatre and Ritual in Švankmajer's Faust
ELISA SEGNINI   153

Poetika Kino (Re)Considered: from Naturschik *to* Film Figure
YANA MEERZON   165

*Golems and Robots in the Theatre and Cinema:
Intermediality, Hybridity and the Prague School*
VERONIKA AMBROS   177

*Anthropomorphic City Horizon: Structuralist's Foregrounding
in Antony Gormley's Sculptures*
SILVIJA JESTROVIĆ   191

(Impossible) Representation in García Lorca's The Public
ANDRÉS PÉREZ-SIMÓN   203

Concluding Remarks
Afterword
LUBOMÍR DOLEŽEL   215

Lubomír Doležel:
Within Structuralism and Beyond

ROLAND LE HUENEN
University of Toronto

Gotthold Lessing once said that the only way to pay homage to artists is to celebrate their work and ignore them as persons. I suppose that this can also be said in a general way about academics, although in some cases their work is stamped with such a forceful and passionate commitment, with such a determination and belief in the progress of human knowledge, with such a dedication to research, that it is impossible to disengage the work from the personal itinerary of its author. The works of Lubomír Doležel belong to this category.

Born in 1922 in the Czech part of the newly established Czechoslovakia, Lubomír Doležel grew up at a time when the young republic, under the presidency of Tomas Garrigue Masaryk, became an oasis of democracy, a highly cultured country and the tenth biggest industrial power in the world. Masaryk was a philosopher, a thinker and a former professor at Charles University. His thoughts mainly centered on the crisis of European civilization which he diagnosed as the product of religious decline, and his views on Russia, which he described as having missed the advent of the modern nation-state in the 17th century, by-passing as well the Enlightenment and the Industrial Revolution. These served as guiding principles in his determination to found and promote a democratic Czechoslovakia. Masaryk greatly contributed to the development of a political system marked by free elections, the authority of law, the separation of powers and the protection of fundamental liberties. There were inevitably shortcomings and mistaken initiatives, especially in the treatment of minorities, but these inadequacies, though real and not to be underestimated, should not make one lose sight of the strong humanist commitment of Masaryk's Czechoslovakia, which became a haven for many who feared persecution in their own countries, namely in the Soviet Union and Nazi Germany. This produced in the 1920s and the 1930s a unique open society with a cosmopolitan culture, tolerant and untouched by any form of fundamentalism, religious or political. It was in this climate of openness and international exchange favorable to intellectual advancement that the Prague Linguistic Circle was founded in 1926 under the leadership of Vilém Mathesius, then the Director of the English Seminar at Charles University, and by Roman Jakobson, co-founder of the Moscow Linguistic Circle in 1915, who had moved to Czechoslovakia in 1920. The Prague Circle grew rapidly into an international association where Russian scholars, most of them former members of formalist groups, constituted a substantial section in addition to Czech scholars such as Jan Mukařovský, Bohuslav Havránek, Bohumil Trnka and Jan Rypka. The programmatic "Thèses du Cercle linguistique de Prague" appeared in the first of eight volumes of the "Travaux du Cercle linguistique de Prague," published from 1929 to 1939, and set out a structural theory of language, literary language and poetic language. If the first contributions were concerned with linguistics, very soon questions of poetics emerge as an equally crucial topic of discussion. According to the functional approach characteristic of the Prague School, literature was described as a form of verbal communication regulated by the aesthetic function.

When the Czech universities reopened at the end of World War II, Lubomír Doležel enrolled at Charles University. He obtained a B.A. in Slavic Philology in 1949, taught for several years in various highschools in Czechoslovakia and then, as a research fellow, joined the Institute of Czech Language of the Czechoslovak Academy of Sciences, an institution modeled after the Soviet Academy of Sciences. Under the supervision of Bohuslav Havránek, a linguist and an early member of the Prague Linguistic Circle, Lubomír conducted his Ph.D. research on modern Czech literature, with a focus on stylistic features, in particular "style indirect libre". Defended in 1959 and published in 1960 under the title *On the Style of Modern Czech Prose Fiction*, this work, in which the spirit of the Prague School is easily noticeable, was awarded a prize by the Czechoslovak Academy of Sciences and attracted international attention. Nineteen-Sixty was also the year of a major conference on poetics organized in Warsaw by Roman Jakobson and Thomas Sebeok. The proceedings published by Mouton in 1961, *Poetics-Poetica-Poetika*, were instrumental in reviving formalist literary criticism in Central Europe. Lubomír's key contribution to the conference focused on the relationship of poetics and stylistics. Throughout the 1960s, Lubomír Doležel continued working as a research fellow in the Czechoslovak Academy of Sciences as well as assistant and later associate professor at the Faculty of Philosophy at Charles University. He was engaged primarily in the application of mathematical models, especially statistical parameters of information theory and cybernetics, to the study of the Czech language and literature. This led to the publication of numerous articles on stylistics, poetics, cybernetics, philosophy of language and also to the creation of a series entitled "Prague Studies in Mathematical Linguistics."

In 1965, Lubomír Doležel, whose reputation in the fields of Slavic linguistics and the statistical theory of Poetics had crossed frontiers, was invited as visiting professor to the University of Michigan. During his stay in Ann Arbor he co-authored *An Annotated Bibliography of Statistical Stylistics* and co-edited, with Richard Bailey, a collection of studies called *Statistics and Style*. On his return to Czechoslovakia in early 1968, Lubomír was appointed research fellow—this time at the Institute of Czech Literature of the Czechoslovak Academy of Sciences. This was to be a short-lived appointment. Following the Soviet invasion of Czechoslovakia in August of the same year, which brought to a brutal end the Spring of Prague, Lubomír Doležel, like many other Czech intellectuals, chose to leave his native land and accepted an invitation to join the Department of Slavic Languages and Literatures at the University of Toronto, first as visiting professor, and from 1970 as full professor.

This marked another and important stage in Lubomír Doležel's academic career, and especially signaled an apparent shift in his scholarly interests. From statistical stylistics and mathematical linguistics, his research now moved toward the field of narratology, still at its early stages in France but a field that had long before attracted the attention of the Russian formalists Shklovsky, Tomashevski and Propp, as well as some members of the Prague School, including Felix Vodička who counted among Lubomír's teachers and mentors at Charles University and who had left a vivid impression upon him. At the time of his dissertation, Lubomír had already demonstrated a definite interest in structural analyses of narrative discourse and in 1967, in a Festschrift in honor of Roman Jakobson, he published a seminal article on the typology of the narrator which was the first systematic attempt to categorize point-of-view in fiction, revealing an astonishing ability to describe and clarify intricate critical issues and elusive concepts associated with the narrating instance. A series of articles written between 1970 and 1974 and a book *Narrative Modes in Czech Literature*, published in 1973 with the University of Toronto Press, confirmed this new trend toward narratology.

Commenting upon the work of Mukařovský, Lubomír Doležel writes: "Some structuralists restricted literary theory (poetics) to the nomothetic study of categories and regularities, but the Prague epistemology is synthetic. It combines an abstract poetics of universal categories and general laws with an analytical poetics of individual literary works. Mukařovský's 1928 monograph (reprinted in *Kapitoly*, vol. 3) already demonstrated this synthesis. A theoretical system is developed in the introduction and then used to describe a particular poem (Mácha's *May*) in the uniqueness of its sound patterning, its semantic organization, and its thematic structure" ("Prague" 594). A similar compositional pattern underpins the central argument of *Narrative Modes in Czech Literature* by combining on the one hand a progressively developed abstract model of narrative functions and verbal structures, and on the other hand finely tuned analyses of literary texts from Czech writers, articulated within the framework of the introductory model. In coupling a functional model which identifies the obligatory and secondary functions peculiar to the Narrator's Discourse (DN) and to the Characters' Discourse (DC) conceived as the two terms of a dichotomy, with a verbal model that originates from Karl Bühler's organon model where the communicative functions of language are described according to their focus on the sender, the receiver or the referent, Doležel produced a narrative typology that constitutes a remarkable synthesis of operating concepts derived from linguistics and more traditional notions such as objective/subjective/rhetorical, third-person narrative or *Er*-form and first-person narrative or *Ich*-form. Such a narrative model is general, flexible and productive, bringing to our reading of literary texts fruitful stimuli, giving the reader the opportunity to view the narrative structure of these texts in their entirety, yet allowing each one of the texts the authority of speaking for itself, of unfolding its own arrangement of structural features and strategies aimed at specific aesthetic effects. "It should be emphasized," writes Lubomír Doležel, "that no theoretical 'solution' will eliminate ambiguity from narrative texts. Discourse ambiguity seems to be an inherent property of the narrative text structure, resulting from the dynamic character of the opposition DN-DC. The very existence of this opposition—which, as we know, is essential for the narrative genre—creates immanent formal and semantic tensions within the texts; in some narrative texts, these tensions are resolved by a rigid separation of DN and DC, in others, by their assimilation ('neutralization'), inevitably leading to discourse ambiguity" (*Narrative*, 12). Whereas most of the narrative theories generated in the 1970s fall into reductionism, viewing the literary text as an example or a mere illustration of theoretical issues, the narrative typology developed in *Narrative Modes in Czech Literature* assigns to itself the role of a tool, of a mechanism of precision and general validation, aimed at revealing the underlying narrative systems which articulate the works of literature. This typology assumes concurrently that the aesthetic functions and effects of a literary text are rooted in its verbal base and must be addressed accordingly, and that a purely linguistic investigation of literature, neglecting supraverbal structures, is rather limited in its scope and validity. This well balanced approach in terms of theory and analysis, highly representative of Prague School epistemology, accounts for the very successful reading of the Czech literary pieces in the second part of the volume. Moreover, drawing directly from Lubomír Doležel's narrative typology, Wolf Schmid wrote in 1973 one of the most brilliant essays devoted to Dostoyevsky, thus conferring to the model he adopted a touch of consecration.[1]

In a second book, *Occidental Poetics: Tradition and Progress*,[2] Lubomír Doležel proposed to elucidate the antecedents of contemporary poetics, by reconstructing the history of this cognitive activity that gathers knowledge about literature and formulates the epistemology of a scientific study of poetic art, as it has to be distinguished from criticism considered as an activity strictly concerned with aesthetic evaluation. This important book, which is the first comprehensive history of poetics, examines in its first part the pre-twentieth century formulations of poetic models and issues, focusing on Aristotle's legacy, Leibnizian Poetics, the Romantic morphological model, and the idea of poetic language based on the discordant aesthetic conceptions of Wordsworth and Coleridge. The second part of the volume, devoted to the structural poetics of the first-half of the twentieth century, details the French sources of poetic semantics and stresses the role of Russian Formalism and Prague School Semiotics. According to Doležel, Aristotle's poetics qualifies as scientific since it develops a mereological procedure, that is, a whole-and-parts model which will reappear in other and later poetics as the study of structures, of emergent properties, of hierarchies linked by derivation and integration, of numerous relationships between parts and parts and parts and wholes. "Aristotle's mereological legacy," writes Lubomír Doležel, "is absolutely crucial for poetics. It is an emphatic reminder that no method, no theory, no model of poiesis, which limits itself to the parts without considering the whole, is ever adequate" (24-25). Moreover, Aristotle's mereology suggests an analogy between structures of poetry and structures of living nature, and thus foreshadows the morphological or organic model which will govern Romantic poetics. Romantic morphology refines the Aristotelian mereological model and constitutes the first theoretical attempt at representing particular poetic works as structures. Replacing the mechanistic model by the organic model, it addresses the formation of complex structures from individual parts, as clearly shown in Goethe's theory of organic structures on the basis of five postulates, the two first postulates—completeness and non-additivity, that is, the whole being more than the sum of its

---

[1] Schmid Wolf, *Der Textaufbau in den Erzählungen Dostoevskijs*, Fink, Munich, 1973. In *Essai de typologie narrative: le point de vue* (Paris, Corti, 1981), Jaap Lintvelt offers an interesting discussion of *Narrative Modes* (see Chapter 3 of Part 3, p. 151-165, "La typologie structuraliste tchèque, Lubomír Doležel").

[2] Translated into Italian, Portuguese, Spanish, German, Serbo-Croatian, Rumanian and Czech.

parts—borrowed from Aristotle's *Poetics*, the three other postulates being: (a) "the structure is a unity of polar opposites"; (b) "the "rank" of a natural phenomenon is determined by the complexity of its structure"; and (c) "organic structures exist in a constant interface with their environment" (56-7). Such a morphological model exerts an interdisciplinary control that extends to biological sciences, philosophy, aesthetics, linguistics and anthropological and cultural studies.

What defines the emergence of twentieth-century structural poetics, according to *Occidental Poetics*, was the epistemological shift initiated in linguistics that replaced the organic model with the semiotic model. In order to discuss Russian formalism, Doležel turns to its connection with German poetics—a link in his view significant, yet neglected. The works of the German poeticians of the "Rhetorical School," Steuffert, Schissel and Dibelius, while mostly ignored in Germany, were well-known in Russia by the 1920s. Although Russian formalism shared with the German "Rhetorical School" many concerns, concepts and general assumptions about literary study, it departed from the latter's interest in traditional rhetoric through the importance given to formal innovation. In discussing the Formalists, Lubomír focuses on peripheral figures in whose work the link with German poeticians is more likely to be established.

Doležel's Prague School in *Occidental Poetics* is presented as opting for a semiotic orientation that stands in contrast to "the formalist, the expressive, the mimetic and the sociological conceptions" (148) of art and asserts the idea of literary communication in agreement with Bühler's organon model to which a fourth aesthetic function is added. However, the Bühlerian schema, even in the more sophisticated formulation introduced later by Jakobson, does not account for the social activity taking place in a verbal exchange, disregarding the social status of the participants, and the possible conflicting effect resulting from power structures. Lubomír Doležel indicates an alternative version of Prague School functional linguistics which, under the impulse of Bohuslav Havránek, attempted to integrate into the communication model the language function corresponding to the social components of the verbal exchange, but failed to provide the necessary theoretical base for it. Meanwhile, the most noticeable achievement of Prague School Semiotics lies in Mukařovský's semanticization of the poetic structure, based on the preliminary distinction between material and formal elements constitutive of any literary structure, and ultimately on the process of semantic accumulation resulting from the meaning-creative value assigned to both material and formal constituents of the structure. However, Lubomír Doležel cannot help but notice in Mukařovský's system the lack of an adequate answer to the question of the reference in literature. He wrote: "Clearly, Mukařovský's repeated attempts to specify 'universal reference' cannot be called successful; the idea remained broad, indefinite, eluding theoretical fixation [...] In other words, Mukařovský does not accept the concept of fictional existence; he rejects as "aesthetic subjectivism" the view that art is "a sovereign creation of a hitherto nonexistent reality" (*Occidental*, 165-6).

I would like to suggest that this theoretical deadlock was largely responsible for Lubomír Doležel's interest in the concept of possible-worlds. He had to find the means to resolve the tensions between the aesthetic and the referential functions of the literary text, using a totally different vantage point. This interest became clearer after 1979 in invited lectures and articles such as "Extensional an Intensional Narrative Worlds," published in *Poetics* 8, "Mukařovský and the idea of Poetic Truth" (1982), and "Pour une typologie des mondes fictionnels", published in 1985 in a volume in honor of Greimas. The second chapter of *Occidental Poetics* is devoted to Leibnizian poetics and its legacy, where the concept of possible-worlds started to germinate. Finally, in 1998 Lubomír Doležel published at the Johns Hopkins University Press the much awaited synthesis of his views on fictional semantics, under the title *Heterocosmica: Fiction and Possible Worlds*. The book was rapidly translated into Italian, Spanish, Portuguese and Czech. This book is a sum, reflecting the previous stages of Doležel's inquiry in literary study and acts as a keystone in binding them together, shifting the emphasis from narrative to fiction when addressing the crucial question of the reference put in brackets by the structuralists. In an evaluation of Doležel's contribution to contemporary literary studies, Thomas Pavel suggests that the central polemical message which runs through his intellectual itinerary is to be found in the rejection of impressionistic literary criticism.[3] This statement is still as valid today as it was fifteen years ago when the article was written. Whatever choices Lubomír Doležel made in his approach to literary study, there is one lesson that students of literature should meditate upon: that literary theory as a tool to apprehend literary meaning remains an empirical enterprise based on a rigorous set of concepts.

For us at the University of Toronto Lubomír Doležel is a figure of legend. He came to this university in 1968 with an aura of prestige from his association with the Prague School at a time when Structuralism appeared to those of my generation as a world of wonders that we had just discovered. He taught for twenty years in the Department of Slavic

---

[3] Pavel, Thomas G., "Lubomír Doležel's Contribution to Contemporary Literary Studies" in *Fiction Updated: Theories of Fictionality, Narratology, and Poetics*. Eds. Calin-Andrei Mihailescu and Walid Hamarneh, University of Toronto Press, Toronto, 1996, 303-309.

Languages and Literatures and, after his retirement in 1988, has continued to teach at the Centre for Comparative Literature which he had joined in 1982. He was Chair of the Department of Slavic Languages and Literatures and Acting Director of the Centre for Comparative Literature. He co-founded in the 1970s the Toronto Semiotic Circle and became its President. This is where I met him for the first time, and I keep to this day vivid memories of the intense, at times heated, intellectual exchanges in which he actively participated. Doležel was also instrumental in the creation of the International Summer Institute for Semiotic and Structural Studies, which he chaired on several occasions. He is a member of the editorial boards of several prestigious journals: *Poetics, PTL, Poetics Today, Canadian Review of Comparative Literature, Essays in Poetics, Semiotics Inquiry, Style, Texte*. He has lectured in many universities all over Europe, in Israel, Canada and the United States. He has been a Fellow of the Royal Society of Canada since 1991. In 1995 he was awarded the F.X. Šalda medal by the Institute of Czech Literature of the Academy of Sciences of the Czech Republic, and in 2002 the Council of the Academy awarded him the Joseph Dobrovsky Honorary Medal for Merit in the Social Sciences.

Lubomír Doležel is a leading thinker in narratology and possible-worlds semantics of fictionality who has modeled and shaped those disciplines over the last thirty years. He is also a wonderful teacher in great demand with graduate students. In the Centre for Comparative Literature, his seminars have always been among the most well attended. One of the distinctive features of the Centre's curriculum is to emphasize the link between research and teaching and Lubomír Doležel has greatly contributed to this trend. What he has passed on to the students is the true spirit of research, that is, the need to maintain the pressure of questioning, to view each result obtained as a springboard toward new questions and issues based on new assumptions. In Lubomír Doležel's mental laboratory there seems to be no room for resting, but rather a tireless curiosity and a genuine quest for knowledge.

Furthermore, Lubomír Doležel's intellectual itinerary shows a definite sense of fidelity to his cultural origins against the odds of History, apprehended undoubtedly as a source of inner tension, as a tearing off and displacement of the self that soon became a dialogue or an encounter within himself, the thinking process and its critical function, and fuelled the irrepressible passion for research.

Works cited

Doležel, Lubomir. *Heterocosmica: Fiction and Possible Worlds.* Baltimore and London: The Johns Hopkins UP, 1998.
—. *Narrative Modes in Czech Literature.* Toronto: U of Toronto P, 1973.
—. *Occidental Poetics: Tradition and Progress.* Lincoln and London: U of Nebraska P, 1990.
—. "Prague School Structuralism." *The Johns Hopkins Guide to Literary Theory & Criticism.* Ed. Michael Groden and Martin Kreiswirth. Baltimore and London: The Johns Hopkins UP, 1994. 592-95.

Foreword

In October 2007, several of the leading figures in literary structuralism as well as a number of graduate students gathered in Toronto to reflect on structuralism today. The proceedings from this conference developed into the corpus of the present volume. As will soon become apparent to the reader, this volume is not a report on the "state of structuralism" as a theoretical trend. Indeed, this is not a report at all. It is, rather, a collection of some of the most exciting and varied work that takes structuralist notions—from Prague, Paris, Tartu, or elsewhere—and integrates them into our contemporary theoretical and literary framework.

You will notice an absence of adjectives such as "Czech" or "French" to describe the structuralisms of the past. This is of course for a number of reasons, historical accuracy being chief among them. But we also did not want to ascribe a certain nationalistic quality to scholarship that clearly transcended political borders. While the literature analyzed tended to come from a particular socio-historical context, Structuralism at its inception were multilingual and multinational. This in a sense was recreated in Toronto by the 2007 conference that sought to evoke, in an age desperately looking to the future for theoretical inspiration, a memory of the *continuity* of the past in contemporary scholarship. We present these papers as evidence that the methodologies advocated by structuralists working in Paris, Prague and Tartu decades ago and recently has been reinterpreted and reinvented in ways that yield fresh momentum for analysis.

Our first section is devoted to "General Aesthetics." Papers in this section range from a discussion of structuralism's place in current theoretical trends to reflections on its place in extra-literary disciplines. Emil Volek writes about the 'scene of theory' after the passing of the French theory superstars. He questions their disputed nexus with the Prague School while exploring the divide between the 'technological' and 'ideological' criticism in the transition between 'structuralism' and 'poststructuralism'. Marcel Danesi writes that the theory of oppositions —a theory fundamental to semiotics but also a model that was extensively employed by Prague School structuralists—has had to struggle against the attacks of generativism in linguistics and post-structuralism in semiotics. He notes, however, that structuralism had begun much earlier to investigate many of the problems posed by post-structuralist critics and suggests that much of structuralism's theoretical framework possesses today the "uncanny ability once again to guide research in interesting and suggestive directions." Both Danesi and Volek attempt to clear up some misunderstandings of structuralism in questioning its appropriation by poststructuralism.

Still focusing on modern trends in literary theory, Tetiana Soviak uses the provocative article by Galin Tihanov, "Why did Modern Literary Theory Originate in Central and Eastern Europe? And Why is it Now Dead?" as a way of revisiting Felix Vodička's conception of literary history. She posits that Tihanov's claims that literary theory had an eighty-year lifespan are erroneous because he fails to conceive of the socio-historical character of literature even within this eighty-year period and because he has conflated the practices of literary criticism and literary analysis. In doing so, Soviak clearly articulates the important contribution of the Prague School to the field of literary studies.

Several contributors consider the use of structuralist concepts in modern theoretical discourse. Uri Margolin writes that the case-studies of formalist and early structuralist writings of the Prague School have been complemented in recent decades by the general socio-historicl theories advanced by Anglo-American poetics and analytic aesthetics. In this way he demonstrates what turns out to be a common thread in many of the following essays—that the vocabulary created by the structuralist tendency has been subjected to successive refinements which continue to yield innovative and enriched reformulations. Margolin points to empirical studies as one such area of innovation of practice. Barbara Havercroft identifies the ways in which Émile Benveniste's concepts of subjectivity operate in recent theories of testimony, most controversially in Giorgio Agamben's claim that testimony is both necessary and impossible. Havercroft questions Agamben's assertion that the subject in the discourse of testimony cannot speak by suggesting that "Agamben's unexpected conclusion concerning the impossibility of speech is contrary, in word and spirit, to Benveniste's theory of enunciation."

In a transition between the first and second sections, between general and applied aesthetics, we find Tomáš Kubíček's article which compares two contemporary interpretations of the semantic gesture, a term coined by Jan Mukařovský. In pointing out the differences between Jankovič and Doležel, Kubíček suggests that the semantic gesture, an important development of the Prague School, was the impetus for "an interdisciplinary analysis of principles…under the functioning of which the literary work designates not only its meaning, but also its literary nature." The semantic gesture transforms the literary work into an aesthetic object and calls into question analyses purely of the work's *poeticity*, instead demanding a reading of the function and value of the literary work from an aesthetic point of view.

The second section termed "Applied Aesthetics" includes topics in narratology and in performance theory currently being undertaken under the umbrella of structuralist criticism. What is most striking about this section is the desire to create a common vocabulary to discuss literary phenomena. In an age when the fragmenting of discourse is held up as evidence of the postmodern period, it is refreshing to see such attention to the precision and elucidation of key analytic terms. Implicit in this desire is a recognition that without a common vocabulary, literary theory becomes a polyphonic but confusing cacophony of individual voices, straining to be heard but destined to be misunderstood. For no dialogue is really possible without common problems, a common framework, and a common vocabulary. Such a community of problems—to appropriate the words of French theosophist Henry Corbin—does not arise suddenly under the pressure of material events, but ripens slowly through a common participation in the questions a discipline or theoretical trend has asked itself.

In the 'narratology' sub-section, then, Wolf Schmid explores Jurij Lotman's 'eventfulness' as a narratological category that remains useful in examining the most modern literature. Emma Kafalenos applies Vladimir Propp's model of narrative functions to a reading and re-reading of the famous Chinese short story "Ah-Q—The Real Story" by Lu Xun. Nancy Felson similarly incorporates Lubomír Doležel's model of transduction and applies it to oral poetics, specifically two passages from the *Iliad*. In doing so, she shows that a study of the fabula of three tale-types—Father's Concubine, King's Wife, and Bride-Prize—reveals their position in a single general category of Parricide-Incest Tales. In the final essay in this part, Wladimir Krysinski reflects on A. J. Greimas' contribution to narratology and on the possibilities for the "pluridisciplinary cognition of the literary work." What all of these essays show are the current modes in which structuralist concepts from the three major schools are apprehended as narratological tools of analysis for both modern and classical literature.

Our final section shows the ways in which structuralist theory illuminates a variety of literary texts from theatre and the cinema. Elisa Segnini approaches the distinction between ritual and theatre made by Jindřich Honzl and finds ambiguity between these two categories in Švankmajer's *Faust*. Adam Grunzke explores Takeshi Kitano's film *Hana-Bi* through the developments made possible by Jan Mukařovský and Gilles Deleuze's theories of cinematic time. Andrés Pérez-Simón explores Mukařovský's fascinating essay on intentionality and unintentionality in art as well as the concept of ostension as it applies to Garcia Lorca's *The Public*. Yana Meerzon suggests in her analysis of *Poetika Kino*, the important subsequent contributions of the Prage and Tartu schools in establishing the semiotic interdependence of theatre and cinema aesthetics. Veronika Ambros writes about the expansion of intermediality and hybridity in modern art, especially in the performing arts. Silvija Jestrovic seeks to take the structuralist concept of foregrounding out of its traditional sphere of literature and apply it to Anthony Gormley's sculptures which engage the relationship between humans and the environment. What we see in these six papers is a statement of belief that structuralist concepts can be used in a variety of studies on cinema and the theatre to penetrating effect. Though the aesthetic artifact under consideration might vary, the terms of discussion, once clarified, continue to give the literary scholar the ability to be innovative while maintaining fidelity to the work of art.

* * *

In terms of acknowledgements, the conference would not have happened were it not for the support of Dr. Roland Le Huenen, Director of the Centre for Comparative Literature; Aphrodite Gardner in her boundless patience and skill at organizing made possible the visit of out-of-town scholars as well as arrangements for the conference; Bao Nguyen designed the posters and was our official tech-support officer; Dr. Marcel Danesi made possible the publication of this volume following the conference; Ioana Cosma was the voice of calm and ensured that the conference ran smoothly. Finally, while the graduate students at the Centre provided the impetus for the conference, the biggest thanks must go to Dr. Veronika Ambros for believing in her students, that they may present their work on structuralism beside well-known practitioners in the field.

Adil D'Sousa
University of Toronto

Futures of the Past: Steps and Mis(sed)steps in Structuralism(s), Semiotics, and Aesthetics from a Metacritical Perspective

EMIL VOLEK
Arizona State University, Tempe

Introduction

The early twentieth-century theory began by searching for one homogeneous and all-encompassing theory, capable of covering the whole field of literary and cultural studies, and yearning for the possibility of putting all facts into one commensurable framework; but it ended up carving this field into several heterologous, mutually irreducible, yet complementary spaces (Figure 1).

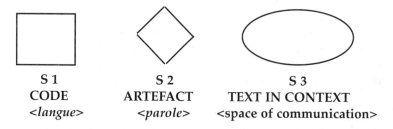

S 1　　　　　　S 2　　　　　　S 3
CODE　　　　ARTEFACT　　TEXT IN CONTEXT
<*langue*>　　<*parole*>　　<space of communication>

Figure 1: *Heterologous spaces explored in modern theory.*

Different geometrical shapes in the Figure 1 underscore the *heterologous* nature of the separate spaces: the logic of the Code (S1) is principally paradigmatic, and the syntagmatic dimension is potential only. The logic of the Artefact (S2) is principally syntagmatic and rhizomatic: in the semantic pathways of the Artefact, crisscrossing its construction, everything is interconnected with everything. In the verbal art, the syntagmatic conducting line is more apparent than in the visual arts. The logic of the Context (S3) is even more complex, since a plurality of languages both for communication and for mapping of communicative situations may contribute to and shape the communicative process. Moreover, 'communicative situation' is not something objectively 'out there', outside of or just 'framing' communication processes; it is an inhabited life-world (Volek, "Habitat"), more concrete or more abstract, where communication is always 'situated' and 'oriented' ('from-to').

Going from the space of the Code all through to the communicative Context, the level of complexity grows exponentially. At the same time, all these separate heterologous spaces are *complementary*: *parole* could not exist as such without *langue*; but *parole* as communicative act could not exist as such without communicative Context either. This goes beyond the fact that verbal language usually plays major role in communication and that communication can reduce its role or substitute for it partially or totally through diverse means. The Artefact (utterance, text in S2) does not arise solely as projection of the Code, but rather from the multifaceted *power struggle* between the generative force of the Code and the already 'inhabited' and resisting space of communicative Context, characterized by the plurality of languages and of positions/orientations within certain specific physical, historical and social situation. (Bakhtinian dialogism models one facet of those conflicts). 'Chaos' invades the straightforward succession Code→ Artefact → Context presumed by the structuralists.

The mechanistic concept of communication processes as a straightforward succession, I am disputing here, extends now through all current poststructuralist, postmodern cultural theory. It is shared by the French structuralism (focusing exclusively on the Code), by Heidegger (language 'speaks through us'), by the Frankfurtian 'Critical Theory' (mass media manipulation), by the Chomskyan generative-transformational grammar, among other deterministic views. One of the consequences is the erasure of the subject as possibly active agency. The Code is hypostasized as an independent force ramming its 'message' through the subject, turned into a passive space of passage. S1 supplants S2 and S3. Viktor Shklovskij has already stated memorably that the subject ("author") is mere geometric point of intersection of external power lines. While interesting as poetics, theory has paid high price for this avant-garde *boutade*.

The specific logic of the space of the Code (S1) was first grasped and explored by structuralism, following upon the insights disseminated in linguistics and pulled together by Saussure. Before, this space existed as a repository of rationalistic scheming and daydreaming (recall Goya's "the dream of reason engenders monsters"), a warehouse of grammatical paradigms modeled on Latin or Greek, or repertory of rhetorical and poetic figures, stored in prescriptive or simply enumerative order. This new logic that transformed the warehouse into a close-knit, tightly ordered and layered, code and system—too neat, indeed—dazzled by its artificial symmetries, and was thrust upon many unsuspecting disciplines.

The constitutive logic of each space allows for most diverse conceptualizations within the particular space. Each space actually subdivides into two halves: one general and one specific. Saussure's contribution falls into the general part of S1: he is not interested in exploring the system of one particular language but rather in the general problems of "systematicity" in languages, i.e. in the emergence of the language system as such. In contradistinction, the post-Saussurean linguistics—with the exception of the Prague phonology—has used his insights to focus on the systemic modeling of specific languages.

In the specific part of S1, we can put side by side different models of the narrative code: the line going from Propp to Lévi-Strauss to Greimas equals passing from surface to depth and, simultaneously, from analogous to digital modeling. These models do not exclude one another, but simply point to different aspects and levels of narrative. While Lévi-Strauss may scoff at Propp, the latter's model of thirty-one steps has proved handy for analysis of all kinds of narratives; yet, once we cross over from the Code (S1) to the Artefact (S2) as a rhizomatous—teleological, semantic and aesthetic—construction, *all narratological and other models worked out in the logic of the code fall short.*

The space of the Artefact (S2) has been explored in its general aspects namely by the phenomenology (Roman Ingarden and later Wolfgang Iser). The construction of specific texts as isolated artefacts has been studied by numerous schools, such as stylistics, Russian Formalism, and the Prague School structuralism. In contradistinction to stylistics, both Russian Formalism and Prague structuralism have pointed through the texts to a kind of general literary, poetic or artistic 'textuality'. Yet the 'literariness' searched for in 'devices', 'dominants' or 'semantic gestures' has proved to be another mirage.

Prague has focused on the *functional* articulation of artefacts in complex, dynamic—semantic and aesthetic—structures, changing over time. The very concept of structure means something different in Paris and in Prague, yet it retains certain identity by referring to a type of 'structured totality', *phenomenic* and *functional* in Prague, *deep, systemic,* and *transformational* in Paris (Volek, Metaestructuralismo 19-20, 220).

The space of the communicative Context (S3) has been usually explored from most diverse perspectives (such as semiotics, communication, hermeneutics, history, sociology, etc.).

The heterologous character of the nodal spaces we have separated in the 'field of theory' has numerous and fundamental implications: 1. Singular spaces are mutually irreducible, yet complementary. 2. The logic of one space is not fully transferable to another (S1 → S2 and/or S1 → S3, as attempted by the French structuralists; or S3 → S1, as done by deconstruction and poststructuralism, both with little success and leaving behind much confusion). 3. This new vision of the 'field of theory' is the product of a specific *metacritical* work (a phenomenological reduction *sui generis,* as proposed in my *Metaestructuralismo*). As a consequence, the established singular spaces function as *heuristic* aids only. They do not imply that theories should be such and such, or that some theories are 'better' just because they focus on one space instead of another, or that a theory x oriented on S_x somehow supplants and makes unnecessary the theory y oriented on S_y (the illusion propagated by the poststructuralists who have centered on S3 and have not only thought that they have overcome structuralism and other theories oriented on other spaces, but have tried to apply the logic of S3, they have not fully grasped, on S1 and S2). 4. The breakdown of the logic of one space when transplanted on another does not mean breakdown of the logic as such (as wrongly implied by poststructuralism). 5. The futile search for one homogeneous and all-encompassing theory does not lead necessarily to unbridled eclecticism and the suicide of 'untheory'.

Once unveiled and explored, the space x can be projected retroactively on previous stages of critical thinking, to "reveal dimensions that went unnoticed in earlier phenomena and systems" (Volek, *Metaestructuralismo* 35). Individual thinkers and schools may focus on one of these spaces only, may move between some or all, may gradually shift from one to another, or may be scattered, schizophrenically, over various of them. Any variation of interest or abandoning of certain space does not mean that that space has disappeared from THEORY; it has only been disregarded from the vantage point of one *particular* and *partial* theory$_x$. The inactive space may continue to exert influence or be "felt" by its absence. Any space may and will be 'reopened' when and if useful new conceptualization is found.

This should help us to focus anew on and to sort out the confusing maze of critical currents and individual "jetties" (as Derrida called them, "Some" 65) in their most diverse conceptualizations and interests, launched from the most diverse epistemic—or *despistemic*[1]—grounds.

The 'scene of theory'

Currently, what the 'scene of theory' has to offer us is a complex and confusing panorama. On the one hand, Theory (with capital T) was recently 'officially' buried in Chicago (in April 2003, Stanley Fish officiating as M.C. in that memorable ritual); on the other hand, hopeful anti-theories and post-theories began to appear even before her alleged demise. What was that Theory, after all? At the Irvine colloquium on The States of "Theory", in 1987, Derrida called her, slyly, "a purely North American *artifact*, which only takes on sense from its place of emergence in certain departments of literature" in the U.S. ("Some"

---

[1] *Despisteme*, from Spanish, 'despistar', to stray, to mislead.

71). And he quotes, approvingly, Jonathan Culler's *Criticism and Institutions* referring to "literary thinkers debating with theoretical movements which are themselves at work in departments of literature," such as linguistics, psychoanalysis, feminism, structuralism, or deconstruction.

Let's skip the circularity transparent in Culler's quote, and note in passing that our topic here—structuralism—is buried there between feminism and deconstruction as part of that hodge-podge U.S. Theory, and let's quote part of Derrida's quotation of Culler:

> A corollary of this has been the expansion of the domain of literary studies...[2] In most American universities today a course on Freud is more likely to be offered in the English or French Department than in the Psychology Department; Nietzsche, Sartre, Gadamer, Heidegger, and Derrida are more often discussed by teachers of literature than teachers of philosophy; Saussure is neglected by linguists and appreciated by students and teachers of literature. ("Some" 82-3; originally Culler 87)

This "miscellaneous genre" of discourse, continues Culler, "whose most convenient designation is simply "theory" … refer[s] to works that succeed in challenging and reorienting thinking in fields other than those to which they ostensibly belong." Derrida then struggles with the feeling of grateful recognition of the fact that this concoction of Theory opened up for him the door to literary fame and glory, and yet strives to decouple his philosophical deconstruction from this "parasitic and small seismic" perversion of (his) Theory he looks upon with the perplexity of a putative father, holding the DNA verdict in one hand and "I have never had sex with that woman," in the other...

Such wholesale extrapolations of theories that may be quite antiquated in their own fields in order to illuminate other fields raise a number of questions: To what degree is their use and abuse metaphorical and amateurish? Alan Sokal's incident with *Social Text* (in 1996) comes to mind. Are not some of those theories pervasive precisely for their straightforward simplicity (e.g. Saussure's *sémiologie*), offering an illusion of simple, far-reaching, and clear-cut 'applications'? Are not others, to the contrary, selected rather for their aura of unfathomable sophistication, as signs of allure of and intoxication with prophetic obscurity (Lacan's and Derrida's "jetties" come to mind)? These specters of outdatedness, simplicity, and studied obscurity are haunting the so-called 'cultural studies' in the U.S. to this day.

If we take into consideration the fact that Derrida and Culler talk

---

[2] In his deconstruction of the traditional conceptual position, Derrida prioritizes —puts— "her" over "him."

already about the "last twenty years' developments," we have now some forty years of stagnation and circularity. It is time to call the time up, to stop this literary theory of exhaustion and seek some food for replenishment.

In my view, the road 'forward'—let's forget for a moment that this notion contradicts yet another exhausted paradigm, that of the so-called 'Postmodernism'—may lead rather through a careful reconsideration of the past, of what was already there latent or even discovered and was later forgotten, or lost in translation (from Russian to French, from Saussure to Derrida, etc.). The past is pregnant with intuitions never born out, so to speak. Some such revision would have to go beyond genealogy as it was coined by Nietzsche and reemployed by Foucault. A careful re-reading would have to venture into a 're-translation' of some of those oldies within the new frameworks, yet avoiding the temptation of simple transvestism of the 'old' as 'new'. Also, at times, a good understanding and re-translation would require a substantial reconceptualization of the new framework.

A kind of 'genealogy in reverse' would then retrace the steps and missteps along that traveled and untraveled road. Questions such as, What can 'poststructuralism' teach us about 'structuralism'?, would have to be asked. But, immediately, Which 'postructuralism' about whose 'structuralism'? The concepts of 'continuity in discontinuity' and 'discontinuity in continuity' would have to be introduced to clarify some non-lineal complexities of historical processes in the twentieth-century literary and cultural theory (Volek, *Metaestructuralismo* 35). These complexities go well beyond Viktor Shklovskij's 'knight's move', passing heritage from "uncle to nephew"; but at least he was the first to showcase the non-lineal processes in literary and critical progression.

When we look at the road of modern theory forking and winding from the Russian Formalism up to the early poststructuralism, Milan Kundera's notion of "laughter and forgetting" comes to mind. Prague continues and improves on the Russian formalists, but Shkovskij's anti-logocentric narratology is lost in translation (this will be repeated in France; see my *Metaestructuralismo*); Paris builds on the Prague phonology, but ignores her structuralism, semiotics, and aesthetics. Deconstruction radically re-reads Saussure, but in some weird infinitesimal key. Other currents of the so-called 'poststructuralism' are generally 'remakes', mostly conscious: Jauß's aesthetics of reception picks up where the Prague structuralism left off, and his colleague from Konstanz, Iser, revives the literary phenomenology of Ingarden; Kristevian intertextuality flattens Bakhtin's live dialogism, and New Historicism waters down Marx's class struggle and deterministic historical materialism.

The structuralism/poststructuralism divide

How did we get into this mess? The short answer is: through structuralism and poststructuralist deconstruction. (For a moment, I will take structuralism as one.) A curious divide is put between these two: deconstruction is apparently 'more philosophical' and resonates with the postmodern turn; even its original group ambiance, the *Tel Quel* circle, is clearly Postmodernist. This characteristic would leave structuralism behind as "still" modern and "less" philosophical. To put this positively, we could say that modern theory up to structuralism was more *technically* oriented. The shadow cast by the nineteenth-century positivism, with its aversion to philosophical speculation, would obviously be longer than presumed.

Heidegger comments on "the growing incapacity for metaphysical knowledge" in modern times (89) and points out, not without sarcasm, the "sense of the miniscule" in the new academic science. It would seem that, in the 1970s and after, metaphysics, ushered by deconstruction, returns with vengeance, but in degraded form: as *ideology*.

However, the divide between 'technological' and 'ideological' theory in the transition between 'structualism' and 'poststructuralism' is not clear-cut either. Within structuralism, the first step towards ideological criticism was made when the structuralism in linguistics, specifically in the Prague School phonology, became the model for the French studies *in culture* (in Claude Lévi-Strauss and later in Roland Barthes's adaptation of Saussurean semiology). While the *Elementary Structures of Kinship* (1949) launches the hardcore technological French structuralism, Lévi-Strauss's other writings such as "Race and History" (1952) or *The Savage Mind* (1962) already announce the coming cultural relativism ('multiculturalism') and postmodernism, and actually open the door for them. *The Savage Mind* strikes several chords at once: it anticipates postmodern questioning of the scientific discourse (the "engineer") and of man himself: "I believe the ultimate goal of the human sciences to be not to constitute, but to dissolve man" (247); in open polemic with Sartre's Marxism, any special status for the dialectic reason is denied, which precipitates crisis in Marxist philosophy; the very possibility of writing history is questioned; and the final chapter, "History and Dialectic," surprises yet with another intuition, that of the end of the modern era, historically oriented towards the French Revolution (254).

On the other hand, deconstruction is intimately enmeshed in French structuralism, even through its partial re-reading of Saussure. While in Prague the Genevan linguist was just one of the impulses for the new linguistics and semiotics, among the Parisian intellectuals, not specifically schooled in linguistics, he was worshipped as the last word in that discipline. Awarding him that status and backtracking French structuralism directly to that 'origin' also helped the French minimize any 'connecting links' and claim structuralism neatly for themselves.

Derrida 'trumps' mere *linguistic* readings of Saussure: while linguists used his intuitions about *langue* to focus anew on grammatical systems of specific languages, or, as in the Prague phonology, proposed a new model for one building block of language, Derrida has been fascinated by the negative and relational processes of construction of values in the language system, and has projected them, metaphorically, to the infinite and on most diverse entities (from here come his whimsical concepts such as *différance,* trace, etc.). For example, the text is shifted from the space of the determined artefact to become an infinite flow of never coalescing "textuality":

> ...what I still call a "text", for strategic reasons ... is henceforth no longer a finished corpus of writing, some content enclosed in a book or its margins, but a differential network, a fabric of traces referring endlessly to something other than itself, to other differential traces. Thus the text overruns all the limits assigned to it so far. (Derrida, "Living On" 83-84)

Unless we understand this overflow metaphorically, as a kind of intertextuality, "text" is confused with the "negative" and relational aspect of the construction of the system and is conflated with the space of *langue*. S2 becomes part of S1. This was a radical, dazzling reading that caught many off guard; unfortunately, Derrida's haste left out the other half of what Saussure had to say about language system as a system of *positive* entities. "But the statement that everything in language is negative is true only if the signified and the signifier are considered separately; when we consider the sign in its totality, we have something that is positive in its own class" (Saussure 120); and a bit later, this *positive fact* "is even the sole type of facts that language has" (121). Back in 1927, Saussure's alumnus Karcevskij would note that pure negativity would not create any system on any partial level (*Système du verbe russe*).

The Yale school would jump to rescue, asserting that any reading is misreading and that the only question then is how productive it proves to be. Yet I would say that here we do not have a case of misreading but that of *missed* reading. While Zen Buddhism and the Avant-Garde have shown that nonsense and absurdity can be productive in spiritual education and in literature, it is less so in literary and cultural theory.

Finally, structuralism and poststructuralism share the "linguistic turn." However, it would seem that the assumed link—language— has been poorly known and understood by philosophers who have proclaimed language as the protagonist of our times, and even less by the literary and cultural theorists, indeed by many linguists. Linguistic turn assumes primacy of verbal language as world modeling system and of the code over discourse. Both premises are wrong, as I argue in my "Habitats of Language" (2007), where I follow the path from 'ostensive language' to the emergence of verbal language and to their entanglement in physical and cultural habitats and in communication.

Returning to the presumed divide, we can see that it is getting fuzzier and fuzzier. Interesting parallels and overlaps emerge, adding to those already mentioned: if the French structuralist narratology rediscovers the 'morphologist' Vladimir Propp (late early Formalist at best), poststructualism finds seminal inspiration in the postformalist Mikhail Bakhtin (in him, the anti-formalist becomes post-formalist when he discovers language, dialogue, and carnival). Derrida, on the other hand, will recover certain dynamism that was characteristic of the Russian Formalism and of the Prague structuralism. The deconstruction of static logical modeling we find in Petrograd and in Prague, coming from the *energeia* and experimentalism of the avant-gardes, actually foreshadows Derrida's deconstruction and his criticism of traditional logocentrism, emerging in the Parisian neo-avant-garde ambience.

Yet the differences between the French structuralism, scattered perhaps schizophrenically over several theoretical spaces, and poststructuralism could not be exaggerated: the former tends to and is inscribed in history for its 'technological' positions; the latter, passing through the erotic and 'philosophical' deconstruction, is ideological, historicist at best (in the *Rezeptionsaesthetik* or in New Historicism).

As far as the pendulum between the technological and ideological theory is concerned, the shift of interest from the Code toward the Artefact and then especially toward the space of communication and to its social and historical contexts does not mean that the spaces S1 and S2, chartered by the Code and by the Artefact, cease to exist. It only shows why the 'post-' in poststructuralism is so misleading, since much of the 'post' has already come before the French structuralism was born. In general, I would say (paraphrasing John Barth, again): If the second half of the twentieth-century has taught us that the technological-oriented theory is not the whole story, then at the beginning of the twenty-first century we cannot fail to notice that the ideological and speculative Theory is not the whole story either, more so if based on simplified and outdated models.

The Prague School and her hidden jewels: semiotics

The Prague structuralism has barely been on the horizon of the French structuralism. Jakobson gets his due as a teacher and friend of Lévi-

Strauss during his war exile in New York, as a linguist and later as a 'grammarian of poetry'—taking the interest in the miniscule to new heights—from the late 1950s through the 1960s. But Jan Mukařovský has been and remains unknown and unacknowledged. An anthology of his works was translated into French in the early 1970s, but its publication, prepared for Gallimard, was allegedly thwarted by Todorov. Structuralism, after all, was buried by then by the student revolt of 68 and its "sentimental journey" was cut short one more time.[3]

Well, if that translation were perhaps as inept as some of Mukařovský's renditions into Spanish and English are (here most notably *Aesthetic Function*, 1936), or as Todorov's own translation of Russian Formalists into French is, it may have been indeed better not to publish than to publish something that might substantially distort author's conceptual system.

The trouble is when an author does it somehow to himself. There is a strange case of missing original for one of Mukařovský's key texts, considered sometimes as the first manifesto of the Prague School autonomous on the Russian Formalism. Written 'originally' in French from some presumable Czech *Urtext*, perhaps just notes or "brain *écriture*" that would delight Derrida, it was retranslated into Czech in the 1960s (for his *Studie z estetiky*, 1966) and not even by the author himself but by the philosopher and later martyr Jan Patočka. Since the early 1930s, 'sign' is the sign of the times, and Mukařovský is developing his own concept of the sign-nature of the arts. Invited to participate at the International Congress of Philosophy in Prague, in 1934, he decides to commit his ideas to paper. God knows how he would have written his contribution in German. But French was the 'politically correct' international language in Czechoslovakia after the World War. So, writing in French and hoping to address the French audience, he produced "L'Art comme fait sémiologique". The trouble was that in the French philosophical and intellectual *milieu* at that time Saussure did not mean anything, and that by this title and by some haphazard use of *signifiant/signifié* in the text Mukařovský perhaps unintentionally disfigured his own conceptual system and, subsequently, misled his readers and even his later followers into believing that his semiotics was just a kind of Saussurean semiology and that *that* was all that was to it in Prague.

A careful reading of "L'Art" reveals that in that text there is much more than, and actually anything but, *sémiologie*. It is in his untranslat-

---

[3] Stalinism buried Russian Formalism (and the avant-garde) in 1929; Hitler and Stalin buried the Prague School in 1939 and in 1948; Brezhnev in 1968. *Sentimental'noje puteshestvije* (A Sentimental Journey, 1923), Viktor Shklovskij's memoir, plays on Laurence Sterne's whimsical novelette about a trip that is cut short as it barely begins...

ed and perhaps untranslatable brilliant piece on Nezval's surrealist poem *Absolutní hrobař* (Absolute Grave-Digger, 1938) where Mukařovský expresses freely his attitude to the current stage of the science of the signs: "semiology, the science of the sign Saussure so clear-sightedly called for, is still in diapers" (*Studie* 285). After the papers he had prepared for his university seminars from the early 1930s were finally published in the 1980s and collected in the 1990s (1995), we now know that at that time he was intimately engaged with phenomenology and with the Husserlian *Bedeutungslehre*, especially through Roman Ingarden's *Das literarische Kunswerk* (1931). His engagement with phenomenology was therefore continuous, and not some 'fortunately brief deviation' from the 1940s, as it was sometimes wishfully characterized.

The suspicion of authorial mistranslation is further corroborated by the subsequent subsumption of "L'Art" into *Aesthetic Function, Norm and Value as Social Facts* (1936), where the self-induced references to *sémiologie* have completely disappeared.

Prague has more surprises in stock in this regard. As early as in 1929, Sergej Karcevskij in "Du Dualism asymétrique du signe linguistique", attacked the sacrosanct monogamy of the signifier/signified relation in the sign, and proposed something like "floating sign" that explains much better what decades later Lacan and Derrida have tried to hint at. The trick is that Saussure conceptualizes the sign within the space of the linguistic system (*langue*—S1) and, therefore, he does not need reference or the referent, while Karcevskij, Lacan, and Derrida think in terms of *communication* (S3 in Figure 1) where "the interplay of signification has ... no limit" (Derrida, "Structure" 250). Derrida's error then is to project this back onto the space of the *langue* and to try to call into question "the concept and the word sign itself"—which is more in harmony with the tenor of his deconstruction than with the functionality of the sign itself. The poststructuralist semiology heralded as "overcoming" of the structuralist semiology looks rather like a comedy of errors, created by shifting of attention from one space to another without realizing it and without taking into account the fact that the sign functions differently in each of those heterologous spaces, without losing its essential identity.

In 1936, the Russian member of the Circle and folklorist Petr Bogatyrev writes a path-breaking study "Kroj jako znak" (Costume as a sign, 1971), inspired by Valentin Voloshinov's semiotics as ideology as explained in his "Slovo i jego social'naja funkcija" (1930). Bogatyrev ponders the "now I see an object, now I see a sign" effect: for example, a stone (natural object) turned into a border marker (sign). Folk costume—or any clothing for that matter—then also becomes a sign without ceasing to be used as a cover for the body (i.e. as an object).

The vacillation between the two states and the transformation of an object into a sign will lead to the still unsurpassed exploration of the semiotics of theater in the Prague School and, later, to Ivo Osolsobě's concept of ostension, defined as "a type of communication where the reality itself functions as the *message*" (1967), or as "the cognitive use of non-signs" (1979). My own work attempts to expand the concept of ostension from the specific use of an object in communication to name the basic language for mapping subject's inner and outer habitat.[4]

Going beyond signs and language, Voloshinov's semiotics, positing an interchangeable relation between natural objects and signs —notwithstanding its crude sociologism and ideologism—, is then yet another important seminal impulse for expanding the scope of the Prague semiotics.

The revolutionary theater semiotics developed in Prague will also lead back, to the rediscoveries and re-appropriations of the path-breaking pre-semiotic semiotics of theater proposed in Otakar Zich's *Estetika dramatického umění* (Aesthetics of the Dramatic Art, 1931). Zich combined acute sense of detail with rigorous formal analysis, but his conceptual framework harks back to the psychological aesthetics in the line of Johannes Volkelt. The key concept here is *Bedeutungsvorstellung* (something like "significant ideation"). Zich further differentiates between 'technical' and 'image' ideations: the first asks "how something is made", the second, "what it means." Zich's theater aesthetics is audience-oriented, and in this it is forward-looking; but it is based solely on the material of realistic theater and art. One set of concepts merits special attention: *herecká postava* and *dramatická osoba*. *Herecká postava* is literally "the figure created on stage by the actor" (Veltruský uses the term "stage figure" since "actor's figure" would be misleading); *dramatická osoba* is the "character", dramatis persona, as represented by the former. The stage figure is created by the actor; the character is what the audience can see and interpret on the stage. In this way, we get an interplay of four intimately connected elements: actor / stage figure / character / audience. And both stage figure and character can be viewed, alternately, from the 'technical' and the 'image' perspective (this could be expanded to the actor as well as to the audience).

Zich's project working with the 'significant' elements in 'ideation' beacons for a semiotic re-reading. We have got three such attempts to

---

[4] See my *Metaestructuralismo* and *Znak*. Osolsobě's and subsequently my concept of ostension differs both from Eco and Sperber and Wilson. In Eco (224-227), it is kept close to the "ostensive definition" in logic ('pointing to'); in Sperber/Wilson (50-54), it refers to behavioral 'pointing to', not as a 'definition' but as a trigger of 'ostensive-inferential communication' within the context and situation of communication.

re-write at least part of his book in semiotic terms. It is a sign of the times that these attempts, written between 1976 and 1981, at home and abroad, are disconnected from each other.

Jiří Veltruský (1976) employs a simple semiologic model, based on *signans* and *signatum*. His *signans* concentrates on the creation of the stage figure and on all that may characterize it, using not only his intimate knowledge of the avant-garde theater but also of most diverse types of world theater. Thus the stage acting goes far beyond the actor's acting in Zich's realistic aesthetics, but the theoretical framework strikes one as very simple and surprisingly unsophisticated. For example, Mukařovský's deconstructive concept of intentionality and unintentionality (1943; Volek 2004) would tease out more implications of Zich's audience-oriented aesthetics.

In his introduction to the reprint of Zich (1931), Oleg Sus (1977) attempts to use a more complex semiotic model, sometimes, however, marred by slippages. He adopts Roland Barthes' two-tier concept of mythological discourse, where the signifier and the signified at one level become the signifier of the higher order, and interprets the stage figure as an 'elemental sign', and the character as a 'complex sign'. Further, he quite wrongly identifies the 'elemental' level with the 'technical ideation' and the 'complex' one with the 'image ideation', transforming alternation in both into their sequence. On the positive side, understanding the stage figure creation as an elemental sign process makes it possible for him to introduce as part of the first-level signifier Osolsobě's ostension as an important contribution to theater semiotics. Finally, Osolsobě himself (1981) points out the latent semiotic nature of Zich's project, relying especially on the 'significant' in the 'ideation', but without proposing any specific model (not even his own) for the re-reading, which then also falls somewhat flat.

Zich's book is precisely a good example of what I mentioned earlier: a pioneering effort beaconing for and yet resisting simple re-appropriation and re-translation into later, 'more modern' conceptual systems, in this case, semiotic, and, at the same time, showing the very limits of those systems and the need for their further development and re-conceptualization. It also shows that the conceptual system goes only so far as does the knowledge of concrete pertinent material, the object of theoretical reflection.

Jan Mukařovský's semiotic aesthetics

Another example of the buried treasures yet to be fully unearthed in Prague, is Mukařovský's aesthetics. His poetic, or aesthetic, function moves well within the Russian Formalist tradition, resonating with the avant-garde poetics, and is repeatedly defined as autonomous, self-centered, in sum, as the dialectical negation of practical functions and values in the aesthetic object. In this way it entered the history of poetics and aesthetics of the twentieth century. However, in the *Aesthetic Function, Norm and Value as Social Facts* (1936), Mukařovský has introduced some strange, alternate logic, working differently 'from the inside' and 'from the outside'.

On the outside, the aesthetic value (and necessarily also norm and function) continues to be seen as 'full' and as 'positively' defined, i.e. as autonomous, as isolationist (isolating the object from and within the social sphere) and as 'purgative' (purifying the artwork from practical functions and concerns). (In his posthumous *Aesthetic Theory* (1973), Theodor Adorno, picking up an insight by Walter Benjamin, would call this line of modern aesthetics 'aesthetics of negativity'.) Mukařovský goes as far as positing that the aesthetic function confers some *sign value* on its object. I think that this is going too far: the concept of ostension would have helped out in this instance, but it was not on Mukařovský's horizon (Volek, *Znak* 66-68).

On the inside, however, the aesthetic value becomes 'transparent', 'it has dissolved into individual extra-aesthetic values, and is really nothing but a general term for the dynamic totality of their mutual interrelationships' (Mukařovský, *Aesthetic* 88). Aesthetic values "assume the role of mere conductors of energies introduced by extra-aesthetic values". "The work of art appears, in the final analysis, as an actual collection of extra-aesthetic values and nothing else". This is a stunning reversal, showing a completely different value on the other side of the coin, so to speak.

This new concept of aesthetics raises numerous questions and needs to be further developed. The 'canonical', formalist-structuralist formulation, falls well within the model of the abstract, modern, negative, Kantian aesthetics, based on disinterestedness; and the other, based on the 'view from the inside', is anti-Kantian, nonreductive, and potentially postmodern. Mukařovský (1937) adds later a significant corrective to the 'transparency' of value: it is now *situated* within several mutually irreducible horizons (social, historical, and individual).[5] What emerges, then, is a situated, oriented and transformative transparency of the aesthetic function, characteristic that puts it closer to

---

[5] Surprisingly, then, individuum becomes in Mukařovský, at that time, an irreducible 'horizon' of activity, and he will subsequently study the role of the individual in literary development (and in other social processes). The individuum pops up as irreducible agency and as possibly transforming disturbance in the system. This 'maverick' –chaotic *avant la letter*— role of the individual contradicts all 'death' warrants written on the 'author' and on the 'subject' at large, emitted from Paris.

what aesthetics has been looking for in these postmodern times, so far without much success.

This facet of Mukařovský's aesthetics is clearly inscribed in the anti-Kantian line of modern aesthetic thinking: we may note echoes of Nietzsche, of Bergson's vitalism, and also certain parallels to Heidegger due to the common connection to Husserlian phenomenology (the positionality of the aesthetic function 'in the world'). Yet this facet, based on the in and out, later fades in and out of the system. Striking as it might be, Mukařovský himself perhaps may not have been fully aware of the revolutionary character of his redefinition of aesthetics 'from the inside'.

Finally, in my view, the whole Prague structuralism needs to be rediscovered yet. First, the major global works dedicated to it were based on materials available through the early 1970s. Second, these works have generally erred on the side of attempted reconstruction of the conceptual system. And closed homogeneous system is precisely what is absent in Mukařovský's *work in progress,* rich in fits and starts... What was left behind, were not only the 'dialectic contradictions' of the Prague structuralist theory, but contradictions *tout court,* including false starts and blind alleys (for fuller account see my *Znak*). It may be precisely these unruly fragments resisting systematization that may lead us to a more fruitful understanding of the Prague School effort and of its possible import for contemporary state of the art.

In conclusion, in my opinion, a change in the current 'scene of theory' is overdue. In the theoretical thinking at the dawn of the twenty-first century, a new paradigm is looming on the horizon, leading hopefully beyond the bankrupt modern and postmodern *despistemes.*

Works Cited

Bogatyrev, Petr. "Costume as a sign." *The Functions of Folk Costume in Moravian Slovakia*. The Hague: Mouton, 1971. Trans. of "Kroj jako znak. Funkční a strukturální pojetí v národopisu." *Slovo a slovesnost* 2 (1936): 43-47.

Culler, Jonathan. "Criticism and institutions: the American university." *Poststructuralism and the Question of History*. Eds. Derek Attridge et al. Cambridge: Cambridge UP, 1987. 82-98.

Derrida, Jacques. "Living On." *De-Construction & Criticism*. Eds. Harold Bloom et al. New York: The Seabury Press, 1979. 62-142.

———. "Some statements and truisms about neologisms, newisms, postisms, parasitisms, and other small seismisms." In *The States of 'Theory'*. Ed. David Carroll. New York: Columbia UP, 1990. 63-94.

———. "Structure, sign, and play in the discourse of the human sciences." *The Structuralist Controversy*. Eds. Richard Macksey and Eugenio Donato. Baltimore: The Johns Hopkins UP, 1970. 247-65.

Eco, Umberto. *A Theory of Semiotics*. Bloomington: Indiana UP, 1976.
Heidegger, Martin. *Nietzsche, I: The Will to Power as Art*. Trans. David F. Krell. London: Routlege & Kegan Paul, 1981.
Karcevskij, Sergej. "The Asymmetric Dualism of the Linguistic Sign." *The Prague School: Selected Writings, 1929-1946*. Ed. Peter Steiner. Austin: U of Texas P, 1982. 47-54. Trans. of "Du Dualisme asymétrique du signe linguistique". *Travaux du Cercle Linguistique de Prague* I (1929): 88-93.
Lévi-Strauss, Claude. *The Savage Mind*. Chicago: U of Chicago P, 1966.
Mukařovský, Jan (1934). "L'Art comme fait sémiologique." *Actes du huitième Congrès international de philosophie à Prague 1934*. Prague, 1936. 1065-1072. Several trans. into English available.
___. *Básnická sémantika*. Ed. Miroslav Procházka. Prague: Karolinum, 1995.
___. *Estetická funkce, norma a hodnota jako sociální fakty*. Prague: Borový. Quoted after *Aesthetic Function, Norm and Value as Social Facts*. Trans. Mark E. Suino. Ann Arbor: U of Michigan, 1970 (a rather poor translation of a key text).
___. "Intentionality and unintentionality in Art." 1943. *Structure, Sign, and Function*. Ed. and trans. John Burbank and Peter Steiner. New Haven: Yale UP, 1978. 89-128.
___. "On the problem of functions in architecture." 1937. *Structure, Sign, and Function*. Ed. and trans. John Burbank and Peter Steiner. New Haven: Yale UP, 1978. 236-250.
___. *Studie z estetiky*. Prague: Odeon, 1966.
Osolsobě, Ivo. "On ostensive communication." *Studia semiotyczne* 8 (1979): 63-75.
___. "Ostenze jako mezní případ lidského sdělování a jeho význam pro umění." *Estetika* 4.1 (1967): 2-27.
___. "Sémiotika sémiotika Otakara Zicha." 1981. *Ostenze, hra, jazyk: Sémiotické studie*. Brno: Host, 2002. 213-238.
Saussure, Ferdinand de. *Course in General Linguistics*. 1916. Trans. Wade Baskin. New York: McGraw Hill, 1959.
Sperber, Dan and Deirdre Wilson. *Relevance: Communication and Cognition*. Oxford: Blackwell, 1995.
Sus, Oleg. "Předmluva. Průkopník české strukturně sémantické divadelní vědy." Introduction to the reprint of Zich (1931). Würzburg: Jal-Reprint, 1977.
Thom, René. *Structural Stability and Morphogenesis: An Outline of a General Theory of Models*. Reading, MA: Benjamin, 1975.
Veltruský, Jiří (1976). "Contribution to the semiotics of acting." *Sound, Sign and Meaning: Quinquagenary of the Prague Linguistic Circle*. Ed. Ladislav Matějka. Ann Arbor: U of Michigan, 1976. 553-606.
Volek, Emil. "Habitats of language/language inhabited: From ostension and *umwelt* to the possible worlds of communication and culture." *Dynamic Structure: Language as an Open System*. Eds. Johannes Fehr and Petr Kouba. Prague: Litteraria Pragensia, 2007. 186-219.
___. *Metaestructuralismo: Poética moderna, semiótica narrativa y filosofía de las ciencias sociales*. Madrid: Fundamentos, 1985.
___. "Revisiones: Nuevas perspectivas, cabos sueltos". *Signo, función y valor: Estética y semiótica del arte*. By Jan Mukařovský. Eds. Emil Volek and Jarmila Jandová. Bogotá: Plaza y Janés, 2000. 387-394.

——. *Znak, funkce a hodnota: Estetika a sémiotika umění Jana Mukařovského v proudech současného myšlení. Zápisky z podzemí postmoderny* (Sign, Function, and Value. Aesthetics and Semiotics of the Arts of Jan Mukařovský within the Contemporary Critical Currents. Notes From the Postmodern Underground). Prague: Paseka, 2004.

Voloshinov, Valentin. "The Word and its Social Function." *Bakhtin School Papers*. Ed. Ann Shukman. Oxford: RTP Publications, 1983. 139-52. Trans. of "Slovo i jego social'naja funkcija". *Literaturnaja ucheba* 5 (1930).

Zich, Otakar. *Estetika dramatického umění: teoretická dramaturgie*. 1931. Prague: Melantrich. Würzburg: Jal-Reprint, 1977.

Avatars of a Research Tradition: From Slavic Structuralism to Anglo-American Poetics and Aesthetics

Uri Margolin
University of Alberta, Edmonton

Some fifteen years ago I had the privilege of participating in a symposium entitled "Fiction Updated" held at the University of Toronto on the occasion of Lubomír Doležel's retirement. At that time I took my cue from Lubomír's work on fictional worlds' semantics and spoke of characters and their versions across story worlds. Today, on another happy occasion, celebrating another milestone in Lubomír's career, I thought that, following the theme of the conference, I should take my inspiration and point of departure alike from Doležel's other major line of research, that of metatheory and history of poetics. In *Occidental Poetics* (1990), Lubomír sets out to "reconstruct the growth of theoretical knowledge in poetics" (viii) by tracing in it one or more research traditions. He goes on to say that logical and epistemological continuity in poetics involve not the re-assertion of the same claims but rather the constant re-examination of its major claims, and that in the course of a research tradition the issues of poetics appear as successive refinements, versions or variations on a limited number of fundamental themata which are being defined and redefined, enriched and reformulated (5).

My aim today is to define and relate to each other two major historical phases of one such tradition, namely, Russian Formalism and the Prague School on the one hand and Anglo-American poetics and analytic aesthetics from the 1970s onwards on the other. Three shared fundamental themata or notions and their transformations will form the focus of our discussion: the work of verbal art, literature or literariness, and the poetic cum aesthetic function. From the point of view of global disciplinary organization, the near identification of the three notions in early Formalism and their resultant interchangeable discussion has evolved in the transition from one phase to the other into three distinct though interrelated sets of concepts and corresponding lines of enquiry.

As for each of them individually, the textual specificity of the *work of verbal art,* initially defined in terms of device and perceptibility and later on as foregrounding, has become the object of a whole new area of enquiry, that of cognitive poetics or stylistics, systematically correlating textual structures with receptional effects.

The assumption of early Formalism that there is a constant, textually inherent quality called *literariness* and that it and it alone should be the object of literary theory was definitely rejected by 1924 by Tynyanov and Eikhenbaum, both of whom advocated instead a view of literature as a historically shifting cultural series whose boundaries at each point in time are determined by participants in the literary system, understood as a social action system. After many trials and errors, American aesthetics arrived at the same conclusion with respect to the notion of art in general, and then went on to develop a whole family of theories of art as an institution, all of them viewing art as essentially historical, situative, contextual and relational, rather than object based. A similar approach with respect to literature specifically has been developed by Peter Lamarque and Stein Haugom Olsen (See Lamarque and Olsen).

Poetic function began with Jakobson's 1921 notion of poetry as a message with orientation on the expression side (*ustanovka na vyrazhenie*), revised by him a generation later in 1958 as the poetic function, and defined as set toward the message as such or focus on the message for its own sake. The Prague school subsumed the poetic function under the broader category of the aesthetic one, with obvious Kantian foundation. But both poetic and aesthetic function remained abstractions in need of *operationalisation* and empirical content. This has been done since the early 1970s in the study of literature as cultural practice (Culler, Lamarque and Olsen), focusing on the codified, yet historically variable norms of literary processing handed down in the educational system and including rules of sense making, evaluation, and the appropriate cultural uses associated with the handling or treating of a text as literature.

Concerning disciplinary scope and depth, one notices that what started as a uniquely literary enquiry has by now acquired a broader and deeper foundation in terms of general textual, institutional and aesthetic theories respectively. What started as presumably inherent to the text in isolation (be it device, foregrounding, literariness or poetic function) is now considered instead as essentially related to individual participants in the literary system or to communities of such participants. It is the text-context crux which is by now the defining focus of all three lines of enquiry. In fact, the redefinition and transformation of this research tradition enables us to define its two poles as the formal-structural and the cognitive-cultural respectively.

Turning our attention to the historical line of development, it is interesting to note that, with respect to all three themata, a significant portion of the Anglo-American work has been carried out independently of, or with at most nodding second-hand acquaintance with the

Slavic work. Nevertheless, its claims definitely constitute a further elaboration, transformation, and often improvement of the general assumptions first formulated by the Formalist and structuralist schools. Such notional continuity and *approfondissment* amidst historical-factual discontinuity may suggest the existence of some inner logic in the elaboration of problem clusters. But what it reveals beyond any doubt in retrospect is the existence of a major research tradition unified in terms of its "set of general assumptions about the entities and processes in its domain of study and [even more so] the approaches and methods to be used for investigating the problems and constructing theories in this domain"((Doležel: 1). Now this definition of a research tradition stems from Larry Lauden's 1977 study *Progress and its Problems* and is adopted by Doležel in his book. The obvious theoretical progress made within this research tradition or paradigm over the last several generations suggests a few additional observations as regards the dynamics of literary theorizing:

— Literary theory is not, or at least not entirely, a chaos of ever changing incommensurable approaches or orientations.
— Theorising in this area need not and probably should not start *ab ovo leda*, clearing the slate from all previous work on a given topic on the grounds that it is supposedly antiquated, irrelevant, biased etc. Rather, it can be, and often is, cumulative in nature.
— Literary theorizing, at least in part, can claim the status of rational enquiry, putting forth claims that can be learned and taught (*Lern- und lehrbar*) and that are subject to standard rules of reasoning and argumentation. It can formulate sets of interrelated general claims which often possess significant empirical content, being open to historical or experimental examination or testing respectively.

Having put all my general cards on the table, I should now heed the Quaker saying that God, or at least scholarly enquiry, is in the details, and provide some further specifications of each thema, all within the limited time frame available.

Work of Verbal Art

Underlying Shklovsky's seminal essay "Art as Device" (1917) are several textual and psychological assumptions. Thus, any message is supposed to have an expression and a content side, and the perception of either can be automatic or controlled, hence requiring mental effort, attention, conscious awareness, and the ability to modify (reconfigure) habitual modes of perception. A message is perceptible only if it is received in a non–automatic manner, and a non-automatic manner of reception, hence perceptibility (*oshchutimost'*) of a message is achieved on the expression side by foregrounding aspects of the verbal medium, thus making them prominent, and possibly central or dominant, in any act of text reception. In the Formalist tradition, a whole array of such prominence enhancing textual patterns has been described and explored. In short verse texts this is accomplished by imposing on the text a whole grid of parallelisms and equivalences on all linguistic levels, a grid which is not required from any communicative-informational perspective. In longer prose texts an architectonic or compositional design of some kind is imposed on the incidents of the text: positive and negative parallelism, staircase, gradation, triple construction, embedding, etc. Maximum perceptibility of the expression side is achieved in short verse in non-sense poetry, and in prose narrative if such patterns are devoid of thematic motivation and are expressly pointed out as a formal game (*bez'sjuzhetnyi roman*, laying bare the device). The other major way of foregrounding textual elements is that of deviation from a previously established inner textual regularity or norm, be it by breaking a metrical regularity, shifting the level of style or introducing a radically different semantic element. This aspect was picked up in the early 1960s by Michael Riffaterre in a series of articles in which he defines as stylistic device any inner textual unpredictable deviation or break which makes the novel element highly prominent and hence perceptible.

On the content level, de-automatisation of content perception (= cognitive de-automatisation) is achieved if an author refuses to call things by their habitual name, refuses to recognize them. In current terms, this is done by authors withholding the standard category name or label known to the reader for an object or action, thereby preventing the automatic activation of the appropriate schema or script stored in long-term memory. Instead, one is supplied with a correct detailed literal description without the overall semantic category, and comprehension is delayed or stymied. This kind of semantic riddling is what de-familiarisation is all about.

The foregrounded elements are considered to be inherently perceivable, and identifiable without reference to any external context. "Work of verbal art", or better, artistry, as employed in this context, functions as a scholarly descriptive, quasi-theoretical term used to designate texts in which the predominance of patterns of formal or semantic foregrounding can be identified supposedly independently and objectively. But both the identification of foregrounded elements and the description of their receptional effects as offered by the Formalists lacked any empirical basis, and were ultimately claims made by the scholars on the basis of their own linguistic and literary intuitions. In addition, there were no theories of textual processing available in the 1920s, and Shklovsky for example had to rely on vague speculations about reading effort and energy involved in text processing. And finally there was the implicit bi-conditional or equation of work of verbal art and work of literature. What was needed was hence (1) the development of experimental methods to test on groups of readers scholarly hypotheses concerning what is perceived as prominent or deviant in a given text; (2) The formulation of cognitive-affective theories regarding the operations involved in text processing on various levels (sound to sense) and sizes (micro and macro patterns); (3) the dissociation of work of verbal art and work of literature, since texts with little linguistic foregrounding are sometimes considered literature, while others with a lot of it, such as advertising, are not.

Current cognitive stylistics or poetics as practiced at Lancaster University (Stockwell, Gavin, Semino), has been developed precisely to address these desiderata. While many of the texts it analyses are taken from what is considered literature in our time and culture, the textual patterns and effects under study are not considered as either necessary or sufficient conditions for making the text in which they occur literary. Secondly, cognitive poetics places itself at the interface between linguistics, literary studies and cognitive science. According to Elena Semino, one of its leading practitioners, "it combines the kind of explicit, rigorous and detailed linguistic analysis of the stylistic tradition with a systematic and theoretically informed consideration of the cognitive structures and processes that underlie the production and reception of language" (Semino ix). What is new here is not so much the study of linguistic choices and patterns, but rather the way in which linguistic choices are related first to cognitive structures and processes and then to perceived effects. And, as Semino claims, this provides a more systematic and explicit account of the relations between texts on the one hand and responses and interpretations on the other. (Semino ix). Finally, informant testing is systematically employed to test the scholars' specific hypotheses. The study of works of verbal art is thus absorbed into general cognitive text theory.

"**Literature**" is understood already by 1924, at least by Tynyanov and Eikhenbaum, as designating a dynamic cultural series, system or institution. One cannot define in a non-historical, once-and-for-all manner either "genre" or "literature," or what makes a work of verbal art a work of literature. Text elements, texts, and text models are neither inherently literary nor are they not. Rather, being literary is a status conferred upon a text or text model by the literary institution of the time (authors, critics, groups of readers belonging to the literary milieu [*byt*], publishers) for any of a number of heterogeneous reasons. Calling something "literature" simply designates its being accepted into the institution, forming part of it. A text does not change over time its nature as work of verbal art(istry), since this can be objectively defined, but its literary status can and does change on and off over time, depending on the criteria employed and the group in question. In logical terms, "work of verbal art" has a rather clear and permanent intension (even if no minimal conditions), and its extension depends on what texts there are out there which satisfy this definition. "Work of literature" on the other hand is in principle purely extensional: whatever has been designated as such by any group within the institution at any time and for any reason, and its intension would be differently defined for each group, as determined by the rules of use of the term adopted by it.

The literary historian does not consequently decide or define what literature is. Instead, he needs to describe what texts and kinds of texts have been considered literature, by whom in the institution, when and where and on what basis (ideal of literature). One focus of literary historiography is hence the study of the changing definitions, ideas and ideals of literature, as expressed in creative works, essays, manifestos and works of criticism of each group and their relations with actual literary production. As a discipline, literary history is also vitally concerned with the inner dynamics of the literary institution: changes in what is produced within the institution and their causes, the relation of centre and periphery, archaists and innovators, canonization of subliterary forms, the movement over time of the literature non-literature boundary as conceived of by participants, changes in the canon, etc. The struggle of innovative writers to be accepted could be understood as their claim to legitimacy because what they write is crucially pertinent to the literary system as it exists at that moment, even if they want to invert it completely.

"Literature" is thus a term designating a historically changing, socio-cultural institution defined by its practitioners, not by scholars, and whose practitioners as a group also decide what past and present works will be seen-as or regarded-as literature, depending on their criteria of membership. The rich line or lines of enquiry I have just outlined are a cumulative project starting with the Formalists, continued and refined in Prague (Vodička) and reiterated in the work of Juri Lotman and the Moscow-Tartu school as a whole. Cumulatively, they represent one of the major and enduring achievements of the Formalist-Structuralist tradition.

Anglo American poetics and aesthetics spent a lot of time and energy looking for intrinsic textual features which could serve as a-historical necessary and sufficient conditions for a text being considered literature. The failure of all such attempts led initially to Wittgensteinian skepticism about the possibility of any definition of art. This was superseded by a radical reorientation, where one believes once again in this possibility, but where the relevant features are now essentially historical, contextual, situational and relational. Art and literature are now regarded as socio-cultural practices that must be understood within the contexts of their time and place (Davies, *Definitions* 111). Art exists only in a community, which determines what kinds of features are criterial or decisive for something being a work of literature. So far, USA 1967 sounds very much like Prague 1937 (Mukařovský: *Aesthetic Function, Norm and Value as Social Fact*). But now comes the innovative part: in the absence of any intrinsic defining properties, the crucial question becomes *who*, at any given historical situation, decides that certain texts should be certified as works of literature, on what grounds, and according to what rules and procedures. Even more crucial is the question *who* decides, and on what grounds, to admit any new work into the literary series, or accept it into the literary domain. The question *what* is literature is replaced by *when* does a text acquire the status of a work of literature, and what are the grounds, practices, mechanisms and institutions involved in such a decision. The anecdotal, case-oriented study of such issues undertaken by the formalists, especially with regard to 19th century Russian literature, is now complemented and given a foundation in terms of general socio-historical theories.

Arthur Danto has pointed out the major role often played by dominant theories, such as normative poetics, in deciding upon which new works the literary status will be conferred and George Dickie has put forth the institutional theory of art. Put in a nutshell, his argument is that there is in our culture a loosely defined but widely recognized socio-cultural institution, the Artworld, with various defined roles, such as writer, critic, editor etc. Some agents within this system are authorized, because of their socially recognized role in it, to confer the status of 'work of literature' upon a new text. These agents have the authority to confer such status on behalf of the artworld because of their acknowledged knowledge and understanding of literature, its history, dominant theories, the current state of practice, and how literature works. Furthermore: such acts of conferral are not arbitrary, and the agents' decisions are taken on the basis of shared conventions or criteria which are time- and place- bound and need to be reconstructed by literary historians. While Dickie's institutional approach focuses on power relations (role, authority), Lamarque and Olsen focus more on the constitutive rules which establish and maintain literature as a cultural practice. To understand the institution of literature, says Olsen, is to master the constitutive rules that create the possibility of literature and regulate the expectations and performances of artist and audience roles (Olsen 2005: 3).

The irreducibly historical nature of any account of art or literature is further stressed by Jerrold Levinson in his intentional-historical theory of art. To him, arthood is projected upon a work when it is regarded or treated in the same way as some earlier objects that are already taken at that point to be works of art. Something thus becomes an artwork by being related to a given tradition or practice, and art making involves an agent intentionally relating his newly created object to the body of already existing art. The theory thus posits a backward looking act of reference which, by linking present objects to past artworks, makes the former artwork as well (Levinson: 25) "The concrete history of artmaking up to a given time is ineliminably implicated in any artmaking undertaking at that time" (28). This backward looking aspect has, curiously enough, been anticipated by Eikhenbaum who, in "Literatura i pisatel'" (*Moi Vremennik* : 63) says: "Every work of literature has not only its fate, but also its past." Stephen Davies, in his discussion of definitions of art, argues in the same vein that "What makes something an artwork is that a historically appropriate reflexive relation, such as reference, continuation, amplification or rejection, holds between it and prior works created in the same artworld. In a phrase, art (now) is determined through its relation to art (past)." (Davies 2001:175).

The historical theory has been given its most explicit and convincing formulation by Noel Carroll (Carroll 1999), who says: "what is crucial is the descent or genetic link of a new work" (Carroll 1999: 257). No matter how different, disruptive etc a new work is, it can legitimately raise the claim to be considered a work of literature if it can be shown to be pertinent or significantly related to the existing (current) artworld context or situation, to constitute an intelligible outcome of or response to it. Says Carroll: "to justify a new work's claim to the status of work of art its proponents need to provide a historical narrative of how it came to be produced as an intelligible response to an antecedently acknowledged art-historical situation" (253). This situation may include current artistic practices but also issues, problems, aims, theories and ideals of art, and the relevant response may consist of continuation and variation, but also of disagreement, repudiation and radical break. Carroll is right in remarking that historical narrative as procedure for identifying works of art can well incorporate the mutations of the avant-garde into the continuous evolution of art, since the avant-garde is of course an extreme reaction to and rejection of the current situation. The view that avant-garde works, no matter how disruptive and different from their immediate predecessors, have a strong claim to belong to the same literary or artistic system since they are created deliberately as a reaction to its existing situation was, of course, central to the Russian Formalists' understanding and defence of the radical innovators of their own time, such as Futurism and *zaumnyi jazyk* [transrational language].

Aesthetic function

Implicit in Jakobson's work is the assumption that the structure and make up of a text dictate what communicative function will be dominant in its reception, and that certain text patterns will dictate that the aesthetic or poetic function be dominant in the reception of the corresponding text. This view, implying textual isolationism and determinism, has by now been replaced by the notion of the work of literature as encompassing text, reader and the historical cultural situation. In each generation there are accordingly literary institutional conventions stipulating that, *ceteris paribus*, if a text possesses certain structures it should be received adopting the aesthetic attitude. But the specific content of this form-function correlation is historically variable (Lotman). Moreover, co-textual, para-textual and contextual factors, in this order, may on particular occasions invalidate a current convention or conversely make the reader adopt the aesthetic attitude towards a text devoid of the stipulated structures (Stanley Fish's famous example of random lines of text on the blackboard in the context of a literature class).

But what does it mean specifically to have the aesthetic function or attitude as dominant in the reception of a text, beyond the general philosophical distinction between intrinsic value and purposefulness vs. instrumental ones? Here too much important expansion and improvement has been achieved in the last 30-40 years. One aspect suggested would be treating the text as display text, framed and decontextualised in terms of person, tense, and deictics. One could further claim that once a text is treated as display text it can model or put on display the working of all other communicative functions or of the communicative process itself, a line of thought begun by Mukařovský in the 1930s and followed independently by Mary-Louise Pratt in the1970s. Or it may mean focusing one's attention during textual reception on the text's formal properties, what Noel Carroll has termed "design appreciation." It may also mean special rules of use, such as setting aside questions of factual truth and practical usefulness, and allowing or even encouraging a multiplicity of different interpretations (S.J. Schmidt's rules of literariness). But the major significance of having the aesthetic function dominate one's reception of a text would be to adopt and apply to it a whole series of special rules of interpretation and evaluation developed in the literary institution and acquired in the process of literary education. Jonathan Culler has suggested several such rules in *Structuralist Poetics* (1975). For example, make semantic capital out of formal features and patterns, treat individual statements as having universal or symbolic significance, etc. To have internalized these rules and to be able to use them correctly means to possess literary competence and be a full fledged participant in the literary action system. But we must remember that these rules themselves are time and place bound, and that they are seldom formulated in an explicit and systematic manner. Rather, in the educational process they are acquired through example and repeated practice, and in critical practice they are presupposed. It is hence the task of the literary historian to extract them from the practice in any period of leading critics and other authority figures in the literary institution, and to make them explicit. Much more could be said on this subject, especially with regard to the particular hierarchy of criteria of value employed in acts of literary evaluation, but *ars longa vita brevis*, and it is time to stop.

Works Cited

Carroll, Noel. *Philosophy of Art*. London: Routledge, 1999.
Culler, Jonathan. *Structuralist Poetics*. Ithaca: Cornell UP, 1975.
Davies, Stephen. *Definitions of Art*. Ithaca: Cornell UP, 1991.
___. "Definitions of Art." Gaut and McIver López 169-180.
Gaut, Berys and Dominic McIver López, eds. *Routledge Companion to Aesthetics*. London: Routledge, 2001.
Dolezel, Lubomir. *Occidental Poetics*. Lincoln: U of Nebraska P, 1990.
Eikhenbaum, Boris. *Moi Vremennik*. Leningrad: izdatelstvo pisatelei, 1929.
Lamarque, Peter. "Literature." Gaut and McIver López 449–461.
___. and Stein Haugom Olsen. *Truth, Fiction and Literature: A Philosophical Perspective*. Oxford: Clarendon P, 1994.
Mukařovský, Jan. *Aesthetic Function, Norm and Value as Social Facts*. Trans. Mark E. Suino. Ann Arbor: U of Michigan, 1970.
Levinson Jerrold. *Contemplating Art*. Oxford: Clarendon P, 2006.
Olsen, Stein Haugom and Andars Petterssson, eds. *From Text to Literature*. Palgrave Macmillan: New York, 2005.
Semino, Elena, ed. *Cognitive Stylistics*. Amsterdam: John Benjamins, 2002.
Shklovski, Victor. "Art as Device." *Russian Formalist Criticism*. Eds. Lee T. Lemon and Marion J. Reis. Lincoln: University of Nebraska P, 1965. 3-24.

The Semantic Gesture – An Invitation to a Journey from the Poetics to the Aesthetics of a Literary Work

Tomáš Kubíček
Czech Academy of Sciences

Introduction

If we speak of structuralism at the present time, we already know that there does not exist a single structuralism—and now I do not mean only those "national versions" of structuralist schools. Within these locally determined structuralisms, there exists a whole range of other structuralist currents that differ not only in detail, but often also in their perspective on key methodological or theoretical questions. From my point of view, the view of "our," that is to say, Prague structuralism, this only testifies to the 'unpetrifiable' capacity of structuralist thinking, its ability to further develop a productive theory; and at the same time the absorption in its very self, in its past success. In theory, and it seems to me, all the more in structural theory, all the past victories should only be a reason for continued noetic scepticism.

In the concept of the Prague school, structuralism in literary science is an index of proposals for an understanding of what a work of art is and how a literary text works. It is an index that needs to be constantly tried and revised. I say an index, not a system. The basic theoretical postulate of the Prague structuralists, that is a conviction as to internal dynamics of a literary work, is reflected also in their reluctance to closing their thinking through the trap of 'systems.' It is as if an apprehension were manifested here that in such cases further theoretical work would be aimed primarily towards the servicing of the system, towards its locking and fixation. The variable reality of the work, its basic value consisting in a tension of the ever-renewed entering into the world, making claims upon the world, and therefore in its communication with the world, would recede to the background if this path were taken. If I say this, I do not mean to suggest that Prague structuralism represents an unsystematic type of thinking. That is contradicted by another postulate of Mukařovský and his followers, that is, the mereological principle, within the scope of which the relation is examined of the whole and its parts and the place of the parts in the whole, their interaction (both constructive and destructive) in the overall semantic construction. However, a closed system immuring itself stands against the conviction of Prague structuralists about the basic dynamic quality of a literary work incumbent in the pulsating interaction of the elements of its construction. The reason is obvious: Mukařovský, Vodička, Červenka, Sus, Jankovič, Doležel and others are not concerned with a mere list and description of elements from which the whole is composed and the mutual relations among these elements, but also with the question of their function, the principles of their effect and the problem of their value—and that is the explosive area of the theory, which will not allow the Prague Structuralists to definitely anchor their thought in the form of a diagrammatising system of semantic construction.

With all the differences, this basic principle of the Prague structuralist school is a constant. Its consequence, among others, is the fact that Czech Structuralism is spoken of as a theory of the unique—because the proposals of its practitioners concentrate much more on the varying reality of a single work and do not tend to create abstract systemic proposals. But even if something like that happens—such as in the case of Doležel's proposal of narrative modes—the author of such a proposal accentuates his clear conviction as to the necessity of the modification of any system to the needs of a unique work (which in fact Doležel always practically executes in the second part of his *Narrative Modes*, in which he applies his system and finalises it in the environment of unique texts of fiction).

Therefore if I have denoted the functional approach and mereological principle as a pivot around which the whole thinking of the Prague Structuralists turns, I am approximating the central concept of the Prague school which appears in Jan Mukařovský's work for the first time in his 1938 "Genetika smyslu v Máchově poezii" [Genesis of the Meaning of Mácha's Work], and which is a permanent part of the theoretical proposals arising from the environment of Prague Structuralism, but also from the environment which made the structuralism of the Prague School the subject or resource of its study.[1] This is the concept of semantic gesture, which Mukařovský in the aforementioned study treats as a conjoint denominator, upon which all the components of the work are merged. While doing this, he is not primarily involved with the investigation of the content, but after the reconstruction of that contentually unspecified (and in this sense—if you want—formal) gesture, with which the poet was selecting and consolidating the elements of his work." It is the question of "unity of a dynamic building principle, which is exercised in the ever so little sec-

---

[1] Here I mean for example the work of Herta Schmid, Wolf Schmid, Peter Burg, Miloš Sedmidubský and others.

tion of the work, and depends on the integral and unifying systemization of the elements ("Genetika" 305).

There is not enough room here to dedicate ourselves in detail to the development of the concept of semantic gesture in Mukařovský and his followers, although to those concerned with the study of a history of the semantic gesture I can promise a driving and truly adventurous journey leading not only through the inextricable pathways of theory, but also through the tempests of historical events and hurricanes of revolutions. A journey in the course of which the semantic gesture turns into a politicum, and only by the way does it causes a very change in paradigm of Czech Structuralist theory.

1. The first phase of constitution of the concept of the semantic gesture and its journey from author to reader

As was evident from the quotation above, in the first treatment of the concept of semantic gesture, Mukařovský relies upon the author's intention, with which he firmly binds it, and the reader's task then is to reconstruct that contentually unspecified gesture "through which the poet was choosing and uniting the element of his work" ("Genetika" 305). Already in the first proposal of the definition, there are three basic dimensions present—three qualities, which will play a key role in the further development of the semantic gesture concept, and in the further development of the Czech structuralism as such: I mean the concepts of text, originator and perceiver. It will be necessary to found a relation among them which will help the understanding of their cooperating role while constituting the meaning. The question of a semantic source is solved in favour of the text at the beginning of Mukařovský's text, and its sense is the result of the author's intention which dynamises and unifies all textual elements. Therefore to grasp the sense it is necessary to identify this intention embedded in the work. But it also means that the reader becomes a rather passive decipherer of the code. However, this escalated initial viewpoint is significantly weakened already by the conclusion of Mukařovský's ample study, which attempted to discern the principles of the semantic construction of a poetic piece by the prominent Czech Romantic poet Karel Hynek Mácha. After having examined the material, Mukařovský discovers the enormous potentiality of the textual element, which he examines (i.e. the motive) and which enters complex contextual relations,[2] in which it constantly modifies its meaning, and this activity

---

[2] And that is a very important observation which further turns the attention of Mukařovský and the Czech Structuralists toward the role and nature of context as a significance-creating element.

(potentiality of the semantic action) has the result

> that—similar to Impressionist art that relied on the co-operation of the spectator's eye —Mácha's poetry relies on the spiritual life of the reader whose task is to realize the connection between the motifs only hinted at in the work. [. . .] The polysemy of the relations among the individual semantic units allows every generation to put the sense into Mácha's work, which it needs itself; every epoch reforms again, and at its own responsibility, the poet's appearance in its own image, characterising thus both the poet and itself. ("Genetika" 375)

Purposely, I emphasize an evident shift, in consequence of which the initial viewpoint of the textual intention moves from the author (poet) toward the reader. The same emphasis must be used while calling attention to the meaning of the words "reforms again" and "at its own responsibility." These are important attributes – within the reach of their activity, a semantic gesture of a work of art is born, and they approximate it (i.e. the semantic gesture) to the situation of the perceiver to whom the recognition of the semantic gesture becomes a creative deed of "responsible" collaboration.

We can see what an unstable concept the semantic gesture is even within the scope of Mukařovský's single study. Yet the unstableness of its definition is one of its characteristic features. Mukařovský keeps returning to the semantic gesture to clothe it again with content. However, his definitions are not linked, as we would wish to, for the sake of lucidity, and therefore there is no gradual perfection and deepening in the place where the previous attempt finished. Mukařovský approaches the semantic gesture from different sides, and always slightly shifts its meaning. This has led to many misunderstandings in later interpretations. Briefly, I will try to illuminate the reasons. The end of the 1930s, when the study "Genesis of the Meaning of Mácha's Work" originated, was an exceptionally important period for Czech Structuralism. This is because of a change of its paradigm. The concept of semantic gesture may be perceived not only as a consequence of this metamorphosis, but also as its possible cause. The attention of Mukařovský and his companions shifts from the poetics to the aesthetics of the poet's work. A need intensifies to understand the work as part of an act of communication among the originator, perceiver and a broadly founded context. There occurs a conceptual determination of the work as a process of signification— i.e. not only as organization, but as a complex system of interactive relations. The work as an active communication unit (with the nature of aesthetic action) appeals to meaning which is determined by broadly determined context. It is a system of relations producing meaning which only surpass the borderlines of the inner context of the literary text—i.e. of relations given by the textual organization of elements, their position in the text of the work. The work, as a product, process and action unifying the sense, calls for the perceiver's creative collaboration:

> A work of art is [nevertheless] a highly complex sign: each of its components and each of its parts is a carrier of partial meaning. These partial meanings compose the general sense of the work. And only then, when the general sense of work is fixed, does the work of art become testimony to a relation of the originator to the reality and an appeal to the perceiver to adopt his/her own attitude towards the reality and relation, cognitive, emotional and volitional at the same time. ("O strukturalismu" 30)

However, not to have the identity of the work disolved in a boundless number of concretisations, it is necessary to found it against something. The semantic gesture seems to be a welcome tool for this "logistic" operation. But it is necessary to configure it with the text, and suddenly it appears that this logistic operation will not be simple at all.

It will be necessary to re-define the semiotic process and its participants. A thorough inspection will be given to the concept of unifying semantic action—i.e. semantic gesture, but also the notions with which the Czech Structuralists try to name the participant of the process of meaning construction, therefore these are not only the notions of text and work, but mainly the notions of subject, creator (poet), perceiver and individuum. Their task is to establish their relation toward the literary work and the text, and their share in the production of sense. The conception of the semantic gesture and its functioning brings Mukařovský to the area in which the literary work professes the world in a certain manner and demands the allocation of sense. The mater of textual intention therefore becomes the most important question. But it is necessary to treat it so as not to close the meaning, but on the contrary—to preserve the dynamic productive tension of the textual structure.

With its decision to inspect the semantic gesture, i.e. the conditions under which meaning is constituted, Czech Structuralism leaves the theoretical "zone of certainty," as characterised by Adorno (464), and enters an uneasy zone of the action of sense. One of the consequences will also be the aforementioned inclination toward the theory of the unique, and misgivings with regard to unduly generalising systems or rather mistrust of them.

2. Jankovič's modification and specification of the semantic gesture

If there was one individual among the Czech Structuralists to really do a great deal for the conception of the semantic gesture, then it was

Milan Jankovič. In his studies that have been published intermittently (due to the totalitarian ban on the publication of his books) since the end of the 60s till the present day, he has constantly returned to the concept of semantic gesture, further circumscribing it.[3] Jankovič has managed to consolidate the semantically unstable and contentually insecure determination provided by Mukařovský. At the same time he kept the basic qualities already allocated by Mukařovský, only highlighting or finalising them. Mainly, there remained the legitimacy of the semantic gesture as a result of the general semantic movement of the work in an interaction between intentionality and unintentionality. For Jankovič, who defends the figurativeness of the name, the gesture is a denotative movement (116) that we are supposed to follow – therefore also the meaning is only an indicated movement inviting to be followed. He finds a fundamental discovery, which was consequent to the treating of the concept of semantic gesture, in an initiative nature (his emphasis) of elements carrying meaning, accentuation of the process of formation and the arising of sense (his emphasis):

> In my opinion, there was – certainly on the axis of the previous tradition, the beginning of which I see in Kant—an essentially specified aesthetic structure as such, and especially its possibilities in the artistic creation. And I assume that the concept of the semantic gesture contributed significantly to this general topic. It avoided the straits of the isolated and static investigation of the aesthetic "circumstances" (forms in the Herbartean sense), from which hardly any path leads to the concrete activity of the work. It related the fact of formative sentiment radically toward semantic and value-based movement. Firstly, it suggested that an intention heading toward values finds its language in art directly in expressive forms and in their reformation. (119)

If we speak of Jankovič's contribution to the concept of the semantic gesture, it is necessary to exactly emphasize the approximation of the semantic gesture to the value of its value attachment and especially the imperative accentuation of an anthropological foundation of sense. To recognise the semantic gesture it is therefore necessary to "appreciate the sense-creating impulses, those intentions towards values, in expressions even more elementary than the value of the formative unification represented by Mukařovský's concept of the semantic gesture" (Jankovič 119). A work concerns us in a certain way —it is the plot on which its pulsating structure works. The concept of the semantic gesture approximates the work to reality, but the semantic action and sense of the work are not its (mirror) image, but a source

---

[3] Parts of these circumscriptions are also polemic contributions to the studies by Herta Schmid or Wolf Schmid.

of energy. Jankovič then mainly emphasizes the processionality of the semantic gesture, the product of which is the sense that is also "an output of the work, and is not a mere acknowledgement of validity to the work from outside" (120). This results in a methodological suggestion:

> An internal examination of the work, if it wants to be consequent, does not end with an establishment of a methodical principle of construction. A deeper, sense-searching reflexion is founded on its observation. It always singles out a seizable sense of the work again from the intimate tension of the "what" and "how." Only in this way does a work of art have a right to its own life, because what the work may mean to us is revealed more in its progress than in its completion. (121)

And eventually, it is Jankovič who stresses the relation between the aesthetic function and the semantic gesture. In his representation, the semantic gesture becomes a "factual realisation of an aesthetic function in the semantic construction of a work of art. Nevertheless, it represents the least definite component in it, i.e. exactly the "meaning-attitude," "meaning-perspective," simply an appeal or direction for the perceiver to adopt a similarly creative attitude to reality as the creator" (132).[4] For Jankovič, the work is therefore an impulse for an intersubjective establishment of sense; the subject of the work—on which a multiple intention participates, is an intersubjective activity, and from that issues also the value foundation of the semantic gesture.

Jankovič opened the semantic gesture to the reader's situation to a maximum extent: The text retains its controlling authority, and as a producer collaborates in the sense, in which an important role is played not only by the capacity of the reader to recognise the textual meanings, but also his/her location in the world. Although the dominant role of the text is vindicated in Jankovič's work on the determination of the semantic gesture, it seems to me that we find ourselves too close to the conception that will accentuate an active role (domination) for the reader over textual meaning. Is it therefore possible to deal with the semantic gesture without the necessity of entering an uncertain and unstable domain of the reader? Is it possible to bind it to the text even more closely?

This is the moment for Doležel's important correction. For Doležel, Mukařovský's conception of the semantic gesture is a proof of the fact

---

[4]Therefore in connection with sense, Jankovič amplifies the inner circle and the outer circles. In the inner circle of the work, there occurs the production of the variably updated work's sense, and here we are a significant, percipient individual. In the inner circle (original intention toward values expressed through the expressive capacity of paradigms) there is a significance-creating work.

that Mukařovský's semiotic poetics leaves no doubt as to who is responsible for the structure and meaning of the literary "message" (*Occidental* 168). How are we to understand this statement from *Occidental Poetics*? Especially if we consider it against the background of the aforementioned reflections. We may be aided by Doležel's treatment of the principle of functioning of the intentional function and the foundation of intentional meaning—i.e. the concept with which he reinforces the textual identity of a work based on what he calls 'texture.' Also the semantic gesture is perceived by Doležel as an intentional phenomenon, and as such

> ...it is fully determined by its texture, it is affected by any textural change; It cannot be paraphrased, it slips through the net of interpretations, it is lost in retelling. Paraphrases or interpretations destroy the intentional meaning by destroying the original texture [. . .]; the intentional meaning of the text cannot be convented otherwise than by repeating that text. (*Heterocosmica* 143-144).

Does there exist an issue from this "narrow lane" in which the intentional meaning, the semantic gesture, logically finds itself outside the area demarcated by Jankovič—i.e. outside the situation of the reader (who could not participate in it in a creative way, which would mean a weakening of the anthrolopological principle of the identity of the literary work that was emphasised already by Mukařovský and upon which Jankovič insists)? Doležel suggests that we look for the way to the indirect study of intentions through the observable, analysis-accessible structuring of texture. This is the central motive of his work on the projection of a theory of fictitious worlds—i.e. the projection of textural intention into the fictional world of the work. He also concentrates on the finding of the initial conditions for the origin of sense. These are more important to him than the very sense (individualisation of meaning), although it is exactly these that refer to (indicate) the "realm of sense."

Doležel's and Jankovič's treatment of the semantic gesture are in a seeming antagonism. In Jankovič, the reader participates in the semantic gesture, and it becomes open to an individual sense. Doležel accentuates more evidently the objectivity of the literary work that bounds the sense of unique interpretation, and the semantic gesture as such as a datum of the texture and resists the concept of creative collaboration. However, the antagonism is only illusive and is washed away by the final allegation from the chapter of Heterocosmica dedicated to the intentional function:

> Fictional macrosemantics observes the reader's reconstruction and doing so, gradually apply three analytic approaches: it apprehends

> the regularities of texture; from these regularities it derives the intentional structuring (and therefore the semantic gesture, if we want) of the fictional world; by applying an extensional metalanguage (e.g. paraphrase) it reconstructs the extensional world structuring. The structure of the world is not a set of separated levels, but a set of transformations converting one level into another. (148)

The reader's reconstruction is therefore a grasping of the semantic gesture by its paraphrase, and due to that it also means individualisation. Both concepts, those of Jankovič and of Doležel, meet, even though Jankovič's is oriented rather towards the aesthetic nature of the act of literary semiosis, connecting the semantic gesture with the constitution of an aesthetic function, which is clearly perceived as a specific human attitude, founded and invited by the aesthetic function. Doležel then concentrates his attention more on the questions of the poetics of text, but he is also aware of the aesthetic "overrun." The mutual encounter of both conceptions is underscored also by the global establishment of the dynamic nature of the structure, and therefore of the durability of the semantic action. However, in Jankovič's concept, as it seems to me, an important role is played by discontinuance of this permanence—the nature of understanding, In other words: individualization of sense.

But it is clear enough to both of them that a theory dealing with a process of literary signification should not study the mental state of every receiver, but only "the conditions for an induction of this state, which are given in the same way in the structure of the work for all the perceiving individuals [and] are objectively detectable" (Mukařovský 1939, 343). And what yet needs to be accentuated—both Jankovič and Doležel reflect, in relation with the semantic gesture, mainly regarding the unique text—unique texture—because generalising of the conception of the semantic gesture could probably lead to unwanted simplification and to its depletion.

3. The actual significance of the semantic gesture

The last question of my paper reads: How can the semantic gesture serve us today? It provides a basis for research which, in attempt at formulating a reply to the question of the semantic construction of a work and its identity, abandon text-oriented theory and deal with questions of interaction between the originator, the text and the perceiver, and it reinforces, or allows us to keep, the central position of the text in the communication model. That means the position in which it is exactly the literary text as an open aggregate of potential meanings that refers to its originator, to its context as well as to its perceiver—i.e. to its inalienating sense.

The development of the concept of the semantic gesture already denotes the principles of constitution of meaning, which must be taken into consideration. This way the semantic gesture approximates the work to the situation of the reader and points at the principles of the happening of sense—the unique and still not definite.

Doležel's closure of the semantic gesture with texture and his grasp of it as an intentional function retains the potentionality of the semantic action. It also shows that meaning is part of paraphrase, but that it is precedent to it. The antagonism between the view of Doležel, who insists upon the textual determination of the semantic gesture, and that of Jankovič, who introduces also the reader's intention into the play (although he does not make it absolute) is beneficial because it opens up the transitional area in which the identity of meaning must be exercised and the constitution of the work as an aesthetic object must be observed.

The semantic gesture conception this way de facto invites an interdisciplinary analysis of principles, as a result of which the literary work retains its actuality; or in other words: under the functioning of which the literary work designates not only its meaning, but also its literary nature.

The conception of the semantic gesture shows that it is exactly the internal potentionality of the literary structure of the work as an aesthetic object, which should make us wary of conceptions that only want to study the poetics of the text and look away from its aesthetics, i.e. from the questions of the effect and value of its elements and the work as a whole—that is, from its unique situation in the world – therefore we must perceive the semantic gesture as a result of a pragmatic situation.[5]

Because the concept of the semantic gesture is one of macro-structural semantics, it directs our attention towards macro-structural processes, e.g. to the question of literary development. Then, through

---

[5] In 2003 the book *What is Narratology?* was published in Hamburg, in Naratologia edition, and through the key question of the theory of narration, which was investigated by prominent contemporary narratologists, a conviction kept returning as a leitmotiv that it is necessary to head from the semiotic research toward a broader semantic research, in which an important role is played also by pragmatics. It is evident that the Prague Structuralists arrived at a similar recognition – for them the semantic gesture is a result of a pragmatic situation. The journey that was necessary to be undertaken, and the important milestones, which always meant amplification of the concept of the work by further aspects (be it the perceiver, the context, the matter of value and conception of the work as a coexistence of the object and the sign), which were necessary to be invited to the symposium on the nature can provide important support to the contemporary research of the nature of narrative action.

its mediation, it is possible, for example, to study metamorphoses in successive stages of reception. So there emerges also the question of standards, their validity, contravention and development. In an equal manner, the question of the relation of the aesthetic function to other functions gains significance. In this sense, Jakobson's appeal is renewed and creatively shifted, for literature to be examined within the scope of the discourse that it produces—i.e. within the scope of its literary nature. At the same time, the semantic gesture leads, or has the capacity to lead, the literary nature from a narrow and isolationist immanentism.

The semantic gesture turns our attention toward the very action of the formation of meaning, to the principles of its construction (and re-construction); it shows that meanings do not lie here at hand, ready to use, but that they must be constructed (re-constructed) by a creative mind. Therefore they are not only a matter of poetics and within the reach of their conceptual tools, but they are also a concern of aesthetics, a relation of the work to reality and its effect. At the same time, the semantic gesture proposed by the Czech Structuralists makes it impossible to understand the relation between an intention and a effect as a consequence of simple irreversible causality. The conception of the semantic gesture frees the reader on the one hand—it gives him/her the possibility to individualise the semantic construction to its momentary situation—but on the other hand, it deprives him/her of the freedom: it is necessary to view the textual readiness of the individual significance and to recognise it as a part of the structural interplay of elements and levels of the literary work. It is a unique meaning, but not the only one. I assume that the Czech School could not do more by means of the concept of the semantic gesture neither for structuralism as such nor for the identity of the literary work.

Through a journey to the semantic gesture and the efforts of its grasping and therefore grasping the roofing sense of a literary work, I wanted to show that the semantic gesture itself is not important as such, as a final tool and a roofing principle of analysis, but also that the journey which leads through history of the Czech structuralism and in the course of which, in consequence of the effort to define the principles of functioning and formation of the semantic gesture, paradigm of structuralist thinking changes. It is a journey from poetics and the formal description of elements of the literary text to aesthetics of the literary work. The semantic gesture then is a product of an effort to seize and reinforce not only the identity of the literary work, but also its vitality, which rests upon its capacity of being ever open to sense. Understanding the principle of the functioning of the work as an action of sense which, however, finds itself within the reach of the work and therefore is controlled and controllable by it, transforms the literary work from an object of pathological literary-scientific analysis into a form of understanding it as a living tissue. Its individual parts are simple elements no more, but co-active organs which provide its function —and that is wedded with its entrance into the world. The semiotic approach and the pragmatic approach to the work are interconnected in this concept. The result can be a glimpse of its essence as a work of art that is open to creative understanding.

Works cited

Adorno, Theodor. *Estetická teorie*. Praha: Panglos, 1997.
Doležel, Lubomír. *Heterocosmica: Fiction and Possible Worlds*. Baltimore and London: The Johns Hopkins U P, 1998.
———. *Occidental Poetics*. Lincoln and London: U of Nebraska P, 1990.
Jankovič, Milan. *Cesty za smyslem literárního díla*. Praha: Karolinum, 2005.
Mukařovský, Jan. "Genetika smyslu v Máchově poezii." *Studie II*. Brno: Host 2001. 305-375.
———. "O strukturalismu." *Studie I*. Brno: Host 2000. 26-38.

Felix Vodička's Legacy for Literary History

Tetiana Soviak
University of Toronto

Galin Tihanov, in an article provocatively titled "Why did Modern Literary Theory Originate in Central and Eastern Europe? And Why is it Now Dead?" locates literary theory, retroactively, in his own words, within a period of eighty years—from the late 1910s to the early 1990s. He writes that in our historical moment we are "at last positioned to recognize and admit the demise of literary theory as a distinct discipline of scholarship" (61). While the death of literary theory and comparative literature has been proclaimed numerous times, it is worthwhile to look at Tihanov's argument.

In Tihanov's article, the early boundary of literary theory is marked by the call of Russian Formalists for literature as an autonomous field with its own methods of investigation. The field of literary studies was conceived, at that time, as closest to the field linguistics while still separate from it. Tihanov writes that "the Formalists were leaving literature to its own devices, uncontrolled by, and irreducible to, ethics, religion, or politics" (62). The later limit of literary theory is marked as the early 1990s. This limit is set by Tihanov as the time of the rise of philosophy and cultural theory in literary studies or the return to precisely that which Formalists tried to separate from the study of literature: "The abandonment of literary theory in favor of projects in semiotics as a form of cultural theory (Lotman), and in favor of forays into philosophical anthropology (Iser), were symptoms of ill health and of a decline in self-sufficiency" (63). If we leave aside the fact that semiotics is part of literary theory "proper," in Tihanov's sense, Tihanov seems to be arguing that literary theory cannot be compatible with social and cultural theory while retaining its own distinct character because the current dominant "regime of relevance" (77), reduces aesthetic uniqueness to practical usefulness (or social and political function)—that simply means that the role of literature in the social context has changed and, therefore, literary theory is no longer relevant. Tihanov's definition of literary theory is premised on appreciation of literature on the basis of literariness and, therefore, literary theory must concern itself, by definition, with artistic originality.

Is this a fair evaluation of the possibilities of literary theory? It is true that there is currently a wide-spread phenomenon of applying the contemporary cultural studies dominant to literature and, moreover, literature from different cultural and historical contexts. This often results in theorizing that, while novel, is ahistorical and seemingly outside of the field of literary theory. In turn, this leads to laments on the demise of literary theory from the contamination from other disciplines.

It might be useful here to look at a literary theory that would fall within Tihanov's time-frame, namely the theory of literary history articulated by Felix Vodička, a literary historian of the Prague Linguistic Circle. Why this particular theory—there is another cliché to be said here, that is to say that Prague School has been neglected and often misunderstood. This is partially due to the school's insistence on investigations of literary structures within their specific socio-historical context. More importantly, they focused on specific linguistic context. Thus, most of the work done by the members of the circle focused on their native literature. Furthermore, since we are now in the "post-structuralist age", revisiting Prague Structuralism is understandably not a high priority.

There is however a more compelling reason. A look at Prague School Structuralism shows a development of the Formalist ideas (the ideas Tihanov considers to be the beginning of literary theory) with eventual incorporation of social and historical context. The Prague Linguistic Circle elaborated on the Formalist concern for the autonomy of literature, and has attempted to turn aesthetics into science with a systematic and dynamic approach. Vodička is a key scholar in terms of synthesizing the Prague School's ideas on literary history. Long before post-structuralism or New Historicism, he was proposing a model of reception that was aware of historical fluctuations of meaning and interpretation based on different socio-historical contexts. Since, according to Vodička's theory of literary history, there is no single correct aesthetic norm, there can be no single evaluation "and a work can become subject to multiple evaluations, in the process of which the shape of a literary work (its actualization) constantly changes in the mind of the perceiver" ("Response" 205). This leads us back to the death of literary theory. Vodička cautions that "Literary history with its evaluative opinions is often the captive of period views whether they are determined esthetically, ideologically, or socially" ("Concretization" 130). But, we should note here, that this does not spell the end or death of literary history. Vodička provides a model for differentiating the task of literary history (or we could even say theory) from the views of a particular historical moment. This is most evident in his distinction between the tasks of the scholar and the critic. In this he provides a useful way of thinking about literary theory's forays into other fields. But first let us look at how Vodička balances the internal and external approaches to literature and shows a way out of oscillation from one extreme to the other.

Vodička explicitly delimitates his approach from the previous two modes of literary reception which he labels "esthetic dogmatism" and "extreme subjectivism":

> Dogmatism has sought eternal and constant esthetic values in a work or has conceived the history of reception as a path toward a definitive and correct understanding. Extreme subjectivism, on the other hand, has seen in all receptions evidence of individual perception and has only exceptionally attempted to overcome this subjectivism by invoking the period ("Concretization" 108).

At the same time, Vodička was one of the first literary scholars who attempted to unite phenomenology and structuralism (the approach that focuses on the subject-object interaction and the one that focuses on the shared codes of that interaction). His theories are in many ways an elaboration of ideas formulated by his mentor Jan Mukařovský – those of dynamic structure, foregrounding, dominant, aesthetic function, hierarchy of values, norms, and the notion of aesthetic object. Mukařovský's concern with history can be traced to what F. W. Galan calls the semiotic turn—the realization that literature is a verbal sign structure and must be analyzed through the new science of semiotics; this takes the investigation of literature into the realm of the social, cultural, and, by extension, historical. Art is a cultural exchange and therefore cannot be understood or evaluated in any other way than in relationship to the system of values within a community.

The problem with the semiotic turn was that it raised the issue of how to distinguish the external and the internal approaches. That raised doubts about the autonomous nature of literature even though Mukařovský was proposing a method of analysis that is dialectical— movement between the internal (literary) and external (social). Mukařovský's groundwork makes possible a literary history as history of reception and of functions but Vodička played a crucial role through his theory of concretization and his methodological reflections on the function of literature.

Vodička accepts the Prague School Circle's definition of verbal art as a semiotic system and, therefore, that art is used to exchange cultural codes in a cultural community within a specific historical moment. He is aware that the aesthetic function of a work of art changes and that users interpret it according to a code. Therefore, he saw semiotics as the principal conceptual framework.

Vodička outlines three interlinked areas of investigation: history of emergence, history of the work of art as a sign structure, and the history of reception. These areas correspond to the three agents that partake in the literary process: the author (originator), the literary practice (that is the existing literary structure), and the society (recipients). Let us briefly outline each task. The history of emergence studies the production of the text as an interaction between the originator, the literary practice of the time, and the social context. This involves a two-way relationship between the internal (literary structure) and the external (socio-historical) elements that partake in the genesis of the text. The second task deals with the history of the text as a sign structure studied within a historical series. The analysis involves not only a reading of the text but also of the historical moment, both in complex interaction. The literary text here is conceived as embedded in a social context while the immanent development of the literary structure is preserved and remains central. The last task involves the reception of the literary text. This involves reconstruction and understanding of reception both in material terms but also in terms of the social and literary norms that mediate the text's actualization. These norms involve the system of norms and their hierarchy within which the text is read and understood by the recipients. The placement of norms in a hierarchy allows the scholar to consider the changes in norms and of literary structure diachronically. It is important to note that the data for the reconstruction of the norms comes from literary criticism and not from other disciplines although these can also play some role in the interpretation. For this final task, the role of the critic is paramount since he or she concretizes the norms of the period.

These three processes are inter-woven and it is this interweaving that creates the actual historical process. Here Vodička refines the dialectical approach of Mukařovský into a more complex system. He cautions against dialectics that simplify the complexity of the literary structure and evolution. Thus, the chief methodological task in these three interconnected tasks of the scholar is to reunite the work of art with the aesthetic object (the sign and its usage) in the analysis.

Vodička recognizes that the literary scholar is never handed down aesthetic objects but must infer them from a literary-historical context. However, the focus on reconstruction of context does not mean turning away from the literary structure. We must distinguish between subjective concretization and 'epochal attitude'. Vodička writes that "all the possible concretizations of an individual reader cannot become the goal of understanding but only those that reflect the encounters between the structure of the work and the structure of the literary norms of the period" ("Conretization" 118). What this essentially means is the re-creation of literary norms in their historical evolution for the purpose of investigating the relationships between that evolutionary series and the specific evolution of a literary structure

At this point it is crucial to discuss Vodička's distinction between the critic and the scholar. Vodička conceives the two roles in structural and functional terms. The critic concretizes art with explicit reference to the current norms and values. He or she places the work within the current hierarchy of values and the literary system. But Vodička writes that the critic "does more than provide one reader's concretization. His evaluation compels a confrontation between the properties of the work and the period's literary requirements" ("Concretization" 112). As Jurij Striedter puts it, the critic is a mediator between "the individual work and the momentary state of literary and social evolution" (127).

The literary historian uses the critic as a source on a meta-level: 'It is the literary historian's business to observe how the critics of a given period fulfilled [their] function, just as it is his task to judge how poets performed their function with regard to given literary tasks' (Vodička "Response" 201). Critical methods, thus, actualize and evaluate a work from the point of view of a given socio-historical moment, whereas the methods of literary scholarship make it possible to understand and interpret a work in connection with other historical phenomena. It is precisely through this investigation that we can grasp and trace the social importance of the aesthetic function while still being mindful of the work as an aesthetic object. Vodička of course recognizes that sometimes scholarly analysis can result in criticism or that the functions of scholar and critic can overlap but we must not identify the methods of criticism with the methods of scholarly tasks.

All of this is not to say that questions asked by cultural studies, for example, are not valid, but that they serve different goals and answer a different set of problematics. From a methodological point of view, Vodička recognizes that literature may be used as a source for other fields of inquiry as literature tends towards pluri-signification but he does insist that such inquiry "no longer appertains to the field of literary historical research proper and instead becomes a matter of cultural history for which the literary work would be a source" ("Response" 203). Jurij Striedter writes that "Vodička's purpose as a literary historian is to place a work, an author, or a literary period in its particular context and thus comprehend it in its historical singularity—and by this comprehension to reveal its significance for the present and raise the issue of the historical contingency of the assumptions on which our own interpretations rest" (144). This is most evident in Vodička's interpretation of the critic and the scholar in structural terms.

Perhaps the biggest 'problem' with Vodička is that he does not provide a step-by-step methodology aside from the works that carry out his theory in practice. He tells us what is to be done just not how to do it. But that is perhaps his biggest strength in the anti-dogmatic spirit of his intellectual predecessors. Prague Structuralists declared that they were providing neither ideology nor methodology. Rather, structuralism is an epistemological stance. That might be a useful way of characterizing Vodička. The best way of thinking about Vodička is in terms of balance: he attempted to mediate between a literary approach, which is intrinsic and immanent (New Criticism), and an extrinsic one which is essentially an approach that uses literature in the service of other disciplines. His purpose was to place the literary work into its context and to comprehend it in its historical singularity. It is here that we can see that interaction of internal and external approaches are already present in a nuanced way in literary theory.

Vodička's theory of literary history is part of the Prague Structuralist project which elaborated on the Formalist ideas and expanded them to include social context and historical concerns. Thus the interaction of the literary and socio-historical is present in these theories. Tihanov's assertion that literary theory (which would include Prague Structuralism) is concerned only with literariness, is contradicted in Vodička's writings. Furthermore, the assertion that literary theory is dead because the role of the literature has changed and, therefore, a study of literary texts has lost its relevance seems to imply that there is an objective criteria for what literature is—as we can see, however, the criteria is historically and socially determined.

At the same time, Tihanov's concern over literary theory's forays into other fields can be untangled with Vodička's separation of the role of the critic and the scholar. As we have seen, Vodička allows for overlapping of the two roles while cautioning that scholarly analysis must not be confused with criticism. This is to say that the 'death of literary theory' is a conflation of the two roles. The death of literary theory, which Tihanov declares, can be countered by careful separation of the critical and scholarly tasks. Perhaps in the current historical moment the literary scholar's role is overlapping with the role of the critic but the task of literary theory and the literary scholar still remains to be done. Thus, cultural theory concerns are providing actualizations of literary works in specific socio-historical context which is the raw material for scholarly analysis.

By separating the critic and the scholar, Vodička is mapping out productive guidelines that a scholar must take into consideration when thinking about what his or her discipline is and what the methodological aims and possibilities of the field are, that is, a productive path to disciplinary and theoretical (self-) reflection. Vodička's and the Prague School's insistence on non-dogmatic methodological rigor cautions against the conflation of methodology and ideology (and I would say of scholar and critic) and systematically attempts to integrate the subject (that is literature) with its use and history. In Jurij Striedter's words, Vodička's theories "by means of careful reconstruction of literary-historical contexts and the tasks associated with them [to] cast doubt upon the one-sided readings that in their moment of timeliness attain the status of dogma" (152).

Works cited

Doležel, Lubomír. "Poststructuralism: A View From Charles Bridge". *Poetics Today* 21.4, (Winter 2000): 633-52.

Galan, F. W. *Historic Structures: The Prague School Project, 1928-1946*. Austin: U of Texas P, 1985.

Matejka, Ladislav. "Literary History In A Semiotic Framework: Prague School Contributions". In *The Structure of the Literary Process: Studies Dedicated to the Memory of Felix Vodiǎka*. Ed. Peter Steiner. Amsterdam: John Benjamins, 1982. 341-70.

——. "The Sociological Concerns of the Prague School". In *The Prague School And Its Legacy (in Linguistics, Literature, Semiotics, Folklore, and the Arts)*. Ed. Yishai Tobin. Amsterdam: John Benjamins. 1988. 219-226.

Striedter, Jurij. *Literary Structure, Evolution, and Value: Russian Formalism and Czech Structuralism Reconsidered*. Cambridge: Harvard UP, 1989.

Tihanov, Galin. Why Did Modern Literary Theory Originate In Central and Eastern Europe? (And Why Is It Now Dead?). *Common Knowledge* 10.1 (Winter 2004. 61-81.

Vodička, Felix. "The Concretization of the Literary Work: Problems of Reception of Neruda's Works". In *The Prague School : Selected Writings, 1929-1946*, Peter Steiner (ed.), 103-134. Austin: U of Texas P, 1982.

——. "Response to Verbal Art". In *Semiotics of Art: Prague School Contributions*, Ladislav Matejka and Irwin R. Titunik (eds), 197-208. Cambridge: MIT Press, 1976. 197-208.

Subjectivity and Language Revisited: Benveniste, Agamben, and Recent Theories of Testimony

BARBARA HAVERCROFT
University of Toronto

One of the most enduring legacies of French structuralism is undoubtedly that provided by Émile Benveniste, whose groundbreaking and innovative insights in *Problèmes de linguistique générale* (1966, 1974) have proved to be of immense importance for research in a number of different disciplines. Indeed, Benveniste's pioneering work on subjectivity and language laid the foundations for all future inquiry into the linguistic theories of enunciation;[1] scarcely a study exists that does not cite or expand upon his fundamental research on deixis, discursive registers, and performative verbs, to name but a few of his multiple areas of scrutiny. Far from being limited to linguistics proper, Benveniste's concepts have also been adopted and adapted by scholars of literature, philosophy, cinema, history, psychoanalysis, and political science (see Havercroft 1993; 2002). More recently, the enduring pertinence of his work has come once again to the fore in the flourishing and interrelated fields of trauma and testimony, in which the oxymoric coupling of the imperative and the "impossibility" of speech in extreme situations draws extensively on certain key notions pertaining to subjectivity and language. While certain scholars of testimony, such as Shoshana Felman and Dori Laub, do not explicitly acknowledge their debt to Benveniste's thought, the links and affinities with the latter are both evident and essential. In his study of testimony, however, Giorgio Agamben specifically addresses and cites Benveniste's work, but in so doing, appropriates it in a theoretical re-enunication that culminates paradoxically in a discursive aporia. In the following article, I shall explore these two contrasting, theoretical enunciative situations, which themselves testify to divergent conceptions of the act of testimony, beginning with an overview of certain major concepts proposed in recent theories of testimony, demonstrating their debt to Benveniste's

---

[1] For post-Benvenistian studies of enunciation, see, among many others, Kerbrat-Orecchioni (1980; 2001); Morel and Danon-Boileau (1992); and De Mulder, Schuerewegen and Tasmoski (1992).

thought, and concluding with a close reading of Agamben's borrowing of Benveniste in *Remnants of Auschwitz : The Witness and The Archive* (2002 [1999]).

Testimony : Conceptions and Characterizations

Theories of testimony are thriving in the contemporary critical context of autobiography studies, in this "age of the memoir" (Miller 537), also known as "the age of testimony" (Felman "Education" 17), an era characterized by the publication of numerous forms of life writing (autofictions, autobiographical novels, confessions, diaries, testimonials, and autobiographies), as well as by the expansion of autobiography studies per se into the interdisciplinary domains of trauma, memory, disability and illness, ethics and law, performance, visual culture, and so on. Given this proliferation of the forms of life writing, one might wonder as to the specificity of testimony: is it a subgenre of autobiography, or perhaps a mode of reading certain personal narratives? According to Carole Dornier, testimony is the "le récit autobiographiquement certifié d'un événement passé […] [auquel le témoin] a assisté" [the autobiographically certified narrative of a past event which the witness-narrator has experienced personally] ("Toutes" 91).[2] Mirna Velcic-Canivez conceives of testimony as the intersection of two types of narratives, the historical and the autobiographical, in which the narrator refers to lived realities with the aim of soliciting a response from the addressee (reader or listener), who then becomes the witness to the original witness (v-vi). Testimonial narratives, like autobiographies and autofictions, presuppose the referential coincidence of author, narrator, and main character, all of whom are designated by the deictic "I". Many theoretical writings on testimony emphasize the ethical nature of such texts, the presence of the witness – often a victim – at the past scene or event in question, as well as the witness' capacity to speak for other victims. The witness addresses herself specifically to an addressee, hence the conative function of testimony, as she seeks the empathy of a reader or listener "prêt à recevoir le message" [ready to receive the message] (Dornier and Dulong xiv). The addressee's role is crucial in testimonial enunciation, as she must believe the witness' narrative to the point of becoming, in turn, what Jacques Derrida terms "le témoin du témoin" [the witness' witness] (32). Given the addressee's absence from the actual scene of the event, the witness frequently has recourse to what Dornier and

---

[2] All English translations from French texts are my own, except for passages cited from Benveniste's *Problèmes*, which have been translated by Mary Elizabeth Meek (*Problems*).

Dulong describe as "pathos, des effets d'héroïsation, d'une dimension épique" [pathos, effects of heroization, of an epic dimension] to secure the receiver's attention and touch her emotions (xiv). Often used by victims of trauma, be it that of the Shoah, World War I, or another extreme situation, the testimonial narrative functions to repair "la fracture que l'événement a souvent provoqué dans l'identité de celui qui raconte" [the fracture in the identity of the speaker, often caused by the event], and to restore the place of the victim within the human community (Dornier and Dulong xvii). A further function is that of the transmission of a "moral message," used to warn and educate the public (Dornier and Dulong xix). In Freudian terms, Dominick LaCapra sees a tension in testimonial texts, as they may oscillate between a working-through and an acting-out of traumatic symptoms, whereby the process of working-through does not entail "full redemption, total recovery, or unmitigated caesura [that] may never totally transcend acting-out or compulsive repetition but that does provide a measure of critical distance on problems and the possibility of significant transformation, including desirable change in civic life with its responsibilities and obligations" (144-145).

From this cursory overview of specific features of the testimonial narrative, certains points of intersection with Benveniste's theories of language and subjectivity can readily be discerned. With its emphasis on the intersubjective nature of communication and most particularly, with its focus on the involvement and receptivity of the addressee, the structure of the testimonial narrative both echoes and enacts Benveniste's conception of enunciation as a reciprocal process necessitating the interaction of the "I" and the "you":

> Le langage n'est possible que parce que chaque locuteur se pose comme *sujet*, en renvoyant à lui-même comme *je* dans son discours. De ce fait, *je* pose une autre personne, celle qui, toute extérieure qu'elle est à « moi », devient mon écho auquel je dis *tu* et qui me dit *tu*. La polarité des personnes, telle est dans le langage la condition fondamentale [...]. C'est dans une réalité dialectique englobant les deux termes et les définissant par relation mutuelle qu'on découvre le fondement linguistique de la subjectivité. (*Problèmes* 260)

> Language is possible only because each speaker sets himself up as a *subject* referring to himself as *I* in his discourse. Because of this, *I* posits another person, the one who, being, as he is, completely exterior to "me," becomes my echo to whom I say *you* and who says *you* to me. This polarity of persons is the fundamental condition in language [...]. It is in a dialectic reality that will incorporate the two terms and define them by mutual relationship that the linguistic basis of subjectivity is discovered. (*Problems* 225)

The testimonial narrative also capitalizes on the referential mobility of pronominal and other deictics, whose particular linguistic nature as "empty signs" was first elucidated in detail by Benveniste, allowing each victim/witness to become an "I", a subject of enunciation, and to target an indefinite number of "you" readers or listeners. As Dornier and Dulong claim, testimony is specifically addressed to receivers; its objective is the transmission of "la vérité sur un épisode historique que l'auteur a vécu [...]; [le message doit] établir et maintenir le contact entre deux sensiblités humaines" [the truth of a historical episode that the author has experienced [...]; [the message must] establish and maintain contact between two human sensibilities] (xiv). In *Poétique et politique du témoignage*, Derrida also insists on the crucial role of the "you" in this type of narrative, stating that testimony communicates the implicit message of *"Vous devez me croire*, parce que je m'engage à vous dire la vérité" [*You must believe me*, because I promise to tell you the truth] (31-32). And, as previously mentioned, the addressee's role greatly exceeds that of a passive listener, merely receiving the message: Derrida points out that this "you" does not see what the witness has seen, has no direct access to the extreme situation of which she speaks, and is only present to it by the memory and narrative of the victim. However, the "you" interlocutor has the responsibility not merely of an empathetic reception, but also of becoming what Derrida calls the witness of the witness, an interactive role which has consequences beyond the actual narration of the testimony in question (32).[3]

This emphasis on the intersubjective nature of testimony, on its perpetual unfolding of the "I"/"you" relationship, makes of testimony a particular type of enunciation which both highlights and depends on the very characteristics which defiine enunciation in general and which even enable it to occur. Testimonial discourse, like all enunciation, is a relational, dialogic process "a signifying transaction" (Silverman 48) through which the reciprocal address to the other enables self-definition for the "I" and "you" dialogue partners. The reversibility of the "I" and "you" subject positions, aptly expressed by the term "echo" in Benveniste's description of enunciation cited above (*Problèmes* 260; *Problems* 225), creates a bond between the two partners in discourse that is nurtured and sustained by the forwards and backwards flow of discourse and the exchange of subject positions. Theorists of testimony insist repeatedly on the crucial importance of the "you" listener in witnessing situations, as Dori Laub explains:

---

[3] François Rastier speaks of the "ethical engagement of the witness", referring to the speaker's *own* critical task, which consists of finding witnesses in the human community for her story" (161).

> To a certain extent, the interviewer-listener takes on the responsibility for bearing witness that previously the narrator felt he bore alone, and therefore could not carry out. It is the encounter and coming together between the survivor and the listener which makes possible something like a repossession of the act of witnessing (69).

It is, then, the shared responsibility of the witness and the listener to make the truth of testimony come forth in this reciprocal process of communicating the story to someone outside the self; further, the witness then reappropriates it, after its reception by the "you" receiver. The "you" subject position is in fact even more complex than these comments would initially indicate, as the narrator-witness, through the dialogic process of testimony, effects a doubling of the referent of the "you": in addition to her discourse partner, the interviewer-listener, she also has access to a listener inside of herself, thus establishing her own position as witness through what Dori Laub terms the "reconstitut[ion] of the internal 'thou'" (70). While maintaining her own separate identity, the listener is the victim's witness, feeling her emotions and responding to her experiences so that they can become testimony, but at the same time, the listener is also the witness to herself listening and reacting to the testimonial narrative. It is precisely this status of the double witness that makes the listener "the enabler of testimony—the one who triggers its initiation, as well as the guardian of its process and of its momentum" (Laub 58).[4]

A further affinity between the testimonial narrative and Benvenistian concepts can be discerned in the very nature of enunciation as an act, as a process of textual production, as a doing (*un faire*) and not as a static, finished product. In a similar manner, testimonial enunciation is itself portrayed as an active doing, as a set of performative utterances with the twofold purpose of therapy for the victim—in telling her story, the victim is doing something for her psychological health—, and of the communication of essential knowledge to the public: in recounting her story, she performs the ethical function of educating her readers or listeners. Derrida develops this performative dimension even further, noting that the witness promises to tell the truth (which does not entail providing proof or evidence) : "le témoin est lié par un contrat, un serment, une promesse, par une fois jurée dont la performativité est constitutive du témoignage et fait de celui-ci un gage, un engagement" [the witness is bound by a contract, an oath, a promise that has been made in good faith and whose performativity is constitutive of testimony and makes of it a guarantee, an engage-

---

[4] So crucial is the listener's role in successful testimonial enunciation that the lack of what Laub calls an *"addressable other"* or an "empathetic listener" results in the "annihilation" of the narrative (Felman and Laub 68).

ment] (36). It is as if the entire testimonial text in question were prefaced by an implicit performative utterance such as "I swear/promise to tell you the truth". What is more, in this performative instance of speech as action, following the vow or promise to tell, the speech itself acts as "material évidence for truth [...] rather than [...] simply formulating a statement" (Felman "Education" 17). According to Shoshana Felman, the performative nature of testimonial enunciation allows it to function like a signature, since witnessing allows the victim to rediscover and reclaim her identity and proper name, thereby reversing the anonymization process that occurred in the camps, where prisoners were interned, enslaved, tortured, and murdered as numbers, bereft of their onomastic identity ("Education" 53).

As the foregoing remarks indicate, the testimonial narrative constitutes a particular instance of the functioning of performative verbs as theorized by Benveniste and others. In his much-cited article entitled "De la subjectivité dans le langage", Benveniste explains the linguistic mechanisms of precisely these two performative verbs, to swear (*jurer*) and to promise (*promettre*). Noting the necessity of the use of the first person in order for the verb to act as a performative, Benveniste describes the behaviour of such verbs in the following manner:

> Or *je jure* est une forme de valeur singulière, en ce qu'elle place sur celui qui s'énonce la réalité du serment. Cette énonciation est un *accomplissement* : "jurer" consiste précisément en l'énonciation *je jure*, par quoi Ego est lié. L'énonciation *je jure* est l'acte même qui m'engage, non la description de l'acte que j'accomplis. En disant *je promets, je garantis*, je promets et je garantis effectivement. (*Problèmes* 265)

> Now *I swear* is a form of peculiar value in that it places the reality of the oath upon the one who says 'I'. This utterance is a *performance* : "to swear" consists exactly of the utterance *I swear*, by which Ego is bound. The utterance *I swear* is the very act which pledges me, not the description of the act that I am performing. In saying *I promise, I guarantee*, I am actually making a promise or a guarantee. (*Problems* 229)

In testimony, this primordial, constitutive, and necessary (albeit at times implicit) performative underlying the entire text is a precondition of its existence, of the text actually belonging to the testimonial genre or mode of discourse. This initial performative then leads to or enables other possible "doings" or textual performances, such as the previously silent (or silenced) *I* finding a voice, thereby conferring a reparative function on the text, in addition to the ethical function of educating the reader or listener, of bringing her into the past world and present memory of the witness, both of which are often traumatic. In this respect, Dori Laub refers to the action of reliving and re-experiencing the traumatic event through speech, which may even cause a retraumatization of the victim. Alternatively, the active performance of witnessing, of accomplishing this performative speech act, may give rise to positive and curative results, as in the case of one of Laub's patients, an Auschwitz survivor, whose reenactment of events through testifying was an affirmation of resistance and survival: "she is breaking out of Auschwitz even by her very talking", hence "breaking the frame of the concentration camp by and through her very testimony" (Felman and Laub 62).[5]

Agamben: Aporia and Desubjectification

Remnants of Auschwitz is the third volume of a trilogy dealing with political philosophy and ethics that Giorgio Agamben began in *Homo Sacer* (1998 [1995]) and *Means Without End* (2000 [1996]). In all three volumes, the basic premise is that only by examining extreme situations—what Agamben calls the state of exception—can one glean the truth of an ethics pertinent to the current state of biopolitics in the Western world. Drawing upon the Greeks' distinction between *zoe* and *bios*,[6] Agamben posits the concepts of bare or naked life (*nuda vita*) versus political and fuller existence, where bare life refers to humanity totally reduced to the state of its basic needs, deprived of what makes it human, beyond bare physical survival. The human being is consequently a remnant, an emaciated corpse that can be killed without being sacrificed or executed. As Debarati Sanyal succinctly describes it, bare life "designates the biological existence of all subjects prior to their investment with political and juridical value, their status as living organisms who are unconditionally vulnerable to elimination" (*Means* 5). The *Muselmann*, a figure which I shall discuss in more detail below, is Agamben's exemplary instance of bare life, but other examples

---

[5] Another much-discussed tenet of theories of testimony, which I shall not explore in greater length here, concerns the poeticization or stylization of certain testimonial texts, particularly in light of Adorno's oft-cited statement regarding the impossibility of poetry after Auschwitz (see Felman 39-40). While some theoreticians argue for the necessity of a strictly factual form of testimony—if such an account were even possible—, believing its authenticity would be compromised by the use of stylistic devices (see Velcic-Canivez), numerous other scholars insist on its aesthetic qualities (see Jeannelle 87-88; Dornier and Dulong xvii; Rastier 157-172; Derrida 9; Blanckeman 211).

[6] Agamben explains these terms in the following manner: *zoe* refers to natural life, the "simple fact of living" (*Homo* 1), or to human beings as "simply living beings, whose place was in the home" (*Means* 138), and *bios* denotes political life, "human beings as political subjects, whose place was in the polis" (*Means* 138).

include *Versuchspersonen* (human guinea pigs, the subjects of Nazi concentration camp experiments), and hopelessly comatose individuals ("neomorts") whose organs may be used for future transplant purposes (Agamben *Homo* 164-165). One of Agamben's major arguments that connects these diverse threads together is that life and politics, formerly divided, have become inextricably linked by the "no-man's-land of the state of exception that is inhabited by bare life" (*Homo* 148).[7] This reasoning leads Agamben to advance the provocative claim that we are currently living in a perpetual state of exception, and that the concentration camp, which appears in the form of various contemporary avatars, has become the basic—if at times hidden—paradigm of the West, "the inaugural site of modernity in which public and private events, political life and biological life, become vigorously indistinguishable" (*Means* 121). Claiming that his research is a continuation of Michel Foucault's work on biopolitics in hospitals and prisons (*Homo* 5-6, 9), as well as on the "process of subjectivation" (*Homo* 119), Agamben proposes to study the intervention of sovereign power in the subject's bodily life through an investigation of how the camp scenario could actually occur, i.e., how such unspeakable crimes against human beings could be committed, depriving them of their basic rights and reducing them to bare life, in a context where these crimes no longer appeared as crimes. In addition to these noble and notable goals, Agamben calls for a new ethics and a new politics, which remain to be formulated (*Homo* 10-11).

Choosing Auschwitz as his state of exception for scrutiny in *Remnants of Auschwitz*, Agamben offers what he terms, in a metatextual preface, a "perpetual commentary on testimony" (13), an effort to "locate the place and theme of testimony, thus providing some signposts allowing future cartographers of the new ethical territory to orient themselves" (13). Drawing heavily upon Primo Levi's writings, particularly *The Drowned and the Saved*, Agamben resorts to a discourse of the sublime in an endeavour to describe the most extreme form of victimization and abjection.[8] One of the book's main claims is that the

---

[7] This idea is expressed in the form of a chiasm which underscores the contemporary overlapping of life and politics: "The novelty of modern biopolitics lies in the fact that the biological given is immediately political, and the political is as such immediately the biological given" (*Homo* 148). For a more detailed discussion of these and other Agambenian notions, see Mesnard and Cahan, Sanyal, and LaCapra. In his recent book *State of Exception* (2005 [2003]), Agamben analyses the unusual and dubious extension of police powers authorized by the Bush government subsequent to 9/11, in its attempt to curtail and control terrorist activities.

[8] Dominick LaCapra questions this use of "a logic of the sublime" in the context of the suffering of others, "when the Shoah becomes the cypher for the

notion of testimony is only understandable or even possible in terms of the witnesses who have perished, of whom the *Muselmann* is the exemplary figure. In a hyperbolic discourse which Dominick LaCapra describes as "elated, seemingly radical [and] breathlessly ecstatic" (166), Agamben paints the dysphoric portrait of a bankrupt, post-apocalyptic, post-Auschwitz world which appears to be characterized by a state of "Auschwitz-now-everywhere" (LaCapra 166), hence the urgent need of a new ethics and politics. Testimony is paradoxically necessary and yet impossible, for at its heart is a fundamental aporia, a lacuna, and that is, the impossibility of bearing witness, since "the survivors bore witness to something it is impossible to bear witness to" (Agamben *Remnants* 13). While one might understand this "something" as a reference to the horrific nature of the events of the Shoah, Agamben subsequently reveals the more precise referent of this expression. The lacuna is in fact the figure of the *Muselmann* (or Muslim), a concentration camp jargon term used to denote the prisoners who had simply given up, who were the living dead, oscillating on the threshold between human and inhuman (or nonhuman). Shunned by their comrades in the camp, dying of malnutrition, utterly devoid of hope, the *Muselmann* becomes for Agamben the extreme instance of traumatized abjection, a synecdoche that functions as "a theoretical cypher to disprove human dignity and to discredit all preexisting (perhaps all presently conceivable) forms of ethics" (LaCapra 180). In terms of testimony, the *Muselmänner* are, according to Levi and Agamben, the only true and complete witnesses, but access to their testimony is impossi-

---

sublime" (155). Further, he is doubtful of the legitimacy of Agamben's human/nonhuman opposition incarnated by the *Muselmann* and the generalization of the state of exception as the rule (166). LaCapra is not alone in his criticisms of *Remnants of Auschwitz*. In a meticulous, careful study of the entire volume, Philippe Mesnard and Claudine Kahan criticize Agamben's over-emphasis on the *Muselmann* (8, 50); his resultant neglect and devaluation of survivor-witnesses and their testimonies (9, 11); his use of the proper name "Auschwitz" as an antonomasia to denote all camps (55)—one might also view this as a synedoche—, neglecting other death camps that were demolished in 1944; his lack of attention to history and to the social (126-7); his misuse of various sources, taking quotations out of context and distorting them (22), hence forcing the interpretation of certain passages (8); and finally, his use of a "sublime" style and a paroxysmic rhetoric (85), garnished liberally with superlatives and terms belonging to the lexical fields of purity and the absolute. Debarati Sanyal echoes many of these criticisms, and formulates a number of her own, such as that of Agamben's conflation of literal and metaphorical survival in the analogy he creates between camp survivors (primary witnesses) and contemporary spectators of television programs and athletic events (secondary witnesses), who share the "anguish and shame of the survivors" (Agamben *Remnants* 26).

ble, as they did not generally survive.

This lacuna, the lack of the true witness or the "drowned" at the center of testimony concerning the Shoah, leads both Levi and Agamben to describe an enunciative situation that is essentially one of ventriloquism or proxy and that illustrates, indeed, necessitates, Benveniste's distinction between the relationship of subjectivity, proper to "I" and "you", as opposed to the third-person pronominal forms such as "he", "she", and "they". Unable to witness, to tell his or her own story using the pronoun "I", the *Muselmann* occupies the linguistic position of Benveniste's *non-personne* (*Problèmes* 256; *Problems* 221), the third person excluded from the instance of discourse uniting the "I" and the "you", the one of whom one speaks (*la personne délocutée*). This non-person, as Benveniste explains, is linguistically incompatible "avec le paradigme des termes référentiels tels que *ici, maintenant*, etc." (*Problèmes* 256-257) [with the paradigm of referential terms such as *here, now*, etc. (*Problems* 222)] that characterize the act of enunciation. How, then, is the voice of the *Muselmann* to be heard? Following Levi, Agamben proposes that this impossible speech can only occur through proxy, a process of speaking *for* the *Muselmänner*, in their stead, in their place. The survivors must speak for the *Muselmänner*, bear witness in their place, in an enunciation which is a sort of ventriloquism, whereby the impossible « I » of the complete witness, no longer accessible, must necessarily be rendered indirectly as a « he » in the discourse of the « I » survivor. Primo Levi describes this phenomenon of enunciative proxy, characteristic of his own writing, in the following manner:

> [W]e, the survivors, are not the true witnesses. [...] Those who did [touch bottom] [...] have not returned to tell about it or have returned mute, but they are the Muslims, the submerged, the complete witnesses, the ones whose deposition would have a general significance. *We who were favored tried [...] to recount not only our fate but also that of the others [...]; but this was a discourse "on behalf of third parties"*, the story of things close at hand, but not experienced personally [...]. Weeks and months before being snuffed out, they had already lost the ability to observe, to remember, [...] and express themselves. *We speak in their stead, by proxy*. (83-84; my emphasis).

To witness, then, requires that one place oneself in one's own language, but "in the position of those who have lost it, to establish oneself in a living language as if it were dead, or in a dead language as if it were living" (Agamben *Remnants* 161). For Agamben, witnessing consequently entails speaking where such speech is impossible. However, Agamben also repeatedly insists on the aporia in such testimony, for when the witness bears witness to the *Muselmann*, she is actually, paradoxically, bearing witness to the breakdown of witnessing itself, to the abject impossibility of witnessing. Agamben's continual insistence on bearing witness to the inability to bear witness, taken to its logical conclusion, would negate or deny the very posssiblity of any testimony on the Shoah, be it on the part of the survivor (who is not a true witness, according to Agamben) speaking of her own experiences, or on that of a ventriloquized "I" speaking for the *Muselmänner*, the drowned, a posture which Agamben initially seems to support as seen in his perpetual preoccupation with Levi, who, as I have stated, assumes precisely this latter enunciative position. Furthermore, Agamben concludes his book on a paradoxical note, for the volume ends with actual testimony, with exact quotations, from former *Muselmänner* who did not perish, but who should not be able to speak or bear witness, according to Agamben's previous contentions.[9] By quoting the *Muselmänner*, by allowing them to speak in their own voices, becoming true and not proxied subjects of enunciation, Agamben contradicts his previous statements and opens himself up to criticism such as that formulated by Dominick LaCapra in *History in Transit*. LaCapra suggests that Agamben is "caught up in a bitter irony, performatively self-deconstructing by bearing witness to his inability to bear witness, and paradoxically, supporting his own abject identification with the *Muselmann* who paradoxically states, 'I was a *Muselmann*'" (177). LaCapra thus finds fault not merely with Agamben's "spiraling, self-consuming paradox" (177) concerning the supposed impossibility of testimony, but also with his problematic stance on subject positions. When Levi as a survivor states that the *Muselmann* is the true witness, and not himself (Levi 83-84), LaCapra considers this to be an acceptable hyperbole. What LaCapra truly finds objectionable, however, is Agamben's tendency to use Levi as a paradigm *and* his act of speaking *for* Levi, "as an object of projective identification whom [he] ventriloquizes, just as he sees Levi ventriloquizing or speaking for the *Muselmann*" (LaCapra 161). As a paradigm, Levi acts for Agamben as a "perfect example of the witness" (Agamben *Remnants* 16). But as a ventrioloquized subject, LaCapra alleges, Levi "serves Agamben as a prosthetic device (not to say a dummy-figure) in

---

[9] In *Homo Sacer*, Agamben admits to having read the testimony of *Versuchspersonen* who survived their ordeal—documents which should not actually exist, given his stance on the impossibility of witnessing – , characterizing the painful reading process as an "atrocious experience" (156). Mesard and Kahan also point out the contradiction of Agamben's inclusion of the testimonies of former *Muselmänner* (45), contending that his conception of testimony as a lacuna is based on an interpretation of testimony as the revelation of a complete, unabridged truth ("une vérité intégrale"), which no testimony could possibily offer (77-78), and which neatly sidesteps the thorny question of fiction as opposed to history in testimonial accounts.

a covert process of identifying with, and speaking for, the ultimate victim and instance of abjection, the *Muselmann*" (161). Further, as Mesnard and Kahan affirm (35), Agamben's paraphrase of Levi's discourse actually goes beyond it at times, as he ignores Levi's critical nuances and almost misappropriates it in order to reconcile it with his own theory. Debarati Sanyal locates one such instance of distortion in Agamben's extension of Levi's concept of the "gray zone"[10] to contemporary society in an attemp to support his contention that we are presently experiencing a state of exception akin to Auschwitz, noting that Levi in fact uses the "gray zone" to underscore the historical particularity of the life of concentration camp internees (Sanyal 7-8). What results, then, is no less than "a disturbing ventriloquism that disregards the survivor's [here, Levi's] explicit injunction against conflating the extermination camp and civilian life" (Sanyal 8).

What we are confronted with here is a highly complex and intricate embedding of speakers by proxy: my own discourse on LaCapra's, Mesnard and Kahan's, and Sanyal's critiques of Agamben speaking for Levi, who is speaking for the *Muselmann*. This is an imbrication of a series of enunciative contexts of which the originary one seems, if one accepts Agamben's argument, to be an aporia that would give the lie to the construction of the very enunciative chain to which it gives rise. In his insistence on the paradox and the impossibility of testimony, in his gesture of seeming to deny the viability or feasibility of speaking by proxy, all the while performing this very gesture himself, is Agamben completely denying testimony's very possibility or existence? How can the third person actually find a voice, albeit indirectly? To consider these questions, let us examine a section of Agamben's text where he specifically evokes Benveniste, engaging him on Benveniste's own ter-

---

[10] Levi uses the expression "gray zone" to refer to an ambiguous, aporetic space of violence in the camps, where subject positions— notably those of perpetrator and victim— become conflated and blurred. He cites a particular example which is emblematic of such confusion (55): a soccer game played in the Auschwitz crematorium courtyard between members of the SS and of the *Sonderkommando*, a special team of largely Jewish prisoners forced to perform tasks related to the functioning of the crematorium. See Sanyal (1-27) for a rigourous analysis of accounts of this match and their ramifications for Holocaust criticism. Levi learned of this event in a French translation of Miklos Nyiszkli's testimony (originally written in Hungarian), but Agamben does not consult the latter text, basing his comments solely on Levi's rendering of the match in *The Drowned and the Saved*, which itself contains some faulty conclusions, according to Mesnard and Kahan (37-39). One could consider these enuciative borrowings as a case of double ventriloquism (Agamben citing Levi who borrows from Nyiszkli) in which the original voice – Nyiszkli's – has been silenced in Agamben's text.

ritory, that of the construction of subjectivity and the role of deictics in the latter construction.

For Benveniste, as he clearly contends in his *Problèmes de linguistique générale*, subjectivity is defined as the speaker's capacity to become a subject through her use of language (*Problèmes* 259), specifically through the appropriation of the deictic "I", which signifies "l'individu qui énonce la présente instance de discours contenant l'instance linguistique *je*" [the person who is uttering the present instance of discourse containing *I*] (*Problèmes* 252; *Problems* 218). The act of enunciation featuring the pronoun "I" is in fact doubly referential, according to Benveniste, for it refers to the act of individual discourse in which it is uttered, and it also designates the speaker in a reference that is momentary and fleeing (*Problèmes* 262; *Problems* 226). Consequently, the basis of subjectivity for Benveniste is solely located in language and more particularly, in the mobilization of shifters, those "empty" signs which temporarily become "full" when appropriated by an "I" speaker in discourse. While these well-known arguments seem clear and straightforward, they acquire a somewhat contradictory character when adopted and adapted by Agamben in *Remnants of Auschwitz*. Although fascinated by Benveniste's insights on deictics and subjectivity,[11] Agamben tweaks and twists them to suit his own purposes, thereby transforming them into specious arguments at best. According to Agamben, subjectivity "constitutively has the form of subjectification and desubjectification" (*Remnants* 112). Defining subjectification as "the production of consciousness in the event of discourse" (*Remnants* 123), a very Benvenistian stance, Agamben then proceeds to claim that "*perhaps*" (*Remnants* 113; my emphasis) every act of speech implies not a coming to subjectivity, but a desubjectification as well.[12] As an example of such an experience, Agamben cites that of speaking in tongues as documented in Paul's first letter to the Corinthians, chapter 14, verse 2, where the speaker, giving way to a divine voice, speaks without understanding what she is saying, and her speech thus becomes for-

---

[11] Agamben has long been interested in Benveniste's theory of enunciation; see, for example, his comments on Benvenistian subjectivity in *Language and Death: The Place of Negativity* (1991[1982]:23-25, 31, 76-77).

[12] For Agamben, this desubjectification is intimately bound up with shame which, in the end, is equivalent to subjectivity itself. See his discussion of the desubjectified experience in the act of speech as it is demonstrated in poetic creation (*Remnants* 113-114). In a close reading of Agamben's discussion of desubjectification, shame, and the poet, Mesnard and Kahan formulate a number of provocative criticisms of his stance and his conclusions, such as their critique of his misreading of an 1818 letter by Keats, in which they see no evidence whatsoever of the "débâcle du sujet" [collapse of the subject] that Agamben locates in this text (Mesnard and Kahan 121).

eign to her (*Remnants* 114). Agamben's use of the singular experiences of speaking in tongues and of poetic creation as the basic paradigms for *all* speech, and his conclusion from this that *every* act of enunciation necessarily involves a desubjectification seem to be rather dubious moves, given the vast heterogeneity of possible speech acts.

Agamben continues his discussion by reiterating Benveniste's concepts concerning the particular and intriguing nature of shifters, as well as the latter's definition of enunciation as the production of a text. Paraphrasing Benveniste, Agamben notes that enunciation refers "not to the text of what is stated, but to its taking place; the individual can put language into act only on condition of identifying himself with the very event of saying" (*Remnants* 116). Although these remarks remain faithful to Benveniste's thought, the two theorists part ways in Agamben's subsequent comments, for he once again maintains that the passage from language to discourse that occurs during an act of enunciation, an act which he deems, in typically Agambenian fashion, "paradoxical", implies *both* subjectification and desubjectification. But here, Agamben becomes more specific as to the precise nature of the desubjectification process: the "psychosomatic individual must fully abolish himself and desubjectify himself as a real individual to become the subject of enunciation and to identify himself with the pure shifter 'I'" (*Remnants* 116). In other words, to take up and use this "empty" sign, since it is "without substantiality and content other than its mere reference to the event of discourse" (*Remnants* 116), the speaker must emulate its very nature and "desubjectify" herself as a "real individual" as a precondition of even uttering "I". Unfortunately, nowhere does Agamben explain **how** the individual can accomplish this act, how he or she actually "abolishes" herself unto herself to assume a shifter-like state. It is in fact the *Muselmann* figure which is the prime example of desubjectification, for the latter is "a figure for a subjectivity that emerges from a process of radical desubjectification" (Sanyal 24), the result of "an extreme condition that questions the very basis of identity" (24).[13]

Furthermore, this notion of desubjectification, which Agamben claims to derive from Benveniste, is absent from the latter's account of language and subjectivity. Contrary to Agamben's divested subject, Benveniste's discursive "I", "la personne qui énonce la présente instance du discours contenant *je*" (*Problèmes* 252) [the individual who

---

[13] Here, Sanyal sees a connection between Agamben's tendency to generalize the desubjectification and "radical dehumanization" of the *Muselmann* figure to all individuals attempting to speak and Caruth's conception of the traumatic subject as an instance of "entanglement", as a constitutive alterity within the psyche of all individuals (Sanyal 24).

utters the present instance of discourse containing the linguistic instance *I*] (*Problems* 218), does not appear subject to a desubjectification. Let us listen to Benveniste himself define subjectivity:

> La "subjectivité" dont nous traitons ici est la capacité du locuteur à se poser comme "sujet". Elle se définit, non par le sentiment que chacun éprouve d'être lui-même [...], mais comme l'unité psychique qui transcende la totalité des expériences vécues qu'elle assemble, et qui assure la permanence de la conscience. Or nous tenons que cette "subjectivité", qu'on la pose en phénoménologie ou en psychologie [...] n'est que l'émergence dans l'être d'une propriété fondamentale du langage. Est "ego" qui *dit* "ego". (*Problèmes* 259-260)

> The "subjectivity" we are discussing here is the capacity of the speaker to posit himself as "subject". It is defined not by the feeling which everyone experiences of being himself [...] but as the psychic unity that transcends the totality of the actual experiences it assembles, and makes the permanence of the consciousness. Now we hold that "subjectivity", whether it is placed in phenomenology or in psychology [...], is only the emergence in the being of a fundamental property of language. "Ego" is he who *says* "ego". (*Problems* 224)

I have cited this passage at length to illustrate my contention that Benveniste's conception of subjectivity bears no traces of the desubjectification process as Agamben portrays it, no obligatory assuming of the dehumanized state of the *Muselmann*. If the "I" is defined only in language, as Benveniste proposes, this does not mean that the referent which it designates (the individual speaker) is herself somehow akin to or synonymous with, the deictic sign, the shifter. Indeed, Benveniste speaks of a psychic unity and the *permanence* of consciousness, not of an oscillating process of subjectification and desubjectification. In a similar vein, Kaja Silverman, in her study of Benveniste's theories, notes that the "individual finds his or her cultural identity only within discourse, by means of the pronouns 'I' and 'you'" (45). Here, it is a matter of the speaker *gaining* her subjectivity and an identity, not one of being *divested* thereof.[14]

---

[14] According to Mesnard and Kahan (68), Agamben takes Benveniste's theory out of its disciplinary context, with grave consequences for the notion of testimony. In addition, as they rightly contend, Agamben makes an error in his recourse to Foucault's work in *L'archéologie du savoir* as a further justification of the *Muselmann* figure as the supreme instance of desubjectification (Mesnard and Kahan 68). Agamben alleges that Foucault was the first to make Benveniste's theory of enunciation an actual object of inquiry, but in *L'archéologie du savoir*, Foucault is not so much concerned with enunciation as a linguistic event in process as with the resulting statement, the *énoncé*. In this instance, Agamben is confusing *énonciation* and *énoncé*, ignoring the essential

The climax of Agamben's argument—perhaps its disappointing dénouement—consists in the following state of affairs: having stripped himself of all substantiality and extra-linguistic meaning to resemble the shifter "I" that she then takes up to become a subject of enunciation, having appropriated what Benveniste terms the "l'appareil formel d'énonciation" (*Problèmes* 79-88) [the formal apparatus of enunciation], the newly constituted subject makes a startling discovery. Agamben describes this unexpected event in the following manner :

> [T]he subject discovers that he has gained access not so much to a possibility of speaking as to an ***impossibility of speaking*** [...]. [H]e is expropriated of all referential reality, letting himself be defined solely through the pure and empty relation to the event of discourse. *The subject of enunciation is composed of discourse and exists in discourse alone. But, for this very reason, once the subject is in discourse,* **he can say nothing; he cannot speak**. (*Means* 116-117; my emphasis; Agamben's italics).

This passage is open to criticism on several fronts. First of all, Agamben's unexpected conclusion concerning the impossibility of speech is contrary, in word and spirit, to Benveniste's theory of enunciation. Pronouns and other deictic signs exist precisely in order that language as a system (*langue,* in Saussurian terms) may be transformed by the speaker into discourse; shifters give the future speaking subject the means of becoming a subject and of speech itself. Rather than confronting the impossibility of speech, I would contend that once the subject discursively appropriates the appropriate shifters, she is always already speaking. As Benveniste explains, language is itself "la possibilité de la subjectivité" (*Problèmes* 263) [the possibility of subjectivity] (*Problems* 227), and it does not inevitably entail silence. Agamben thus creates a semantic cluster where desubjectification, silence, and death necessarily circulate together around the ontological figure of the *Muselmann*. While the Holocaust certainly causes a crisis in representation, is silence truly the only possible or fitting response? What are the consequences of such a stance for testimony? Agamben's position would appear to negate the very existence of testimony, for in "situating the 'truth' of testimony as somewhere between the speaker and the unspeakable, Agamben ultimately privileges the desubjectified and silenced Muslim as the bearer of the essential lacuna of testimony ('the drowned who has much to say but cannot speak') over the survivor 'who can speak but has nothing interesting to say'" (Sanyal 25-26). Dominick LaCapra rightly describes this particular passage in Agamben's text as "vastly oversimplif[ying] the problem of language

---

distinction between these two related terms, a distinction Foucault takes pains to uphold (Foucault 134).

in use" (172-173); I would also qualify it as a highly questionable conclusion based on Benveniste's ideas.

A further dimension of Benveniste's theories, one which Agamben completely ignores in *Remnants of Auschwitz*, is the linguist's reflections on reference and the referent. Whereas Saussure limited his notion of the sign to the signifer and the signified, Benveniste considers both the sign and its referent. In "La forme et le sens dans le langage" (*Problèmes* 215-238), for example, he distinguishes between the reference of a sentence—"l'état de choses qui la provoque, la situation de discours [...] que nous ne pouvons jamais, ni prévoir, ni deviner" [the state of things which gives rise to it, the discourse situation which we can never foresee or foretell] (*Problèmes* 226-227)—and the referent of a word, which is the "object particulier auquel le mot correspond dans le concret de la circonstance ou de l'usage" (*Problèmes* 226) [the particular object to which the word corresponds in the concrete circumstances of its usage]. For Benveniste, "la notion de référence est essentielle" (*Problèmes* 226) [the notion of reference is essential], and this statement has obviously obvious and significant consequences for testimonial enunciation, where reference to actual, extra-discursive historical events and realities experienced by the subject of witnessing is crucial. Indeed, testimony does not take place within a solipsistic, self-referential discursive vaccuum, devoid of any reference to circumstances beyond itself; the speaker's testimonial address to the "you" necessarily involves the reference to realities within and beyond herself. Furthermore, in the conversion of *langue* to *parole* that is effected when a speaker performs an act of enunciation, during this discourse-as-event, when the speaker avails herself of the deictic signs proprer to the category of person ("I", "you", "now", "here", etc.), the shifter "I" refers to the speaker, as well as to the current instance of discourse. This does not mean that the deictic "I" has a fixed referent; on the contrary, it is this particular sign's very referential mobility which allows an endless number of different speakers to appropriate it and use it in innumerable, unique enunciative situations. The capacity of language to refer also does not mean that the subject is "in control" of her subjectivity; as Silverman explains, "the subject's discourse is constrained by the rules of language" and "the subject's autonomy is further qualified by the inclusion of the unconscious" which bears upon each discursive situation (50).[15] In *Remnants of Auschwitz*, Agamben's neglect

---

[15] According to Benveniste, discourse has its origins in a split subject, is produced by a conscious and unconscious speaking subject, and is composed of manifest and latent levels, the latter of which is accessible only through the former. See Benveniste's "Remarques sur la fonction du langage dans la découverte freudienne" (*Problèmes* 75-87).

of the referent is related to his messianic elevation of the *Muselmann* to a sublime figure of desubjectification and bare life, a rhetorical move which simultaneously disregards specific historical circumstances and obfuscates real bodies, including the corporeal remnants of "ceux qui allaient directement à la chambre de gaz" (Mesnard and Kahan 58) [those who went directly to the gas chamber], and that of the *Muselmann* himself. As Mesnard and Kahan assert, there is no referent here: the real body of the *Muselmann* vanishes in a privileging of the image, or the signifier, for Agamben's reading "libère le *musulman* de son corps" (89) [frees the *Muselmann* from his body].

Furthermore, the problems with Agamben's notion of the impossibility of speech, no doubt formulated to accompany and to support that of the impossibility of testimony, are not limited to his (mis)appropriation of Benveniste's theories. In the context of a book on testimony, a process based on speech, language, and its reception, the impossibility of speech poses a major dilemma, specifically, the evacuation of agency, as LaCapra is quick to point out : "Such a formulation deprives one of an ability to ascribe responsibility and agency" (172). Indeed, how is one to speak, either for oneself, or by proxy for the silenced ones, if speaking is an utter impossibility? A contradiction appears to exist here in Agamben's argumentation on several levels, for not only does he claim that Levi speaks for the *Muselmann*, but, as previously mentioned, his own text contains testimony from surviving former *Muselmänner* who have obviously spoken, who *have* borne witness. In wrestling with Agamben's paradoxes, aporia, and contradictions, LaCapra proposes a view of testimony that would admit the extreme and manifold difficulties inherent in witnessing, yet that *would* permit it to occur, despite the possibility of breakdown, when such breakdown "occurs in the witness's attempt to recount traumatic experience and perhaps in the commentator's empathic attempt to render such an attempt" (174). Rather than being "fixated on breakdown or aporia", LaCapra's view of testimony would be "alert" to it (174), and would include a space for agency in the process of witnessing, where speaking or writing would provide the survivor-victim with the means of living, of surviving, partly by virtue of her own testimony. Herein lies the essential agentic dimension of testimony: if, as Felman declares, testimony cannot provide a "completed statement, a totalizable account of [the] events" (66); if, as Laub contends, witnessing is impossible in the sense that the witness can never extricate herself from the event's "dehumanizing frame of reference" (66) in order to behold it objectively, she is nonetheless faced with the imperative to recount her experiences, an imperative which Laub aptly expresses in the following chiasm : "The survivors did not only survive so that they could tell their stories; they also needed to tell their stories in order to survive"

(63). Testimony, then, provides the survivor simultaneously with the means of survival itself and with the possibility of transforming her status from silenced victim into active agent. If agency is the *modus operandi* of the subject (Druxes 9), how can we ignore the necessary agentic dimension, performative in nature, by which the subject acts in and on her own life – albeit tentatively and with the utmost difficulty – by her act of testimony? In his perpetual return to the aporias of witnessing, especially to that of bearing witness to the impossibility of bearing witness, Agamben conceals and consequently undervalues such curative or redemptive effects of testimony.

It is with this more positive presentation of the precarious act of testimony in mind that I would like to conclude my reflections. Agamben's complex engagement with Benveniste is at best a case of questionable borrowing, at worst a misuse of Benveniste's theories. Is Agamben making Benveniste say things he never actually uttered? Is this an instance of ventriloquism gone wrong, where Benveniste, as the ventriloquist's dummy, becomes subjected to Agamben as ventriloquist, thereby compelled to witness his own discourse on subjectivity culminate in the silence of desubjectification? Keeping all of Agamben's aporia in mind, we could perhaps do best to espouse a vision or version of testimony such as that which Derrida proposes, which admits of speech, tentative and tremulous though it may be, in the performative and curative act of fulfilling the promise of recounting a truth to empathetic listeners such as ourselves, prepared to accept the challenge of becoming the "you" to the victim's "I", becoming the witness of the witness.

Works Cited

Agamben, Giorgio. *Language and Death: The Place of Negativity*. 1982. Minneapolis: University of Minnesota Press, 1991.
___. *Homo Sacer: Sovereign Power and Bare Life*. 1995. Trans. Daniel Heller-Roazen. Stanford : Stanford University Press, 1998.
___. *Means Without Ends: Notes on Politics*. 1996. Trans. Vincento Binetti and Cesare Casarino. Minneapolis: University of Minnesota Press, 2000.
___. *Remnants of Auschwitz: The Witness and the Archive*. 1999. Trans. Daniel Heller-Roazen. New York: Zone Books, 2002.
___. *State of Exception*. 2003. Chicago : University of Chicago Press, 2005.
Benveniste, Émile. *Problèmes de linguistique générale*. 2 vols. Paris: Gallimard, 1966-74.
___. *Problems in General Linguistics*. Trans. Mary Elizabeth Meek. Coral Gables, Florida: University of Miami Press, 1971.
Blanckeman, Bruno. "Mourir en direct: les cas Hervé Guibert". Dornier and Dulong 203-212.
Caruth, Cathy, ed. *Trauma: Explorations in Memory*. Baltimore: The Johns Hopkins University Press, 1995.

De Mulder, Walter, Franc Schuerewegen and Liliane Tasmowski, eds. *Énonciation et parti pris*. Amsterdam: Rodopi, 1992.
Derrida, Jacques. *Poétique et politique du témoignage*. Paris: Éditions de L'Herne, 2005.
Dornier, Carole. "Toutes les histoires sont-elles des fictions?". Dornier and Dulong 91-106.
Dornier, Carole and Renaud Dulong, eds. *Esthétique du témoignage*. Caen: Éditions de la Maison des sciences de l'homme, 2005.
___. Introduction. Dornier and Dulong xiii-xix.
Druxes, Helga. *Resisting Bodies: The Negotiation of Female Agency in Twentieth-Century Women's Fiction*. Detroit: Wayne State University Press, 1996.
Felman, Shoshana. "Education and Crisis, or the Vicissitudes of Teaching". Caruth 13-60.
Felman, Shoshana and Dori Laub. *Testimony: Crises of Witnessing in Literature, Psychoanalysis, and History*. New York: Routledge, 1992.
Foucault, Michel. *L'archéologie du savoir*. Paris: Gallimard, 1969.
Havercroft, Barbara. "Énonciation/énoncé". *Encyclopedia of Contemporary Literary Theory*. Ed. Irena R. Makaryk. Toronto: University of Toronto Press, 1993. 540-543.
___. "Énonciation et énoncé". *Le Dictionnaire du littéraire*. Eds. Paul Aron, Denis Saint-Jacques and Alain Viala. Paris: Presses Universitaires de France, 2002. 179-181.
Jeannelle, Jean-Louis. "Pour une histoire du genre testimonial". *Littérature* 135 (2004): 87-117.
Kerbrat-Orecchioni, Catherine. *L'énonciation: de la subjectivité dans le langage*. Paris: Armand Colin, 1980.
___. *Les actes de langage dans le discours*. Paris: Éditions Nathan, 2001.
LaCapra, Dominick. *History in Transit: Experience, Identity, Critical Theory*. Ithaca: Cornell University Press, 2004.
Laub, Dori. "Truth and Testimony: The Process and the Struggle". Caruth 61-75.
Levi, Primo. *The Drowned and the Saved*. Trans. Raymond Rosenthal. New York: Random House, 1989.
Mesnard, Philippe and Claudine Kahan. *Giorgio Agamben à l'épreuve d'Auschwitz*. Paris: Éditions Kimé, 2001.
Miller, Nancy K. "The Entangled Self : Genre Bondage in the Age of Memoir". *PMLA* 122.2 (2007): 537-548.
Morel, Mary-Annick and Laurent Danon-Boileau, eds. *La deixis*. Paris: Presses Universitaires de France, 1992.
Rastier, François. "L'art du témoignage". Dornier and Dulong 157-172.
Sanyal, Debarati. "A Soccer Match in Auschwitz : Passing Culpability in Holocaust Criticism". *Representations* 79 (2002): 1-27.
Silverman, Kaja. *The Subject of Semiotics*. Oxford: Oxford University Press, 1983.
Velcic-Canivez, Mirna. *Prendre à témoin*. Paris: Éditions Ophrys, 2006.

The Theory of Opposition Revisited

Marcel Danesi
University of Toronto

Introduction

The theory of opposition, which has found its way into everything from the commutation test in linguistics to content analysis in media studies, was the staple technique and, arguably, the primary theoretical framework within which the Prague School operated. Although the idea originated with Aristotle as a principle of logical structure (Hjelmslev 1939, 1959, Benveniste 1946), and although it was used implicitly by Saussure (1916) to carry out the analysis of signs, it became the basis of structuralism only after the Prague School linguists gave it a formal articulation (Trubetzkoy 1936, 1939, Jakobson 1939). Along with Gestalt psychologists (Ogden 1932), the Prague School linguists saw opposition as a pivotal tool for examining meaningful distinctions at various levels of language and for understanding the relationship between linguistic and social structures.

However, starting in the mid-1950s with the advent of both post-structuralism in semiotics and generativism in linguistics, the theory of opposition suffered a setback, as scholars in both these disciplines made a temporary break from structuralism. But the theory has recently resurfaced in various disciplines, such as media and cultural studies, showing its uncanny ability once again to guide research in interesting and suggestive directions. My objective here is to revisit the theory of opposition, which has shown itself time and time again to be one of those notions which continues to flesh out seemingly hidden patterns of human cognition—patterns which manifest themselves in all representational and expressive systems, from language to art and science.

Theory or Technique?

There is little evidence to suggest that the early structuralists saw opposition as anything other than a useful technique for fleshing out significant differences in linguistic forms and units. Its theoretical validity was never overtly justified or even debated, as far as I can tell. Opposition was seen essentially as an analytical tool for identifying phonemes, morphemes, and other meaningful or meaning-bearing units in languages. But it certainly had all the earmarks of a theoretical notion and, indeed, many have utilized it as a full-fledged theory, rather than just a technique.

As is widely known, basic to Saussure's (1916) plan for the study of *langue* was the notion of *différence* ("difference, opposition")—the view that the structures of a language do not take on meaning and function in isolation, but rather in differential relation to each other. For example, the linguist determines the meaning and grammatical function of the word *cat* in English by opposing it to the word *rat* or some other minimal form. This opposition will show, among other things, that the initial consonants /k/ and /r/ are cues in English for establishing the differential meanings of the words. From such oppositions we can see, one or two differential features at a time, what makes the word *cat* unique in English, allowing us to pinpoint what *cat* means by virtue of how it is different from other words. At this microlevel of structure, opposition is clearly a technique that allows linguists to sift phonemic signals out from the phonic stream that constitutes the chain of speech. As a technique, opposition was elaborated by a number of linguists, many of Russian origin, who congregated in the Prague Circle in the early 1920s. In addition to opposition theory, the Circle developed crucial notions, such as that of *distinctive features* and *markedness*, which have remained central to semiotic and linguistic analysis to this day. These had the intent of elaborating and expanding upon the concept of *différence*, by giving it a more concrete methodology. Trubetzkoy, for example, introduced the concept of *minimal pair*—a pair of words, such as *cat* and *rat* that differ by only one sound in the same position. The minimal pair thus identifies the source of any *différence*, allowing the linguist to test empirically what oppositions are significant in a language (Trubetzkoy 1968). Jakobson (1942) went a step further, arguing that the notion of opposition could be used to explain features of language development. He noted, for example, that sound oppositions that occur rarely in languages are among the last ones learned by children. Nasal consonants—for example, /n/ and /m/—exist in all languages. Not surprisingly, they are also among the earliest sounds acquired by children. On the other hand, consonants pronounced near the back of the throat (such as laryngeals) are relatively rare and, seemingly, among the last sounds to be acquired by children. In other words, the theory of opposition would seem to predict the sequence of acquisition in children. Jakobson's work was truly revolutionary in this domain.

However, the Prague School linguists also realized early on that extending the technique of opposition to levels of language beyond the phonological is fraught with problems. Opposition was envisioned as a specific form of controlled comparison, as the minimal pair technique made saliently obvious. So, it seemed logical to use the same notion to compare higher-level units. Opposition could be used, for example, to examine semantic relations such as synonymy (*big-large*), antonymy (*big-little*), taxonomy (*rose-flower*), part-whole relations (*handle-cup*), and so on. Although it was immediately obvious to the Prague School scholars that it provided once again a useful format for establishing the denotative or basic differential meanings of lexical items, they soon realized that it also produces anomalous results. For example, in terms of distinctive-feature analysis, the opposition between, say, *heifer* and *dog* can be given as either [+bovine] versus [-bovine] or [-canine] ~ [+canine]. There really is no way to establish which feature is, conceptually, the differential trigger in the opposition. Moreover, when certain words are defined in terms of features, it becomes obvious that to keep them distinct one will need quite a vast array of such features. The whole exercise would thus become artificial and convoluted, since one might need as many features (if not more) as words. Moreover, a term such as *bitch*, which still exists in English to refer denotatively to a "female dog," is rarely if ever used any longer because of the connotations it has taken on in the social domain. Thus, an opposition such as *(male) dog* versus *bitch* could hardly be used to differentiate gender in canines.

These questions however did not impugn the technique of opposition in any serious way. On the contrary, they led to further inquiry into the nature of meaning, emphasizing, above all else, that connotation was a pivotal semiosic force in language and other representational systems. Abstract concepts, such as "motherhood," "masculinity," "friendship," and "justice," for instance, are particularly high in connotative content. But how does one flesh out their culture-specific connotations with the technique of opposition? In 1957, the psychologists Osgood, Suci, and Tannenbaum answered this question rather ingeniously by expanding opposition with the technique they called the *semantic differential*. This was designed to flesh out the connotative (culture-specific) meanings that abstract concepts elicit, by posing a series of questions to subjects about the concepts—*Is X good or bad? Should Y be weak or strong?* etc. The subjects were asked to rate a concept on a seven-point scale, with two end points constituting the oppositional poles. The ratings were then collected and analyzed statistically in order to sift out any general pattern they might bear.

Suppose that subjects are asked to rate the concept "ideal American President" in terms of the following scales: for example, *Should the President be young or old? Should the President be practical or idealistic? Should the President be modern or traditional?* and so on (Danesi 2007):

young	−1	−2	−3	−4	−5	−6	−7	old
practical	−1	−2	−3	−4	−5	−6	−7	idealistic
modern	−1	−2	−3	−4	−5	−6	−7	traditional
attractive	−1	−2	−3	−4	−5	−6	−7	bland
friendly	−1	−2	−3	−4	−5	−6	−7	stern

A subject who feels that the President should be more "youngish" than "oldish" would place a mark towards the *young* end of the top opposition; one who feels that a President should be "bland," would place a mark towards the *bland* end of the *attractive-bland* opposition; and so on. If we were to ask a large number of subjects to rate the President in this way, we would get a "connotative profile" of the American presidency in terms of the statistically significant variations in evaluations that it evokes. Interestingly, research utilizing the semantic differential has shown that the range of variations is not a matter of pure subjectivity, but forms, rather, a socially-based pattern. In other words, the connotations of many (if not all) abstract concepts are constrained by culture: for example, the word *noise* turns out to be a highly emotional concept for the Japanese, who rate it consistently at the ends of the oppositions presented to them; whereas it is a fairly neutral concept for Americans, who tend to rate it on average in the mid-ranges of the same scales. Connotation is not, therefore, open-ended; it is constrained by a series of factors, including conventional agreements as to what signs mean in certain situations. Without such constraints, our systems of meaning would be virtually unusable.

The semantic differential was not, clearly, a radical break from opposition theory. It simply indicated that gradations might exist in the interpretation of binary oppositions that are culture-specific and, thus, connotative. The weakness of pure binary opposition in fleshing out meanings beyond the denotative was also noticed by semiotician Algirdas J. Greimas, who introduced the notion of the "semiotic square" involving two sets of oppositions forming a square arrangement (Greimas 1987). Given a sign s_1 (for example, *rich*), we determine its overall meaning by opposing it to its contradictory -s_1 (*not rich*), its contrary s_2 (*poor*), and its contradictory -s_2 (*not poor*). Greimas' technique seems to have borne particularly useful results in the analysis of narrative. It is beyond the purpose here to delve into the merits of the semiotic square. Suffice it to say that, along with the semantic differential, it suggests that there may be levels and scales of opposition that determine how we recognize signs. In the same time frame, anthropologist Claude Lévi-Strauss entered the debate on opposition theory by showing that pairs of oppositions often cohere into sets forming recognizable units. In analyzing kinship systems, for instance, Lévi-Strauss (1958) found that the elementary unit of kinship was made up of a set of four oppositions: *brother* vs. *sister, husband* vs. *wife, father* vs. *son*, and *mother's brother* vs. *sister's son*. Lévi-Strauss suspected that similar sets characterized units in other cultural systems and, thus, that their study would provide fundamental insights into the overall nature of human social organization.

But despite such elaborations, modifications, and elaborations, the basic notion of opposition remained intact. Whatever its format, its validity seems to lie in the psychological fact that signs have value only in relation to other signs. The relation can be binary, as are phonemic oppositions in language (*cat* vs. *rat*); it can be four-part, as are some semantic distinctions (*rich-not rich-poor-not poor*); it can be "graduated," as the semantic differential technique has shown with respect to connotative meaning; or it can be cohesive (set-based) as anthropologists such as Lévi-Strauss have discovered. These types of opposition are not mutually exclusive, as some have argued in the past. They are, in effect, complementary. The type of opposition that applies in any context of analysis, therefore, depends on what system (language, kinship, etc.) or subsystem (phonemic, semantic, etc.) is involved.

Markedness and Opposition

The attack on the notion opposition by post-structuralists surfaced in the 1950s shortly after markedness theory came onto the scene within the Prague School as a correlative notion. Just for the sake of argument, it is worth going over the theory rapidly here. The original idea behind markedness was to distinguish the role played by linguistic structures within the language (Tiersma 1982, Eckman 1983, Andrews 1990, Battistella 1990, Corbett 1991). Consider as a simple example, the indefinite article in English, which presents a case of morphophonemic variation:

(1) /a/	(2) /æn/
a boy	an egg
a girl	an island
a friend	an apple
a mother	an opera
a father	

By comparing the forms in (1) and (2), it can be seen that the allomorph

/a/ occurs before a morpheme beginning with a consonant and that its complementary allomorph /æn/ occurs before a morpheme beginning with a vowel. The Prague School linguists referred to a form such as (1) as the *unmarked* form and (2) as the *marked* one, because, they argued, the former is the representative (nonspecific) morph of the indefinite article category, while the latter is the exceptional morph. In the area of phonology the question arose as to which of the two phonemes in a minimal pair would be identified as the unmarked form and this led to truly fascinating debates about the nature of sounds, their frequency distribution in specific languages, their emergence in childhood, and so on. It was this pattern of discussion that led to an implicit acceptance of the notion of opposition as a theory of mind, because markedness features seemed to mirror social phenomena. In Italian, for example, the masculine plural form of nouns referring to people is the unmarked one, referring (nonspecifically) to any person, male or female; whereas the feminine plural form is marked, referring only to females. The fact that the unmarked form in Italian is the masculine gender, as it was (and often still is) in English, is a cue that Italian society is historically male-centered, leading to speculation that in societies (or communities) where the masculine gender is the unmarked form, it is the men who tend to be in charge of social processes (family lineage patterns, surnaming patterns in marriage, etc.); while in societies (or communities) where the feminine gender is the unmarked form, the women are typically the ones in charge. Research has tended to bear this out, suggesting that grammatical structure mirrors social structure. As King aptly puts it, in societies where the masculine is the unmarked form in grammar, "men have traditionally been the political leaders, the most acclaimed writers, the grammarians, and the dictionary makers, and it is their world view that is encoded in language" (2).

In effect, markedness theory has raised critical questions about social inequalities and the structure of the language that encodes them—an event that the Prague School linguists could certainly not have anticipated but would likely have welcomed. In English, sexist terms like *chairman, spokesman,* etc. were often cited in the not-too-distant past as examples of how the English language predisposed its users to view certain social roles in gender terms. Feminist critics maintained (correctly) that English grammar was organized from the perspective of those at the center of the society—the men. This is why in the recent past (and even to some extent today) we would say that a woman married into a man's family, and why at wedding ceremonies expressions such as "I pronounce you man and wife," were used. Similarly damaging language was the kind that excluded women, such as "lady doctor" or "female lawyer," implying that doctors and lawyers were not typically female.

In woman-centered societies the reverse seems to be true. Investigating grammatical gender in the Iroquois language, Alpher (1987) found that in that language the feminine gender was the unmarked one, with masculine items being marked by a special prefix. Alpher related this to the fact that Iroquois society is matrilineal. The women hold the land, pass it on to their heirs in the female line, are responsible for agricultural production, control the wealth, arrange marriages, and so on. Iroquois grammar is clearly organized from the viewpoint of those at the center of that particular society—the women.

The foregoing discussion suggests that "linguistic activism" is likely to be an effective way for setting things right. Can we potentially change social structure by changing linguistic structure? Consider job designations as a case-in-point. Over the past sixty years, as women increasingly entered into traditionally male-based occupations, their presence was perceived (at first) to be a deviation from tradition. Logically, their job titles were marked linguistically by adding suffixes such as *-ess* to male-referencing words: for example, *waitress* or *actress*. It has taken decades to get across the point that the females in such jobs are worthy of the same word-forms as those used for males *(waiter, actor)*. And to this day, it is a battle to get such language changed to reflect the new realities. Moreover, changes in language do not always indicate the same kinds of social consequences. It all depends on the specific situation. Francophone feminists, for example, "advocate separate male and female terms because gender is an inherent feature of the French grammatical system" (King 27). Therefore, adding *-e* to the word *advocat* (male lawyer) to create *advocate* (female lawyer), is a linguistic validation of women's place in the professional workforce.

By the late 1950s the theory of markedness started stimulating more and more debate, leading to a revisitation and ultimate rejection of the notion of opposition—a rejection that was given the designation "post-structuralism." This counter-movement rejected the implicit premise on which opposition was built, namely that meaning differences could be computed by assuming that signs related to each other through contrast and that the resulting contrasts reflected patterns within human cognition. This is why oppositions such as *good* vs. *evil* are found encoded in all kinds structures and units, from words that objectify them to myths that explicate them. Simply put, they mirror a dichotomy felt universally by human beings—a dichotomy that finds its way into other linguistic oppositions such as *order* vs. *chaos* and *God* vs. *the devil*.

Post-structuralism is associated primarily with the late French philosophers Michel Foucault (1926-1984) and Jacques Derrida (1930-2004), who bluntly refuted the classic notions of Saussurean structuralism (Foucault 1972, Derrida 1976). Arguably, the central idea that set off this movement was that signs do not encode reality, but rather construct it. According to Derrida all sign systems are self-referential—signs refer to other signs, which refer to still other signs, and so on ad infinitum. Thus, what appears stable and logical turns out to be illogical and paradoxical. Many semioticians have severely criticized this radical stance of post-structuralism. It has nevertheless had a profound impact on many different fields of knowledge, not just semiotics, including the sciences, reflecting two larger twentieth-century intellectual trends known as absurdism and existentialism. So what do post-structuralists analyze and how does post-structuralism differ from traditional structuralist practice? From many points of view, post-structuralism is really nothing more than structuralism expanded to include a few radical ideas (at least for Saussurean theory). One of these was logocentrism—the view that all human knowledge is constructed by linguistic categories. It was also claimed that this very same logocentrism characterized semiotic practices themselves, rendering them virtually useless. Derrida maintained, in essence, that linguistic forms encode "ideologies," not "realities." And because written language is the fundamental condition of knowledge-producing enterprises, such as science and philosophy, these end up reflecting nothing more than the writing practices used to articulate them. In hindsight, there was nothing particularly radical in the early post-structuralist position, at least for linguists, because at the time structuralism itself was undergoing a serious self-examination and reevaluation—a fact that the post-structuralists seem conveniently to have forgotten or ignored. Already in the 1920s, Jakobson and Trubetzkoy started probing the "relativity" of language oppositions in the light of their social and psychological functions. Basing their ideas in part on the work of German psychologist Karl Bühler (1879-1963), the Prague School linguists posited three main relative functions of language—the cognitive, the expressive, and the conative (or instrumental). The cognitive function refers to the employment of language for the transmission of factual information; the expressive to the fact that language allows the speaker (or writer) to convey mood or attitude; and the conative to the use of language to influence the persons being addressed or to bring about some practical effect via communication. A number of Prague scholars (such as Jakobson) even suggested that these three functions correlated in many languages, at least partly, with grammatical categories. In effect, grammar does not exist independently of cognition and culture.

Questions related to markedness and opposition at levels above the phoneme quickly followed. In pairs such *night* versus *day* it is probably easy to identify *day* as the unmarked form and *night* as its marked counterpart. This does not mean that one is more basic than the other, but rather that it is perceived to be that way for whatever historical or even evolutionary reason. In effect, we perceive *day* as the positive pole in the opposition and *night* as its derivative or counterpositive one. Now, what about the *male* vs. *female* opposition? In this case, the choice of one or the other as the unmarked pole would clearly reflect a cultural (not an absolute) emphasis. In patrilineal societies the unmarked form is likely to be *male*; but in matrilineal ones, as the Iroquois society mentioned above, the unmarked is just as likely to be *female*. More research is clearly needed in this domain. So, rather than discard the technique of opposition as biased towards certain ideologies, as the post-structuralists maintained, it turns out to be actually a critical investigative tool for correlating linguistic forms with social structure and organization. Moreover, since opposition operates across a vast array of nonverbal codes—in the musical code at the level of tones and harmonies (for example, major vs. minor); in the mythical code at the historical-conceptual level (for example, good vs. evil)—it is obvious that it has the capacity of identifying points of contact among the various codes, not to mention pointing to universal structures of cognition across codes and across cultures.

Is Opposition Valid Today?

For the sake of historical accuracy, it should be mentioned that the concept of opposition is hardly an invention of linguists and semioticians. It is an ancient notion. Aristotle, for instance, developed his philosophical system on the basis of a set of existential oppositions: Unity vs. Multiplicity, Being vs. Non-Being, and others. Opposition is a widespread intuitive notion, surfacing in the philosophical, religious, and other writings of cultures across the world. The following oppositions seem to be universal, occurring in representational traditions of societies around the world:

Masculine	vs.	Feminine
Light	vs.	Dark
Good	vs.	Evil
Self	vs.	Other
Subject	vs.	Object
Sacred	vs.	Profane
Body	vs.	Mind
Nature	vs.	History
Positive	vs.	Negative
Heaven	vs.	Hell
Beginning	vs.	End
Love	vs.	Hate
Pleasure	vs.	Pain
Existence	vs.	Nothingness
Left	vs.	Right

As an example of how a single binary opposition might be encoded in various systems, consider the Left vs. Right one. This is derived, obviously, from the fact that we have a left hand (and foot, leg, ear, and eye) and a right one. Here are a few of the ways in which this opposition surfaces culturally.

- It intersects with other oppositions—Right is associated with Good, Light, etc. and Left with Evil, Dark, etc. The English word *sinister* derives from Latin *sinistra* "on the left, unlucky," linking left-handedness with connotations of evil and misfortune.
- In the fresco of the *Last Judgment* painted by Michelangelo in the ceiling of the Sistine Chapel, Christ is depicted as condemning Evil sinners to Hell with his left hand but permitting passage to Heaven for Good people with a blessing of his right hand.
- The word *right* is used commonly in English-speaking societies (and others) to convey concepts of "correctness," "truth," "justice." In the United States, *The Bill of Rights* is a legal document that lays out the *rights* to which each person is entitled. Canada has a similar document called *The Charter of Rights and Freedoms*.
- A *righteous* person is defined as someone moral, and thus without guilt or sin.
- A *right hand man* is someone with considerable power and authority.
- English has adopted the French word *gauche*, which literally means "left," to describe someone who lacks social polish or who is tactless.
- Offering a handshake, saluting, or taking an oath with the left hand is considered improper and wrong.

The list of the manifestations of the Right vs. Left opposition is a huge one. The plausible reason why we have come to assign positive connotations to the Right member of the opposition and negative connotations to the Left one probably stems from the fact that the majority of human beings use their right hands to carry out routine tasks. It is estimated that only about 10% of the population is left-handed. As a consequence, the right hand is perceived to be the default form of human handedness. However, as mentioned several times, markedness is hardly a phenomenon of Nature. Nature makes no social distinctions between right-handed and left-handed individuals; people do. As can be seen by examining the opposition sets above, determining which member of a pair is the unmarked form and which one the marked one is more a matter of tradition and history than it is of anything else. Good, for example, has always been assumed to be the default form of human behavior in many societies, while Evil has always been perceived to be its antagonistic counterpart. In sum, one cannot underestimate the importance of markedness, and more generally, of opposition, in unraveling the reasons behind certain social behaviors and perceptions. The oppositions encoded in language and other semiotic systems are culture-specific ways of reacting to contextualized realities.

Concluding Remarks

In conclusion, in my view at least, structuralism is not finished. It has survived truly devastating attacks from generativism (which have not been discussed here because they are beyond the scope of the present discussion) and post-structuralism, coming out of the attacks intact and even stronger. The theory of opposition remains the implicit working principle in contemporary linguistic and semiotic analysis. Even the truly interesting work going on in cognitive linguistics on metaphor and figurative language generally was always intrinsic to structuralist inquiry—I mention Jakobson's key work in this domain as well as that of the structuralist-Gestalt psychologists (see Danesi 2004 for a summary). As one of the most important achievements of the Prague School linguists, the technique of opposition, continues to have validity in showing the relation of form with content, both internally within a system such as language and externally to the larger psychological and social domains. It has allowed semiotics and linguistics to broaden the way in which meaning can be studied. In the end, the post-structuralist movement was, arguably, nothing more than a reaction to Saussureanism in its most radical forms. It was (and continues to be) of little or no interest to semioticians who work primarily within the framework of the Peircean sign, which emphasizes the interpretive component in semiosis. Ultimately, it might turn out to be a theory of mind after all, in the same way that archetype theory in Jungian psychology has turned out to be such a theory, starting rather simply as a way of understanding the recurrence of symbols and rituals in cultures across the world. Opposition theory is to linguistics and semiotics what archetype theory is to psychology and philosophy. It is one of those notions that has always been implicit in human affairs, but which needed articulation by someone to confirm its existence. That articulation crystallized in Prague in the 1920s.

Works cited

Alpher, B. Feminine as the unmarked grammatical gender: Buffalo girls are no fools. *Australian Journal of Linguistics* 7, 1987. 169-187.

Andrews, E. *Markedness Theory*. Durham: Duke U P, 1990.

Battistella, E. L. *Markedness: The Evaluative Superstructure of Language*. Albany:

State U of New York P, 1990.

Benveniste, E. Structure des relations de personne dans le verbe. *Bulletin de la Société de Linguistique de Paris* 43, 1946. 225-236.

Bühler, K. [originally 1908]. On Thought Connection. In *Organization and Pathology of Thought.* Ed. D. Rapaport. New York: Columbia UP, 1951. 81-92.

Bühler, K. *Sprachtheorie: Die Darstellungsfunktion der Sprache.* Jena: Fischer, 1934.

Corbett, G. *Gender.* Cambridge: Cambridge UP, 1991.

Danesi, M. *Poetic Logic: The Role of Metaphor in Thought, Language, and Culture.* Madison: Atwood Publishing, 2004.

Danesi, M. *The Quest for Meaning: A Guide to Semiotic Theory and Practice.* Toronto: U of Toronto P, 2007.

Eckman, F. R. et al. (eds.) *Markedness.* New York: Plenum, 1983.

Greimas, A. J. *On Meaning: Selected Essays in Semiotic Theory*, trans. by P. Perron and F. Collins. Minneapolis: U of Minnesota P, 1987.

Hjelmslev, L. Note sur les oppositions supprimables. *Travaux de Cercle Linguistique de Prague* 8, 1939. 51-57.

Hjelmslev, L. *Essais linguistique.* Copenhagen: Munksgaard, 1959.

Jakobson, R. Observations sur le classement phonologique des consonnes. *Proceedings of the Fourth International Congress of Phonetic Sciences,* 1939. 34-41.

Derrida, J. *Of Grammatology*, trans. by G. C. Spivak. Baltimore: Johns Hopkins Press, 1976.

Foucault, M. *The Archeology of Knowledge*, trans. by A. M. Sheridan Smith. New York: Pantheon, 1972.

Jakobson, R. *Kindersprache, Aphasie und algemeine Lautgesetze.* Uppsala: Almqvist and Wiksell, 1942.

King, R. *Talking Gender: A Nonsexist Guide to Communication.* Toronto: Copp Clark Pitman Ltd, 1991.

Lévi-Strauss, C. *Structural Anthropology.* New York: Basic Books, 1958.

Ogden, C. K. *Opposition: A Linguistic and Psychological Analysis.* London: Paul, Trench, and Trubner, 1932.

Osgood, C. E., Suci, G. J., and Tannenbaum, P. H. *The Measurement of Meaning.* Urbana: U of Illinois P, 1957.

Saussure, F. de. *Cours de linguistique générale*, ed. by C. Bally and A. Sechehaye Paris: Payot, 1916.

Tiersma, P. M. Local and general markedness. *Language* 58, 1982. 832-849.

Trubetzkoy, N. *Introduction to the Principles of Phonological Description.* The Hague: Martinus Nijhoff, 1968.

Trubetzkoy, N. S. Essaie d'une théorie des oppositions phonologiques. *Journal de Psychologie* 33, 1936. 5-18.

Trubetzkoy, N. S. Grundzüge der Phonologie. *Travaux du Cercle Linguistique de Prague* 7, 1939. (entire issue).

Eventfulness and Context

Wolf Schmid
Universität Hamburg

1.

"Eventfulness" (*sobytijnost'*), a category that has been introduced into the discussion by Iurii Lotman, designates an important narrative phenomenon and is a major narratological tool. But it is not an objective category that can simply be applied to texts. It is at least in some of its parameters a hermeneutic, subject-dependent and context-sensitive category indicative of interpretation.

However, subject-dependency and context-sensitivity is no harm for narratology. Narratology should do more than design clinically pure, aseptic analytical tools whose purpose is to generate objective descriptions that stand alone and have nothing to do with context and interpretation. In fact, there is little merit in the dichotomy between objective description and subjective, context-sensitive interpretation. For example, the task of recognizing a change of state is, more often than not, heavily dependent on interpretation, either because the explicit properties of the initial and final states are not equivalent and thus require suppositions to be made if they are to be comparable, or because the difference between the states themselves is not clear. It might be suggested that the categories of narratology as such are pure, and that a certain degree of subjective contamination occurs only when they are applied to individual texts, if at all. But what about categories such as the *implied author, free indirect discourse,* and others, whose status and delimitation have been the theme of scholarly controversies for decades?

In so far as it can be assumed that eventfulness is indeed a narratological category, my aim here is to consider its usefulness, the range of its applications and the way it depends on context and interpretation.

2.

Let us begin by clarifying the basic terms (for details see: Schmid 2003; 2005: 11–17, 20–27; see also Hühn):

1. *Narrativity*: narrativity implies a temporal sequence representing changes of state.

2. *Change of state*: a state is to be understood as a set of properties

which refer to an agent or to the external situation at a particular point in time. The minimal condition of a story is that at least one change of state must be represented. Edward Morgan Forster's famous example of a minimal story is still too extensive. Forster (82) had coined the example: "The king died and then the queen died". As Gérard Genette (15) pointed out, for a minimal story it is sufficient to have the simple "The king died".

A change of state that gives rise to narrativity implies at least the following:
(1) a temporal structure with at least two states, the initial situation and the final situation (the king alive and the king dead),
(2) an equivalence of the initial and final state, that is, the presence of a similarity and a contrast between the states (being alive and being dead form a classical equivalence),
(3) both states, and the change that takes place between them, must concern one and the same acting or suffering subject (in our case this is the poor king).

3. *Event:* an event is a special type of change of state that presupposes factivity and resultativity. *Factivity* means that changes of state that are only wished for, imagined, or dreamed of are not events (the real acts of wishing, imagining, or dreaming can, of course, qualify as events). *Resultativity* is a correlate of an event's factivity. The change of state that constitutes an event is neither inchoative (begun) nor conative (attempted) nor durative (confined to an ongoing process). Instead, it must be resultative in that it reaches completion in the narrative world of the text.

Reality and resultativity are necessary conditions of an event in the strict sense. However, it is clear that these requirements alone are not sufficient to turn a change of state into an event, for they can both be fulfilled by trivial changes of state.

In the following, I shall describe five features which I believe a change of state must display if it is to be described as an event. These features are listed in a hierarchical order because of their different levels of importance:
(1) *relevance*, the significance of the change of state in a narrative world,
(2) *unpredictability*, the extent to which the change of state deviates from the doxa of the narrative (that is, what is generally expected in the narrative world),
(3) *persistence*, the consequences for the thought and action of the affected subject in the narrative world,
(4) *irreversibility*,
(5) *non-iterativity*.

We will return to these requirements below. (Ockham might have argued that this is too plentiful a list of features and that some overlap with others; unpredictability, for example, seems to imply non-iterativity. But this is not so. The features have been obtained by means of induction rather than by means of deductive reasoning. They are derived from the prose of the Russian post-realist Anton Chekhov, in which they are independent of each other.)

The fourth basic term is *eventfulness*: eventfulness is a scalable property of events. This means that events can have varying levels of eventfulness depending on the prominence of the five features described above. Among them, the first two, namely relevance and unpredictability, are the most important. If a change of state is to be called an event, it must display both these features to some degree at least.

The fifth and last term is *tellability*: this term, introduced by William Labov (1972), designates something that is *worth* telling, the *raison d'être*, the *point* of a story. In a narrative with a high degree of eventfulness, the eventfulness will, as a rule, coincide with tellability. In narratives with low eventfulness or no eventfulness at all, tellability can stem from the absence of an event that the reader might have expected. Though the non-expectedness of a change of state is an important prerequisite for an event, the non-fulfilment of an expectation is not, as such, an event. But it can be the point of a narrative. This can be seen from *Povídky malostranské* ("Tales of the Little Quarter"), a collection of stories by the nineteenth-century Czech writer Jan Neruda. In one of them *(Jak si nakou il pan Vorel p novku)*, the hero attempts to establish a new grocery somewhere in the Little Quarter of Prague where there has never been a shop before.

Iurii Lotman would have called this the "movement of a literary character across the borders of a semantic field" (*peremeščenie personaža čerez granicu semanti českogo polja, Struktura* 282) or the "crossing of a forbidden border" (*peresesčenie zapreščajščej granicy, Struktura* 288). Those are the two definitions of an event Lotman gives in the seminal chapter *Problems of the syuzhet* of his *Structure of the Artistic text*. Lotman uses topological terms as the basis for his definition, but he stresses the normative relevance of the definition by pointing out that normative values tend to be described using spatial images and oppositions. Thus, Lotman's spatial semantics should be understood as a metaphor for non-spatial, normative values.

Let us return to Neruda's tale. The grocer's attempt to establish a new grocery is doomed to fail because of the reluctance of the established bourgeoisie to accept change in their lives. The boycott of the new shop leads to the border violator's bankruptcy and eventual suicide. The death of the grocer is therefore not completely unexpected for reader and narrative world. It is a somewhat foreseeable consequence of what precedes it and is therefore a change with a relatively low degree of eventfulness. The actually 'tellable' thing in this story is the failure of an intended border crossing or the lethal consequences of a completed border crossing. The whole collection of stories in *Tales of the Little Quarter* is devoted to the uneventfulness of this microcosm, to the impenetrability of its borders. This is symbolized by the oft-mentioned city walls that surround the Little Quarter (for details see my "Jak si nakon").

3.

At least two of the five features listed above, namely *relevance* and *unpredictability*, are not objective ones, but rather depend on interpretation and context.

Relevance is a heavily subject-dependent and context-sensitive category. Not only the characters of a narrative world, but also the narrator and implied semantic entities such as the abstract author and the abstract reader, can evaluate the relevance of a narrated change of state in different ways. Moreover we need to take account of the fact that real readers can have individual concepts of relevance that do not conform with those of the fictitious and implied entities—not to speak of the different assessments of relevance by real authors and readers, or by abstract entities and fictitious characters on the one hand and real readers of later times on the other.

That the idea of relevance is a relative one is illustrated by Chekhov in a story with the narratologically promising title "An Event" (*Sobytie*). The story is, apparently, about nothing more than how a cat gives birth and Nero, an enormous dog, eats all the kittens, but, in Chekhov's hands, it illustrates the subjectivity which can influence how we evaluate relevance. The birth of the kittens is a happening of great significance for the little children Vanya and Nina. Then, while the adults readily accept Nero's eating the kittens and feel nothing more than surprise at the dog's insatiable appetite, the children feel that the world has come to an end.

A similar subject-dependency and context-sensitivity applies to *unpredictability*. Eventfulness increases in proportion to the extent to which a change of state deviates from the doxa of the narrative. (The doxa of the narrative is, as has been already mentioned, what is generally expected in the narrative world). This does not mean that the event must rest, as Lotman suggests, on the breach of a norm or the violation of a prohibition. Instead, the essence of the event lies in the fact that it breaks with expectations. A highly eventful change is 'paradoxical' in the literal sense of the word: it is not what we expect. (Aristotle, *De arte rhetorica* 1412a 27, defines paradox as that which contradicts general expectation.) The 'doxa' refers to the narrative world and its protagonists and is not equivalent to the reader's 'script' (that is, what the reader expects in the action on the basis of certain patterns in literature or the real world). A change of state that comes as a surprise to the protagonists in a narrative world can be perfectly predictable for an expert reader if it is a genre characteristic. It follows that the reader's script concerning the course of a work and the protagonists' expectations concerning the course of their lives must be treated as distinct and separate notions.

A change of state that can be seen to follow the normal rules of a narrative world is predictable and thus will have a low level of eventfulness, even if it is of great importance to the individual protagonists involved in it. If a bride marries her groom, it is not, strictly speaking, eventful. But it is likely to be surprising for everyone involved, including the bride herself, if, as in Chekhov's story "The Betrothed" (*Nevesta*), she dumps her prospective husband just before the wedding, after all the arrangements and plans have been made. If this happens, the failure to marry is far more eventful than the marriage every-one expects would be.

Another of Chekhov's marriage stories, "The Teacher of Literature" (*Učitel' slovesnosti*), illustrates how unpredictability is not a constant feature but can change during the course of a narrative. Maša Šelestova seems unattainable to Nikitin, the teacher of literature, and declaring his love for her means gathering all his courage and taking a truly heroic step, for it seems completely impossible to him that he will ever be able to marry this charming girl. The reader, however, can tell from Maša's behavior that she is not likely to resist the proposal with any great conviction; and, after the hero takes the decisive step, he must himself recognize that what he supposed to be a border crossing was actually a perfectly nor-mal act that everyone expected (for the problematization and reduction, but not absence of eventfulness in Chekhov's stories see Schmid 1992; 1997).

As we have seen, relevance and unpredictability are heavily dependent on the subject evaluating the change of state. Each of the depicted, narrating and reading entities is a subject on its own and has its own social and axiological context that determines its norms and expectations.

4.

Such references to context-sensitivity and the suggestion that eventfulness is dependent on context provoke the question: what is context anyway? What does it mean to be context-sensitive? At least three meanings of 'context' can be distinguished.

1. First, 'context' means the system of the general social norms and values of the author's time or of the time depicted in a work. The force of social perspectives on literature in the 1970s, however, led to a tremendous overestimation of the relevance of reconstructing the social context of the author's epoch or of the epoch depicted in a work. To understand the eventfulness of *Madame Bovary*, there is no need to study the social order of France at those times or the curriculum of French convent schools or the state of medical science. It is clear that Emma's expectations of happiness have been spoilt by reading too many bad love novels and that Bovary is a poor surgeon. It is a happy truth that literary works provide, more or less overtly, information about the norms and values in terms of which their eventfulness should be understood. This is the reason why we can understand medieval narratives not having studied the social norms of the time depicted.

2. Second, more specifically, 'context' means the individual social norms, ideologies etc, that are attributed to the depicted, narrating and implied sending and receiving entities of a narrative to motivate their behavior. The intersection of contexts in a narrative is a challenge to the real reader. He can't simply immerse himself in the depicted world and take the position of a hero but is rather invited to check the relevance and unpredictability of an event against the background of the different contexts.

3. Very important is the reconstruction of another context, that is to say, the concept of the event in different genres and literary movements in a given period. Genres and movements are characterized by certain concepts of what is eventful. In Russian literature of the 1830s, for example, epic poetry developed event concepts quite different from those of contemporary narrative prose, and late romanticism allowed for forms of border crossing different from those of contemporary early realism. To understand eventfulness, it is necessary to know the event code of the genre and movement in question.

4. Considerably important but often underestimated is the *intertextual* context. I have already pointed out that a change of state that comes as a surprise to a character may not be surprising at all to well-read readers because they are prepared by pretexts. On the other hand, eventfulness may emerge in view of the pretexts.

Let me give an example. In Pushkin's novella "The Stationmaster" (*Stancionnyj smotritel'*) the title hero drinks himself to death through grief about the presumable ruin of his daughter who, as it seems to him or as he wants to believe, was abducted by a young hussar. But after her father's death the daughter seems to have made her luck. Both the changes of father and daughter emerge as highly surprising and thus eventful when perceived against the background of pretexts. The daughter's happiness contradicts the sad fate of all the poor Lizas, Marfas and Mashas, the peasant heroines of Russian Sentimental literature who, having been seduced by a young nobleman, eventually drown themselves in the village pond. The father's behavior contradicts the generosity of the father in the Parable of the prodigal son, a pretext that is presented by four illustrations adorning the walls of the Russian stationmaster's humble room. Instead of patiently waiting for his presumably prodigal daughter the father, the real prodigal one, drinks himself to death (details in Schmid 1991: 103–170).

Following Viktor Shklovsky (1925), it can in general be said that literature is perceived against the background of preceding literature rather than against the background of real life. This is why the intertextual context is so important.

5.

Where, then, lies the usefulness of the category of eventfulness? Eventfulness is a culture specific and historically changing phenomenon of narrative representation. The category is therefore particularly important when it comes to dealing with problems of cultural typology and the history of literature and thought. Let me give some examples of different concepts of eventfulness in Russian literature.

In Old Russian literature, that is, Russian literature up to the seventeenth century, which was strongly influenced by religious thought, eventfulness does not present itself as a positive quality. There is no unpredictability in hagiography, the leading genre of the time. Of course, hagiographical texts as a rule represent changes of state, and they often culminate in miracles. Miracles are not really surprising and unforeseeable in this textual world, though, for they follow holy models and affirm the Christian world order. Essentially, the hagiographical world does not admit fundamental surprises.

Eventfulness in our modern sense appears in Russia only in some 'secular tales' (*svetskie povesti*) of the seventeenth century that were influenced by western European novellas of the Renaissance. These secular tales tell of morally dubious heroes and their border crossings that are no longer punished at the end as was the case in religious tales. The hero in *The Tale of Frol Skobeev*, for example, is able to rise in society and then marry the daughter of a dignitary whom he has cunningly seduced earlier, all without prospect of worldly retribution.

This phase of secular narrative, of course, was never more than an episode; it was not returned to in the subsequent development of Russian literature. In the eighteenth century, the classical concept of literature pushed eventful narration aside. The classical episteme is defined by the idea of order and seeks to classify all phenomena. This leads to the predominance of description over narration. Varying predications are not the basis of changes but characterize things in terms of their nature and possibilities, both of which serve to predetermine development as something essentially non-contingent (see Dehne 56–78). This means that eventfulness in the modern sense is impossible, since the unpredictability and border crossing that are its constituent features have no positive place in the eighteenth century's shape of the world.

Eventfulness gained the upper hand only with the prose of sentimentalism and romanticism around 1800. The event was increasingly modeled as a change in the internal, mental state of a character. This development culminated in the realist novels in which a variety of event concepts are deployed. In Ivan Turgenev's novels, people are basically portrayed as unchangeable (Markovič, 1975); Tolstoy and Dostoyevsky, on the other hand, give form to mental processes that have been described as cases of insight, illumination, and sudden understanding. The realist event concept culminates in Rodion Raskol'nikov's 'resurrection' in *Crime and Punishment*, the sudden understanding of the meaning of life gained by Konstantin Levin in *Anna Karenina* and Pierre Bezukhov in *War and Peace*, and in the Karamazov brothers' final acknowledgement of guilt. It should be remembered that in both authors the internal change is linked with transcendental forces. Clear enough in Tolstoy, this is clearer still in Dostoyevsky, who uses the saint's life as a model when crafting the chain reaction of conversions in *The Brothers Karamazov* (Schmid 2005). Not by chance is the story of the first conversion, namely that of Markel, Zosimas' atheist brother, told in the language of hagiographical style throughout. This reflects Dostoevsky's attempt to reconcile hagiography and realism, to write a realistic vita, and thus move realism to 'a higher level'.

While the novels of the two realists show people who have the capacity to undergo fundamental transformations and transcend the boundaries of morality and the logic of personality, Chekhov's post-realist narratives place a major question mark over the eventfulness of the world and the ability of people to change. Chekhov's narration is centered on interrogating the idea of a mental event, an existential or social insight, an emotional switch, or an ethical/practical reorientation. If an event does not occur, the tellability of the stories lies in how they represent its prevention, in how they illustrate the reasons that lead to the intention of change and prevent it from being realized. Chekhov's post-realist poetics thrives on the fact that tellability and eventfulness are no longer congruent. Consider, for example, the famous play *The Three Sisters*. The heroines, who lead an unfulfilled life in rural Russia, seek a fundamental change, as expressed in the repeated phrase 'to Moscow' (v Moskvu). The tellability of the play lies in the impossibility of crossing the topographical, occupational, existential and, last but not least, the characterological borders involved.

Socialist realism appears at first glance to have been a development in which eventfulness thrived. The conversion of the doubter or miscreant into a liberator of the people who supports the right side in the struggle was one of the most popular scripts in this kind of literature. On closer examination, however, this way of thinking, with its similarities to salvation history turned out to limit the possibility of border crossings just as much as the Church literature of the Middle Ages.

The picture in the literature of post-communist Russia is extremely varied. In the neo-realist, neo-mythic, and postmodern movements, the eventful stories of 'high' realism are continued, are transposed into mythic iteration, or have their illusory nature exposed. In all cases, though, event and eventfulness are useful narratological categories that can help us describe even the narrative structure and thought that define the most modern literature.

Works cited

Dehne, Marianne. *Der Wissensumbruch um 1800 in der russischen Lyrik*. Frankfurt a. M.: Peter Lang, 2006.

Forster, Edward Morgan. *Aspects of the Novel*. London: Edward Arnold & Co, 1927.

Genette, Gérard. *Nouveau discours du récit*. Paris: Seuil, 1983.

Hühn, Peter. *Event and Eventfulness. Handbook of Narratology*. Berlin/New York: Walter de Gruyter. (forthcoming).

Labov, William. *Language in the Inner City: Studies in the Black English Vernacular*. Philadelphia: U of Pennsylvania P, 1972.

Lotman, Iurii M. *The Structure of the Artistic Text*. Trans. G. Lenhoff and R. Vroon. Ann Arbor: U of Michigan P, 1977.

___. *Struktura xudožestvennogo teksta*. Moskva: Iskusstvo, 1970.

Markovič, Vladimir M. *Čelovek v romanach I. S. Turgeneva*. Leningrad: Izd. Leninradskogo universiteta, 1975.

Schmid, Wolf. *Puškins Prosa in poetischer Lektüre. Die Erzählungen Belkins*. München: Wil-helm Fink, 1991.

___. Čechovs problematische Ereignisse". *Ornamentales Erzählen in der russischen Moderne. Čechov – Babel' – Zamjatin*. Frankfurt a. M.: Peter Lang, 1992. 104–134.

___. "Jak si nakouřil pan Vorel pěnovku. Událostnost v Nerudových 'Povídkách malostranských'". *Čechá literatura* 42 (1994): 570–583.

___. "Modi des Erkennens in Čechovs narrativer Welt". *Anton P. Čechov– philosophische und religiöse Dimensionen im Leben und im Werk*. Eds. V. B. Kataev, R.-D. Kluge, and R. Nohejl. München: Sagner, 1997. 529–536.

———. "Narrativity and Eventfulness". *What is Narratology? Questions and Answers Regarding the Status of a Theory.* Eds. Tom Kindt and Hans Harald Müller. Berlin and New York: Walter de Gruyter, 2003. 17-33.

———. "Ereignishaftigkeit in den 'Brüdern Karamasow'". *Dostoevsky Studies. The Journal of the International Dostoevsky Society*, New Series 9 (2005): 31–44.

Šklovskij, Viktor B. *O teorii prozy.* Moskva: Federacija, 1925.

Reading Functionally Polyvalent Events

Emma Kafalenos
Washington University in St. Louis

In the abstract he provided for the 2007 *Structuralism(s) Today* conference, Uri Margolin perceptively analyzes Lubomír Doležel's method in *Occidental Poetics*. As Margolin recognizes, Doležel translates earlier theories "into contemporary vocabulary." The effect of that, Margolin further discerns, is to make the earlier theories "actual, accessible, and easier to assess in terms of present day relevance and value." Although I have been well aware for a long time that Lubomír Doležel's analysis of Vladimir Propp's theories provided a bridge across which I discovered an aspect of Propp's work that seems relevant and valuable today, Margolin's analysis has helped me understand why Doležel's work was so useful in the development of my thinking.

In *Occidental Poetics*, in the section devoted to Propp, Doležel introduces two terms that led me to perceive a new use for a closed set of functions like Propp's thirty-one. Doležel's two terms are "functional equivalence" and "functional polyvalence" (144). According to the principle of functional equivalence, one function can be expressed by a number of different events. According to the principle of functional polyvalence, one event can represent different functions. The two principles are interdependent and complementary, but the latter, functional polyvalence, more directly underlies the analytical method I have developed from Propp's work. If a given event can represent one function in one context and another function in another context, then our interpretations of the function of the event will depend on the context from which we perceive it and thus can vary from perceiver to perceiver. I illustrate using an example I borrow from Tzvetan Todorov: a feud (64-68). If family A has had a family member killed by family B, and then family A kills a member of family B, from the perspective of family A revenge has been successfully accomplished and equilibrium regained. For family B, however, the death of a family member disrupts the equilibrium and incites plans to kill someone in family A. Functional polyvalence explains how contradictory interpretations of the causality of an event can logically occur.

A closed set of functions—whether Propp's thirty-one or the more concise ten-function model I have constructed—provides a uniform vocabulary for naming interpretations of the function of events by people perceiving events in our world, by readers perceiving fictional events, and by narrators and by characters perceiving events in fictional worlds. Because the vocabulary is uniform, interpretations can be compared. In addition, the vocabulary of functions enables tracing the shifts in interpretation that occur when new information changes the context in which an event is perceived—whether the new information becomes available to readers during the process of reading a narrative, or to fictional characters as they learn about continuing and previously unrevealed events in their world, or to us as we learn about both ongoing and earlier events in our own world.

In my book *Narrative Causalities*, I argue that causality is an interpretation and that narratives guide readers' interpretations of the causes and effects of reported events by establishing the set of events in relation to which these interpretations are made. But just as the finite set of events that a narrative reports provides the context in relation to which readers interpret the reported events, so too does the broader socio-political-cultural system from the perspective of which a text is read. In a recent study of translation in anthropology, Paula G. Rubel and Abraham Rosman describe translation as "a matter of comparing systems of contextualization of one language and culture with systems of contextualization of another" (15). Even more specifically, Aram. A. Yengoyan defines "the job of the translator . . . as taking the message or idea that someone has expressed in language A and rendering the message in language B in a way that speakers of B will understand readily" (32).

While it is now generally recognized that one's socio-political-cultural situation influences one's understanding of perceived events, detailed analysis of the effects of a perceiver's situation on her or his interpretation of as basic an element as cause and effect is not so common and can provide support for other theorists' broader findings. To explore the effects of a perceiver's situation specifically on interpretations of causality, I propose to compare my initial naïve misreading of a story written in Chinese, which I can read only in translation, with my somewhat better informed interpretation after reading an early article by Martin Weizong Huang, who grew up in China, received his Ph.D. from Washington University, and is presently professor of Chinese at the University of California at Irvine. The story to which I am analyzing my response is "Ah Q—The Real Story," written in 1921, by the famous, early twentieth-century Chinese writer Lu Xun (1881-1936).[1]

---

[1] I am grateful to my colleague at Washington University Robert E. Hegel, the Liselotte Dieckmann Professor of Comparative Literature and Professor of Chinese, for his support of this project, his guidance in selecting a translation of Lu Xun's story, and his reassurance that my interpretations that I label "somewhat better informed" are not unlike those of contemporary Chinese specialists.

The story offers a satiric representation of a protagonist, Ah Q, for whom nothing goes well. On two occasions recounted in the story he has money in his purse. On the first occasion Ah Q has been gambling and is actually winning. But he is indiscreet. He draws attention to himself in a crowd of strangers by loudly yelling out the very large bet he is making—and as a result he is beaten and robbed. On the other occasion he returns to Wei Village, where he lives, with money and with possessions to sell for more money, after spending time in the nearby town. The villagers assume he is a thief and place orders for items they want. But when asked he explains that he was unable to climb walls or to enter buildings and that his role as a thief had consisted of standing outside to receive the stolen goods. Even that was more than he could handle. Hearing a commotion inside one night he lost his nerve and ran away, package in hand: the package he had brought to the village that contained the items he has been selling. Moreover he admits that he no longer dares engage in theft.

Shortly thereafter, the revolution reaches first the town and then Wei Village. This is the 1911 Revolution that unseats the last Emperor and brings the Qing dynasty to its end. Ah Q tries to join the revolutionaries because, after his experience as a thief, he perceives the revolutionaries as engaged in theft. He wants to be a revolutionary because he wants his share. But his efforts to join come to naught. He is turned down; the village leaders chase him away. Several days later, with his usual bad luck, he is arrested as an accomplice in a robbery in which he was not involved, and then executed for being a revolutionary, which he was not, and for a theft that he did not commit.

In *Narrative Causalities* I present my ten-function model and demonstrate the usefulness for analysis of all ten functions. For comparing my naïve to my better-informed interpretations of Lu Xun's story, the five key functions are sufficient:

Figure 1: Functions

    Eq   Equilibrium (automobile runs when turned on)
    A   destabilizing event (automobile destroyed in an accident)
or a   re-evaluation that reveals instability (automobile looks worn, may need repairs)
    C   C-actant's decision to attempt to alleviate A or a (decision to buy another automobile)
    C'   C-actant's initial act to alleviate A or a (test-driving potential models)
    H   C-actant's primary action to alleviate A or a (deciding on a vehicle and completing the deal
    I   success of H (automobile is acquired)
    EQ Equilibrium (automobile runs when turned on; is no longer a problem)

Function A represents an event that disrupts a prevailing equilibrium and brings on a period of instability. Let us take as an example of an equilibrium one's ongoing relationship with an automobile one has had for a while. It is always there when one needs it and one doesn't think about it much. But then something happens that disrupts the ongoing equilibrium. My model distinguishes between two kinds of disruptive events. Capital-letter A represents an event that changes the narrative world: one's automobile is destroyed in an accident and suddenly needs to be replaced. Lower-case a represents a change in someone's interpretation of the narrative world: one day one recognizes that the upholstery in one's automobile is torn in spots, and then one remembers that it is about time to buy new tires and that maybe the clutch is going to need to be replaced. Either situation can motivate buying a car.

Function C represents the decision to ameliorate the function-A situation, in this case to buy a car. If test-driving potential models is the first step in the process, that action is represented by function C' [C prime]. Deciding on a particular vehicle and completing the deal fills function H, and function I marks the success of the endeavor and the establishment of a new equilibrium. Having bought a car, the function-A situation is resolved. One no longer needs to buy one.

In my initial reading of Lu Xun's story, I can conceive that Ah Q's motivation is his perceived lack of money. According to that interpretation (Figure 2 below), his lack of money can be perceived as a motivating lower-case function a. Deciding to do something about it (function C), he joins a group of gamblers (function C'), and as his winnings grow he stakes increasingly large amounts of money (function H). But instead of succeeding and taking home the money he has won (function I), which would resolve his initial lack of money and bring about a new equilibrium, he is beaten and robbed, a capital-letter function-A event, which leaves him still without money (lower-case function a_2).

Similarly, because he needs money Ah Q joins a band of thieves and engages in thefts. Perhaps we consider him successful (function I), but his money is soon gone and he recognizes that he is too much of a coward to get more money through theft: a third function-a situation. This time Ah Q conceives that becoming a revolutionary will bring him profit (function C) and sets out to become one (function C') but to no avail (function I_{neg}). He is arrested (function capital-letter A) and executed (function capital-letter A).

Figure 2: "Ah Q – The Real Story," detailed uninformed interpretation

a_1		Ah Q lacks money
C		Ah Q decides to gamble
C'		Ah Q joins a group of gamblers
H		Ah Q continues to play, wins, yells loudly how much money he is staking
A		Ah Q is beaten and robbed
$A = I_{neg}$		Ah Q does not gain money by gambling
	a_2	Ah Q continues to lack money
	C	Ah Q decides to become a thief
	C'	Ah Q joins a band of thieves
	H_{neg}	Ah Q is a coward, runs away
	I_{neg}	after Ah Q sells his loot and spends his money, he has none
		a_3 Ah Q continues to lack money
		C Ah Q decides to become a revolutionary
		C' Ah Q tries to join the revolutionaries
		I_{neg} the revolutionaries chase him away; he's not allowed to join
		A_1 Ah Q is arrested for a theft he did not commit
		A_2 Ah Q is executed for a theft he did not commit

Other interpretations of a function-a lack in Ah Q's life are also possible. In addition to money he wants respect. But to gain respect he makes claims that are not true, and when his lies are discovered, as they easily are, he is looked upon with even less regard than before. Similarly, he wants heirs (specifically sons), but his dealings with women are always misguided. In other words, Ah Q's life as depicted consists of one or another thing missing in his life, a function lowercase-a lack that he tries to satisfy, but his efforts are in vain and his situation more often becomes worse than improved.

Although my analysis thus far may suggest an unhappy situation that tragically does not improve, a reader like me may have difficulty caring what happens to Ah Q. The character is a ne'er-do-well who misreads situations and suffers the consequences. Ah Q has no regular job, no family, no home. To earn money for food and wine he does odd jobs for people and he bunks down at night in a temple in the village.

In addition, Ah Q is a particularly unattractive character. In spite of his lowly position he has a high opinion of himself. He looks down on everyone in his village, including even the two young literati (the scholars who study for years in order to pass official tests that lead to positions in the government) and their well-to-do fathers. After trips to the nearby town, he becomes even more conceited. Because the townspeople use a different word to denote a bench, and season their fried fish somewhat differently from the Wei Villagers, Ah Q considers the townspeople ridiculous, but at the same time thinks of his fellow villagers as "a bunch of hicks" (108) who don't know how things are done in town. He regularly picks fights with people and just as regularly loses. Afterward he consoles himself by engaging in an extremely convoluted thought process. I quote from the story:

> [Ah Q's tormenters] would seek out the nearest wall and give [Ah Q's] head four or five resounding thumps before walking away, fully satisfied and fully victorious—and convinced that *this* time they had done him in once and for all. But before ten seconds were out, Ah Q would also walk away, fully satisfied and fully victorious, for he was convinced that of all the 'self-putdown-artists' this old world had seen, he was number one. Take away 'self-putdown-artist' and what do you have left? *Number one*—that's what! What was a *Metropolitan Graduate*? *Number one* —that's all. 'Who the hell do these jerks think they are anyway!' Having subdued his foes with such ingenious stratagems, Ah Q would go happily off to the wineshop and down a few bowls. (111)

Ah Q's self-deception, which this passage illustrates, in combination with his conceit and his total lack of accomplishments, leads me to see him from my uninformed perspective as thoroughly uninteresting. As my analysis in Figure 2 indicates, I can recognize that Ah Q feels the lack of money, of prestige, of a family, and that he makes some attempts to better his situation although those attempts are generally misguided and always, in the end, unsuccessful. Figure 2 represents an interpretation that takes into consideration the details of his unhappy life.

But how much detail one takes into account in interpreting a set of events depends both on what those details are and on the interpreter's degree of interest. In fact, in my uninformed reading of the story, I find the reported details about Ah Q's life repetitive and too trivial to be interesting and I keep wishing for something to happen that will break the tedium. In other words, when I analyze my initial response to the story, I see Ah Q as going about his daily life in which nothing gets much better but nothing gets much worse either—and then he is dead. Figure 3 represents this interpretation. Ah Q's life seems to me an equilibrium, which is broken only by his death, the manner of which seems unfair, although I find it difficult to care.

Figure 3: "Ah Q – The Real Story," second uninformed interpretation

EQ   Ah Q goes about his daily life
A   Ah Q is arrested and executed

Then recently I happened upon and read Huang's article on Lu Xun's story. Considering my initial uninformed interpretation, one can imagine my surprise when I learned that according to his research "It has often been observed that the power of 'Ah Q' lies in its special ability to force readers to identify with the protagonist" (434). Moreover, Huang specifies "that in other writings, Lu Xun mentions how some readers of 'Ah Q' (all well-educated intellectuals) were made uneasy because they suspected that Lu Xun had modeled aspects of Ah Q's character on them to ridicule them" (446 n7). In other words, as I understand these comments, "Ah Q—The True Story" presents a satirical account of Chinese intellectuals some ten years after the 1911 revolution. So I go back to the story to see what I have missed, this time looking for clues to which I initially failed to pay attention because I was reading the story as pertaining only to Ah Q.

The one specific reference to Ah Q as a representative of China comes in a passage in which the narrator summarizes possible attitudes in response to a victory. We are told that there are victors who take no pleasure in their victory unless their adversaries are fierce, and victors who after a victory recognize that no foe, rival, or friend is left, rendering them melancholy. But Ah Q, the narrator continues, "was not so feckless as any of the above. No, he was *always* full of himself. Perhaps we have here yet another proof that the spiritual civilization of China is superior to any other on the face of the earth" (122). If in fact Chinese intellectuals—the literati—of the early 1920s saw themselves in Ah Q, the ease with which he recovers from the minor mishaps that regularly beset him may offer an example. Similarly, at another point the narrator refers to Ah Q's "'forgetfulness'—that priceless medicine handed down to us by our ancestors" (119), as an explanation for Ah Q's habitual rapid recovery of his high opinion of himself, for instance after a beating. Then too, there are certain words that Ah Q considers taboo and will not use. In his case he bears scabies scars on his scalp that turn red when he is angry. So he avoids the words "scabies," "bright," "shiny," "lamp," and "candle" (108).

These characteristics create an unpleasant portrait, one that explains my initial reading of Ah Q as an unlikeable character: his avoidance of words that make him uncomfortable, his ability to forget, his ease in recovering his high opinion of himself. If the intellectuals of the decade after the 1911 revolution saw this portrait of Ah Q as a portrait of themselves, one can understand that they would have considered it an indictment of their own behavior. Figure 4 illustrates this interpretation. The revolution is a disruptive function A. But the situation will not improve—function C will not occur—because the intellectuals, who might be expected to try to bring resolution to the situation, work to forget and avoid discussing the post-revolutionary government and instead devote their energies to maintaining their good self-opinion. In this reading, which is very different from my initial reading, Lu Xun's story is a call to action to his readers to act responsibly.

Figure 4: "Ah Q—The Real Story,"
first somewhat better informed interpretation

A   the 1911 Revolution disrupts a prior equilibrium
C_{neg} the intellectuals avoid what might be considered their responsibilities
I_{neg} without efforts from the intellectuals, the situation will not improve

Furthermore, when the revolution arrives, first in the town and then in the little village, Ah Q, as we have seen, perceives the revolutionaries as engaged in theft and tries to become a revolutionary because he wants his share. But Ah Q is not alone in his response to the revolution as a circumstance to use to increase his material wealth. There are three characters in the story who are identified as members of the literati. Two of these are the young scholars in the little village, Old Master Zhao's son, who is referred to as "*Budding Talent* Zhao," and Old Master Qian's son, who has studied abroad and whom Ah Q calls "Fake Foreign Devil." These two, deciding that the revolution is "a time for people from all walks of life to unite in national renewal" (154), join forces. They take themselves to the local Buddhist convent, smash a tablet dedicated to the emperor, beat the old nun in charge because they consider her a representative of the Qing government, and steal a valuable antique censer from the convent.

The third member of the literati in the story is Old Master Selectman in the town. His response to the revolution is to send his possessions for safe-keeping to Old Master Zhao in Wei Village. So when the Zhao family is robbed, his belongings also are lost. This is the theft for which Ah Q is condemned to die. But the decision to execute Ah Q comes only after a quarrel between the literatus Old Master Selectman, who maintained that Ah Q should continue to be questioned because "the first order of business was recovery of the stolen property" (168), and the newly appointed lieutenant in the Revolutionary Party, who prevails, who "insisted that the most important thing was to make a public example of Ah Q" (168) to deter further thefts. Given this representation of the literati as more interested in amassing and protecting their personal wealth than in governing, the story becomes an even more scathing account of the post-revolutionary situation. In Figure 5, the revolution is the initial disruptive event and the behavior of the literati is a second event that further disrupts the situation. What initially seemed to me a rather uninteresting account of a ne'er-do-well's minor ups and downs becomes, once I am guided to look for reasons that the intellectuals of the period might identify with

Ah Q, a scathing indictment of the intellectuals' behavior.

Figure 5: "Ah Q – The Real Story,"
second somewhat better informed interpretation

A_1 the 1911 Revolution disrupts a prior equilibrium
A_2 the intellectuals devote their energies to their personal material gain rather than to governing

Of course there are reasons in addition to my lack of information about China in the early twentieth-century for my initial misreading of this extremely subtle story. The narrative shaping, for instance, diverts attention from the centrality of the political situation by introducing the revolution only in the last third of the discourse, in section seven of nine sections. The narrator's distancing ironic stance toward Ah Q discourages concern for the protagonist and his activities. That ironic stance is supported by the use of direct discourse (at least in the translation) and occasional free indirect discourse to represent the words with which Ah Q formulates to himself his self-deceiving logic that allows him to remain self-satisfied, whatever happens.

But our interpretation of causes and effects depends on the set of events in relation to which we are gauging what is cause and what is effect. In my initial reading of "Ah Q—The Real Story," looking only at the depicted events in the life of the protagonist, I see only minor alternations, none of which seem to count as real disruptions, between days in which he has plenty of food and wine and other days when he is hungry. But given the information that the intellectuals who were the story's first readers see themselves in Ah Q, I incorporate the revolution and the response of the literati to the revolution into the set of events in relation to which I interpret causes and effects. As a result I read the story as a devastating account of the situation in China in the decade after the 1911 revolution and of the inaction or worse of the intellectuals who might have been expected to bring about improvements.

The impossible task that a translator undertakes has long been recognized. Linguists have demonstrated the differences from language to language—both in the concepts that words convey and in the syntactical relations that can be specified—that make it impossible to say exactly the same thing in any two languages. Scholars in a number of fields have drawn attention to our misreading of cultural events and situations with which we are unfamiliar. The principle of functional polyvalence explains even more specifically the effects of context on interpretations of causality and thus why native speakers may interpret even the causal relations among reported events differently than readers of a translation do.

The initial readers of a given fictional narrative who read it in the original language of the story and in the period in which it was written will be apt to include in the context in which they interpret the reported events any events in their own world they deem pertinent. Those readers whose self-identification with Ah Q, Whang reports, serve as examples. Even later readers who read the original language may well have acquired, either in school or more generally from the culture that surrounds them, information about the earlier time period that they too may include in the context in relation to which they interpret the reported events. Readers of translations rarely possess comparable information.

The effect of reduced context can be seen in my own grossly different explanations of causality between my naïve interpretations, when I read only the story, and my somewhat better-informed interpretations, when I read the story along with Huang's article. The events the story reports stay the same, but the context in which I view the events changes when I read the two texts—the story and the essay—together. When we are reading fiction, the effect of context on interpretations of causality may be of only academic interest. But even with fiction, I have argued, a narrative—because it provides the context in relation to which we interpret events—shapes readers' interpretations of the reported events. The real-world danger to which this phenomenon draws attention is that, as individuals, we may not recognize the extent to which the reports through which we learn about events can shape—and are shaping—our interpretation of the causes and effects of those events.

Works cited

Doležel, Lubomír. *Occidental Poetics: Tradition and Progress*. Lincoln: University of Nebraska Press, 1990.

Lu, Xun. Ah Q—The True Story. In *Diary of a Madman and Other Stories*, William A. Lyell (trans.). Honolulu: U of Hawaii P, 1990. 101-172.

Huang, Martin Weizong. "The Inescapable Predicament: The Narrator and His Discourse" in 'The true Story of Ah Q.'" *Modern China* 16 (4), 1990. 430-449.

Kafalenos, Emma. *Narrative Causalities*. Theory and Interpretation of Narrative Series. Columbus: Ohio State UP, 2006.

Margolin, Uri. Unpublished abstract provided to participants in the *Structuralism(s) Today* conference, 2007.

Rubel, Paula G. and Abraham Rosman. "Introduction: Translation and Anthropology." In *Translating Cultures: Perspectives on Translation and Anthropology*. Eds. Paula G. Rubel and Abraham Rosman. 1-22. Oxford: Berg, 2003.

Todorov, Tzvetan. *Grammaire du Décaméron*. The Hague: Mouton, 1969.

Yengoyan, Aram A. "Lyotard and Wittgenstein and the Question of Translation." In *Translating Cultures: Perspectives on Translation and Anthropology*. Eds. Paula G. Rubel and Abraham Rosman. Oxford: Berg, 2003. 25-43.

Plot Structures and Semantic Resonances in Ancient Greek 'Almost Incest' Narratives

Nancy Felson
University of Georgia

Authors form characters based on types and . . . , given certain cues, we subsume characters under types. [Whether] the character structures activated in watching a film are the same ones that are activated in watching the world [or] . . . are particular to the film, our view of a character's ideas, motives, likely behaviours, our evaluation... and, our feelings about that character, are a function of both direct information and schemas—or, more likely, prototypes—cued by that information.

(Hogan 129)

[E.g., in the film Titanic,*] the fact that Rose is marrying Cal for his money and is clearly disdainful of him...might very well trigger a gold digger prototype [or] ... even a "whore" prototype... or the feminist prototype, "independent woman." Thus, even in this case, the same elements in the narrative may fit into quite different cognitive structures, yielding contradictory assessments and feelings, depending on the propensities of the particular viewer.*

(Hogan 132)

Blends can be constructed if two stories can be construed as sharing abstract structure.

(Turner qtd. in Hogan 111)

...the text's meaning can be grasped without identifying the intertext but is enriched, often quite substantially, by its discovery.

(Doležel, *Heterocosmica* 201)

In *Heterocosmica: Fiction and Possible Worlds* Lubomír Doležel presents a diagram that depicts 'transduction' as an open, unlimited chain of transmission between Text 1, Text 2, and Text n (204). Doležel draws on Vodička's notion of concretization as he explores intertextuality in terms of possible world semantics. In an interactive literary communication, he argues, Reader 1 constructs a fictional world [W(F)1] that corresponds to the one constructed by Author 1: Text 1. Another Reader 2 constructs a fictional world W(F)2 that corresponds to the one created by Author 2—Text 2—but it contains allusions to W(F)1, by which it is shaped in part.

I would like to test the usefulness of transduction in the context of oral poetics, in cases where there is no concrete Text 1 to serve as the intertext, but there is evidence of a story pattern (a type, a Gestalt) lurking beneath the surface of a second and third narrative. The pattern on which I will focus, Parricide-Incest ("P-I"), would have been familiar to Homeric audiences from a number of stories from the traditional repertoire of Greek mythology and saga. I will demonstrate how an interpreter attuned to the P-I story pattern might respond with richer associations and stronger emotions to two passages from Homer's *Iliad*, Phoenix's autobiographic narrative in Book 9, 446-484 and Glaukon's narrative of his ancestor Bellerophon in Book 6, 152-211.

In archaic Greek literature the P-I pattern finds expression in a number of tales of intergenerational strife within divine and human families. In Homer's *Odyssey*, for example, Odysseus tells his Phaeacian hosts of all the heroines he met in his trip to the Underworld:

> 'I saw the beautiful Epicasta, Oedipus' mother,
> who in the ignorance of her mind had done a monstrous
> thing when she married her own son. He killed his father
> and married her, but the gods soon made it all known to mortals
> But he, for all his sorrows, in beloved Thebes continued
> to be lord over the Kadmeians, all through the bitter designing
> of the gods; while she went down to Hades of the gates, the strong
>   [one,
> knotting a noose and hanging sheer from the high ceiling,
> in the constraint of her sorrow, but left to him who survived her
> all the sorrows that are brought to pass by a mother's furies.'
>
> (*Odyssey*. 11. 271-280)

Explicit in Odysseus' tale within his Adventures are the motifs of parricide and incest. So is the suicide by hanging of Epicasta (= Jocasta) and her ignorance, when she committed the monstrous deed, of her son/husband's identity. What the gods' eventually reveal to mortals anticipates by nearly 300 years Sophocles' treatment in *Oedipus the King*, ca. 426-420. In the early Homeric version, Oedipus is not exiled but continues to rule the Kadmeians (= Thebans) despite his sorrows brought about by his mother's furies (avengers of family crimes). Odysseus, as narrator, seems to present Epicasta's focalization: her ignorance, her suicide, her furies—all reflect his reprisal of her first-person account of events when he encountered her in the Underworld. As narrator, he captures her focalization.

A fuller and still early P-I narrative appears in the Succession Myth of Hesiod's *Theogony* of ca. 700 BCE, albeit with many expansions and adaptations to suit the purposes of this cosmogonic poem. The narrative is told in segments by the Muse-inspired Hesiodic narrator. Whatever the relative chronology between the *Iliad* and the *Theogony*, we can assume that both Hesiod and Homer were drawing their fabulae for their respective tales from a larger oral tradition, and we know that Hesiod's narrative is indebted to its ancient Near Eastern antecedents (see West). Hesiod's text, though not an ideal comparandum, strengthens my argument that the two *Iliadic* passages under consideration can be understood as transductions of the well-attested P-I pattern.

In the *Theogony* Gaia begets Ouranos equal to herself; then, after mingling together, mother with son, they produce three sets of offspring: the twelve Titans, the three Cyclopes, and the three Hundred-Handers. Ouranos hates the Cyclopes and the Hundred-Handers and hides them inside their mother's womb. Enraged and in pain, Gaia asks the Titans for aid, using *oratio recta* in her three-line appeal. In a matching three-line speech the youngest Titan, Kronos, volunteers. Mother and son join forces against Ouranos, as Kronos embraces Gaia's plan and, with the tooth-edged sickle she has fashioned, castrates the father whom he hates. Then he becomes king of the gods. He mates with his sister Rhea, and they produce the six Olympians. Much to Rhea's dismay, Kronos swallows each child as it emerges from her womb—except for the youngest. Gaia helps Rhea trick Kronos into swallowing a swaddled stone instead of baby Zeus. Meanwhile, rescued from obliteration, Zeus grows to manhood in Crete and then, in his prime of youth, he returns and wins the Titanomachy, a ten-year war against Kronos and his allies, with help initially from the Cyclopes and later from the Hundred-Handers, whom he has liberated from imprisonment in Tartarus (or in Gaia's womb). He gains their allegiance in a second *oratio recta* exchange. After his victory, which devastated the earth, Zeus effectively exiles Kronos and his allies to Tartarus and binds them there in jail, to be guarded by the Hundred-Handers. Mating with Tartarus, Earth produces a final 'youngest son', the dragon Typhon, who would have become king of the gods and men, had Zeus not taken note. Zeus defeats him in a deadly battle that again scorches the earth. Only then, at Earth's urging, do the gods elect Zeus king. At this point, he has not only displaced his father Kronos with finality but has eliminated a series of potential threats to his supremacy as well.

From this story I abstract a fabula that accommodates the three separate segments or moves of the story: Gaia – Ouranos – Kronos; Kronos – Rhea –Zeus; Zeus – a series of females culminating in Gaia – a series of challengers culminating in the dragon Typhon:

1. The father sires a series of sons.
2. He hates and/or fears some of them.
    i. because of their excessive manhood, size, or monstrosity (hybridity).
    ii. because he has learned from an oracle that one of them will displace him.
3. He tries to obliterate those dread sons
    i. by repressing (= obliterating) them.
    ii. by swallowing them as each is born.
    iii. by swallowing the pregnant mother.
4. With this act he dishonors/violates their mother.
5. He also dishonors/violates their sons.
6. The mother is enraged and in pain.
7. She betrays her spouse
    i. by enlisting the aid of their youngest son.
    ii. by rescuing the threatened son and instructing him to retaliate later at the peak of youth (*hêbê*).
8. The youngest son embraces her plan and punishes (= displaces) the father.
    i. by castrating him.
    ii. by defeating him in a battle or contest after he grows up in hiding, away from his natal home and returns at *hêbê*.
    iii. He may receive aid from an ancestress (mother or grandmother).
9. The victorious son becomes king, takes a bride, and sires sons.
10. The defeated father curses or threatens his youngest son or all his sons.
11. The victorious son exiles or murders his father (= parricide).
Alternatively, instead of 9-11:
9b. The father defeats his son(s) and eliminates him/them as a threat (through murder or exile).
10b. The father retains his kingdom and his wife as queen.

This version of the story anticipates by nearly 300 years Sophocles' treatment in *Oedipus the King*, ca. 426-420. Odysseus, as its narrator, captures and presents Epicasta's focalization on these events: her ignorance, her suicide, her furies. All reflect the narrator's reprisal of her first-person account of events when he encountered her in the Underworld. Explicit are the motifs of parricide and incest, as well as the mother/wife's suicide by hanging and her ignorance, when she committed the monstrous deed, of her son/husband's identity. After her death, in this early account, Oedipus is not exiled but continues to rule the Kadmeians despite his sorrows brought about by his mother's furies.

At slot 9-11 in Sophocles' *Oedipus the King*, the victorious son, after committing parricide and solving the riddle of the sphinx, wins his father's kingdom and his own mother as queen and bride. In Hesiod's divine Succession Myth Ouranos, who is fatherless from the start, possesses his mother Gaia already and without any contest. Kronos weds Rhea, his sister, while Zeus mates with a series of females, culminating in his marriage to his sister Hera. Only Zeus of the three male figures in the Succession Myth both defeats his father and fends off a series of challengers who might have displaced him.

The PI pattern, I suggest, underlies a number of familiar 'almost incest' myths, among them the Father's Concubine, the King's Wife (usually labeled Potiphar's Wife), and even the Bride-Contest, where the father-in-law and son-in-law play out the conflictual paternal and filial roles. Knowledge of the PI pattern (as outlined above) shapes an interpreter's reception of two passages from the *Iliad*, to which I now turn.

Father's Concubine Tale

The defining feature of this plot-type is a son's act of sleeping with his father's concubine. This occurs in Phoenix's autodiegetic tale at *Iliad* 9.446-484, which is the earliest 'Father's Concubine' narrative in extant Greek literature.[i] Here, within the famous embassy scene, Phoenix is the second of three speakers sent by Agamemnon to bring Achilles back to battle, and he uses two stories and a parable to persuade his youthful ward (whom he raised almost as his own child) not to be stubborn and unyielding. At this moment, the Achaians are in desperate need of their best warrior, and Phoenix adapts his narrative accordingly. Nevertheless, the logic of the story as a recasting of the traditional P-I tale comes through.

> Therefore apart from you, dear child, I would not be willing
> To be left behind, were not the god in person to promise
> He would scale away my old age and make me a young man blossoming
> As I was that time when I first left Hellas, the land of fair women,
> Running from the hatred of Orchemenos' son Amyntor,
> My father, who hated me for the sake of a fair-haired mistress (*pellakis*).
> For he made love to her himself, and kept dishonoring his own wife,
> My mother; who was forever taking my knees and entreating me
> To lie with this mistress instead so that she would hate the old man.
> I was persuaded and did it; and my father when he heard of it straightway
> Called down his curses, and invoked against me the dreaded furies
> That I might never have any son born of my seed to dandle
> On my knees; and the divinities, Zeus of the underworld
> And Persephone, the honored goddess, accomplished his curses.
> Then I took it into my mind to cut him down with the sharp bronze,
> But some one of the immortals checked my anger, reminding me
> Of rumor among the people and of men's maledictions repeated,
> That I might not be called a parricide among the Achaians.
> (*Iliad*. 9. 444-53)

From this text I abstract the following fabula:

1. Father kept loving a concubine and kept dishonoring his wife by sleeping

with the concubine (implication, not with the wife).
2. She retaliated by frequently beseeching their son to sleep with the concubine, so that she would hate the old man (*gerôn*).
3. The son, in his prime (*heboôsa*), repeatedly refused.
4. Finally, the son obeyed his mother and slept one time with the *pallakis* (two punctual aorists).
5. The father found out.
6. He cursed his son to sterility and impotence or blinded him.
7. The son wanted to kill his father but restrained himself, or some god checked his anger, so he might not be called a parricide.
8. Kinsmen kept beseeching him (not to be angry?).
9. They put him under house arrest and kept watch.
10. He escaped and went into (voluntary) exile far away, running from the hatred of his father.
11. He became childless, probably impotent; the gods answered the father's prayer.
12. No outcome is specified for either the unnamed *pallakis* or the unnamed mother or for the father.

Here the second move begins, as the son finds a new home in Phthia on the estate of Peleus, known for his generosity to strangers, who gave him his love, even as a father loves his own son, and made him rich. There Phoenix raised Achilles and made him, as it were, his own child.

The fact that Phoenix is recounting his life-experience to the very one whose father welcomed him as a young fugitive and gave him a second home guarantees the reliability of his first person narrative. The addressee, Achilles, already knows its essential features. The story is further authenticated by Phoenix's childlessness at Troy (i.e., in the fictional world of the text), which confirms what he says as a character-narrator, that the gods fulfilled his father's curse. Phoenix slants the tale to mitigate his own blame while at the same time, in the hope of persuading Achilles to relent and rejoin the Greek forces, he offers his impetuous young self as a negative exemplum for Achilles to avoid.

Phoenix's autodiegetic story, like all PI narratives, is a powerful tale of a transgression that occurs at the critical moment in the life of the son. He begins by telling Achilles he would not abandon him, "even were the god in person to promise he would scale away my old age and make me a young man blossoming / as I was that time when I first left Hellas...". Thus he emphasizes his age-grade difference from Amyntor, who will be designated by his mother as a *gerôn*, an old man, while he was in the prime of youth (*heboôsa*) when these events transpired. Compare how Zeus too in the Succession Myth was at the peak of his youth when he returned to vanquish his father and claim the throne, and so was Oedipus in Sophocles' version of the Theban saga, *Oedipus Tyrannos*. In fact, all such P-I stories contain such intergenerational conflict, as we shall see below.

A mother is dishonored here as in all P-I tales. Amyntor kept dishonoring Phoenix's mother by his preference of the concubine and his implicit refusal to have sex with her. Compare how Ouranos, Kronos, and Zeus dishonor Gaia, Rhea, and Metis, respectively, by either appropriating or assaulting their procreative function. In addition, collusion against the father by a mother-son pair is a motif throughout. Such collusion is isomorphic with mother/son incest: it reiterates, with a difference, the initial uncontested incest between Earth and Sky.

As the secondary narrator and focalizer, Phoenix stresses that he transgressed only once, but each of his parents did so repeatedly. Thus he exculpates himself to the degree possible, despite the paternal curse. In particular, the three frequentatives in close proximity for the parents' actions (*phileesken, atimeske* and *lissesketo*) are answered by two aorists for his own: *pithomên* (I obeyed) and *edraxa* (I did it).

A curse or a threat is present here as in all the P-I tales: Once Amyntor learns of his son's deed of supplanting him in bed, he responds *as if* Phoenix had in fact committed incest. His paternal curse of childlessness is the strongest punishment for such a sexual crime. Moreover, in later versions of the story—Euripides' *Phoenix*, fr. 86N2, Ar. *Acharnians* 421, Apollodorus, *Biblioteca* 3.13.8, Tzetzes on Lyc. 421 — Amyntor blinds Phoenix, a metaphor for castration (Devereux 36-49), in Apollodorus on the false accusation of the concubine. Compare Ouranos' reaction to Kronos's betrayal: he threatens the Titans with eventual vengeance (210: *tisin*), which Rhea ultimately facilitates through her rescue of Zeus, an act specifically designed to avenge her father and her offspring (cf. 472: *teisaito*). Laius, on the other hand, has no opportunity to curse Oedipus before the murder at the crossroads; but the motif of the paternal curse resurfaces in the next generation, when Oedipus (in Sophocles, *Oedipus at Colonos*) curses his two sons, who eventually commit 'autoctony', killing each other at the same instant (cf. Aeschylus, *Seven against Thebes*).

Phoenix's wish to kill his father invokes the actual parricide committed by Oedipus (*Odyssey* xi.273 and later in Sophocles' *Oedipus Tyrannus* 800-813) as well as Zeus' banishment of the immortal Kronos to Tartarus, a kind of death. While the son displaces the father in all these tales, in Father's Concubine his victory is less conclusive. Phoenix triumphs in bed, but he never realizes his desire to commit parricide, and he, not his father, goes into exile, albeit voluntarily; moreover, he is childless and probably impotent as a result of the paternal curse. Amyntor's outcome too is mixed, at best. His 'triumph' over his son evokes the alternative ending of the P/I tale (expressed in Zeus' sequential victories over potential usurpers) and yet his curse reverts to him as well. Amyntor will have no *grand*son to dandle on *his* knees, no son, no heir. As the story continues, in a second move, Phoenix experiences some restitution: after losing his native land and natal family, he gains a new home and Achilles as a surrogate child.

In the PI tale-type, the father's dread occurs twice: at birth, in anticipation of the later displacement, and again at *hêbê*, when the son has come of age and returns to claim the throne and queen. Since Phoenix begins his narrative at his *hêbê*, eliding his birth and childhood, we do not know if his father, like the divine fathers in the *Theogony*, anticipated his own displacement. In fact Amyntor's perspective—on his wife's betrayal, for example—is absent from Phoenix's account. We do not even know what specific information Amyntor had when he cursed his son for sleeping with his concubine.

A few other distinctive features of the Phoenix tale deserve mention. The role of Amyntor's wife is split off from that of the Amyntor's concubine and current sexual partner. From the focalization of Amyntor and perhaps of Phoenix, the unnamed concubine (whom Apollodorus calls Phthia) is indeed a surrogate for the unnamed wife. Moreover, like Gaia in the *Theogony*, the mother/wife exercises extraordinary agency: both females are trying to restore equilibrium, aided by their sons. Phoenix's mother exploits her son's sexuality to reclaim her husband. Phoenix does not volunteer, like Kronos, but complies reluctantly, after repeated entreaties. Both Phoenix and Kronos implement their mother's scheme and, in both narratives, their alliances undermine the sexuality of the father—either simply through displacement in bed or through castration and jailing in Tartarus. This outcome resembles Oedipus' double displacement of his father –as the king of Thebes and as the husband of Epicasta/Jocasta.

Phoenix assigns a motivation to his mother, "so that she [the concubine] will hate the old man". This implies that, in setting up the competition between old father and virile son, she expected her son to win. The assigned motive is never authenticated: we only have Phoenix's words, focalized through his adolescent or adult lens, or both. In contrast, in the first move of the Succession Myth the narrator quotes Gaia's first-person speech to her Titan children: she wants to get even with Ouranos, since he was the first one to commit an evil. In Homer's account Epicasta has no specific motive: she acts in ignorance of her genealogical relation to the newcomer who wins her hand (Edmunds 13-31, see espec. 16-17).

King's Wife Tale and Bride-Contest

The second Iliadic passage is a more peripheral or marginal member, in Eleanor Rosch's sense, of the category I'm calling Parricide-Incest. But the structure of its narrative and a number of its elements bear a family resemblance to the P-I tale type that, I am arguing, lurks beneath its surface. This passage at *Iliad* 6.152-211 has two prominent episodes or moves: the King's Wife's Tale and the Bride-Contest. The narrator Glaukon, a Lykian ally of the Trojans, explains his genealogy to the Achaean Diomedes as they meet on the battlefield. His narration is thus part of a vaunt: I am the grandson of the hero Bellerophon, once of Argos, whose life, fraught with dangers not of his making, was mended when he settled in Lykia, and then (for unspecified reasons) became fraught again.[ii] Whatever the vicissitudes of Bellerophon's fortunes, his grandson as internal narrator focuses on the endpoint most relevant to him, the fact that his father, one of the hero's offspring, survived to beget him and instruct him in heroic values; inspired by these, he has come forward to engage the formidable Diomedes. In other versions of this story, such as Euripides' *Sthenoboia*, which survives in fragments, revenge against the lying queen constitutes a later move, replacing the successful bride-contest in Lycia.

The first move of the Bellerophon story exemplifies the King's Wife Tale, usually labeled Potiphar's Wife after *Genesis*, ch. 39, while the second articulates the Bride-Contest, in which a father sets up various contests, often with hostile intent, and promises to give his daughter in marriage to the winner. In the first move, the king's wife tries to seduce a young man, fails, and invents a lying tale in which she maligns him to her husband, the king: he raped her, or tried to, as a piece of his clothing proves. If the alleged intruder/seducer/rapist is the queen's step-son, as in Euripides' *Hippolytus*, the incest motif in the lying tale becomes overt. The step-mother is then isomorphic with the concubine in the previous story type.

In answer to Diomedes' query, "Who among mortal men are you?" Glaukon responds first with the famous simile at 146-150 ("As is the generation of leaves, so is that of humanity.") and then he narrates the biography of his ancestor Bellerophon:

> To Bellerophon the gods granted beauty and desirable
> manhood; but Proitos in anger devised evil things against him,
> and drove him out of his domain, since he was far greater,
> from the Argive country Zeus had broken to the sway of his scepter.
> Beautiful Anteia the wife of Proitos was stricken
> with passion to lie in love with him, and yet she could not
> beguile valiant Bellerophon, whose will was virtuous.
> So she went to Proitos the king and uttered her falsehood:
> "Would you be killed, o Proitos? Then murder Bellerophon
> who tried to lie with me in love, though I was unwilling."
> So she spoke, and anger took hold of the king at her story.
> He shrank from killing him, since his heart was awed by such action,
> but sent him away to Lykia, and handed him murderous symbols,
> which he inscribed in a folding tablet, enough to destroy life,

and told him to show it to his wife's father, that he might perish.
Bellerophon went to Lykia in the blameless convoy
of the gods; ...
Then after he had been given his son-in-law's wicked symbols
first he sent him away with orders to kill the Chimaira
none might approach; ...
He killed Chimaira, obeying the portents of the immortals.
Next after this he fought against the glorious Solymoi,
...
but third he slaughtered the Amazons, who fight men in battle.
Now as he came back the king spun another entangling
treachery; for choosing the bravest men in wide Lykia
he laid a trap, but these men never came home thereafter
since all of them were killed by blameless Bellerophon.
Then when the king knew him for the powerful stock of the god,
he detained him there, and offered him the hand of his daughter,
and gave him half of all the kingly privilege. Thereto
the men of Lykia cut out a piece of land, surpassing
all others, fine ploughland and orchard for him to administer.
His bride bore three children to valiant Bellerophon,
Isandros and Hippolochos and Laodameia.
...
But after Bellerophontes was hated by all the immortals,
he wandered alone about the plain of Aleios, eating
his heart out, skulking aside from the trodden track of humanity.
...
But Hippolochos begot me, and I claim that he is my father;
he sent me to Troy, and urged upon me repeated injunctions,
to be always among the bravest, and hold my head above others,
not shaming the generation of my fathers, who were
the greatest men in Ephyre and again in wide Lykia.
Such is my generation and the blood I claim to be born from.
(*Iliad*. 6. 156-210)

Interpreting Bellerophon's life-story, as Glaukon tells it to Diomedes at *Iliad* 6.152-211, against the background of the P-I tale-type enriches our understanding of this epic passage. Diomedes responds to the tale by initiating a gift-exchange in lieu of engaging in battle. This outcome resonates thematically not only with several other exchanges in Book 6 but also with the reconciliation between Priam and Achilles of *Iliad* 24 that ends the poem (Fineberg 1999: 14).

Bellerophon's biography is a triangulated tale articulated in two moves that unfold at two locations and with two sets of characters. Only Bellerophon participates in both. In the first encounter the two kings are doublets of one another, as are the two sisters, daughters of the Lykian king.

The age-grade difference between the king of Argos and the youthful Bellerophon marks this tale as an intergenerational struggle over the elder's wife; the difference in their power is marked as well (6. 158-159). Other distinctive features include the wife's initiative; the young man's refusal; her rage; and her lying tale, to which the husband reacts as if it were true. Moreover, some of his reactions invoke the PI tale, in particular, the fact that he treats the young alleged rival as if he were a wayward son: he exiles him and sends him on a dangerous mission in the hope that he will die.

In the first move of this tale, which takes place in Argos, Bellerophon is *not* the suitor of Anteia but rather the object of her pursuit. She desires and pursues him, even though she is a *gunê* and not a *parthenos*, and when rejected, she alleges, in his absence, that he wanted to sleep with her against her will. At this plot juncture one might expect a duel or a murder or a judgment (as on the shield of Achilles in *Iliad* 18), and indeed "kill or be killed" is the option Anteia offers Proitos. (Cf. the Gyges story in Herodotus, Book 1, 8-15, where Candaules' unnamed wife makes a similar offer to Gyges, when he has seen her naked.) The Argive king rejects such an alternative and instead, as Glaukon recounts it, invents a subterfuge—the folded tablet with a message inscribed on it. The tablet functions like the curse in oedipal tales but is also isomorphic with the ambush (189: *lochos*) in move 2.

At the center of this narrative is strife between two men over a woman, the kind of 'trafficking in women' identified by Gail Rubin (1975) (see Felson/Slatkin). In this case, however, the woman sets the trafficking in motion through her lie. Proitos, taken in by his wife's deceit and believing her accusation against Bellerophon, *becomes* the 'sender' (Greimas' term)—i.e., the established king who sends the young hero on a perilous mission, usually intending his death. Underlying his aggressive act of exiling Bellerophon with a damning message on the tablet is the principle that 'he who sleeps with the queen becomes king'. At stake in the triangle in Argos are a bride and half the kingdom. In the Argive move, Proitos retains his wife and his kingship by exiling and perhaps dooming his alleged competitor.

In the second move, which takes place in Lykia, the father-in-law of Proitos initially tries to implement his son-in-law's intentions, in response to what is inscribed on the tablet. As Anteia's father, he is protecting his daughter's honor. The tablet's message activates him to devise a series of three perilous tasks, and when Bellerophon completes them all, he sets up an ambush—an overt attempt to kill him. When Bellerophon, having succeeded at all three bridal tasks, also defeats the ambush, the king relents and gives him his rewards. In this way Bellerophon attains in Lykia exactly what Anteia accused him of wanting in Argos and what he could not have, because of zero-sum. He ends up marrying the sister of the woman who accused him of making overtures toward *her*. Anteia's father gives away his second daughter to and shares his kingdom with the very man with whom Proitos could share neither wife nor kingdom. And so what *was* a story of usurpation and cuckoldry in Argos (according to Anteia's punitive lie) not only precipitates the hero's exile; it brings about a second chance for him to win a bride-contest in Lykia. Here we have a Proppian folktale![iii]

The Lykian king expected Bellerophon to die. In this he resembles many fathers in Bride Contest, who want each suitor to die so that they can have their daughters to themselves, Compare his tyrannical manner to that of Oinomaos, king of Elis, who was reluctant to marry off Hippodameia to the hero Pelops and caused the deaths of every previous suitor. In the two narrative moves of this story, the king functions both as the tool (or extension) of Proitos and as a father/king who protects two daughters and, in a sense, two kingdoms. Ultimately, however, despite the message on the table, Bellerophon triumphs.

In one important respect, the propositioned male in the King's Wife tale-type differs from the more usual male adulterer—like Paris—and from unsatisfactory, spurned suitors. He is an *alleged* male intruder, the undeserving victim of a verbal trick. The pattern is well known from the story of Potiphar's wife, where Joseph is the alleged seducer, and in a number of Greek myths (see Jouan); these appear in Euripides' *Hippolytus* (both versions), *Peleus*, *Phoenix*, and *Stheneboia* and in Pindar's *Nemean* 5 (Hippolyte, and Peleus) and, in a modified form, in Herodotus' Gyges tale, as cited above. In such tales, the spurned queen tells her husband a lying tale, causing him to treat the alleged intruder as if he did indeed seduce his wife. In the lie, the two men vie with one another over the queen and (implicitly or explicitly) the kingdom.

Bellerophon's mastery of the 'impossible tasks' set by the Lykian king causes the tale-type to shift. 'Exile' becomes 'Resettlement in a New Land' once the king makes Bellerophon his new son-in-law and agrees to share half his kingdom. Ironically, Bellerophon becomes Proitos' equivalent: both are sons-in-law of the Lykian king. They are linked by kinship much as Agamemnon would have liked for Achilles to be when, at *Iliad* 9.142-284, he offered his daughter's hand in marriage and part of his kingdom in his effort to appease Achilles.

The Bellerophon folktale sets the tone for reconciliation between Diomedes and his natural adversary, the Lykian Glaukon. It also provides a model for the resolution of other conflicts in the poem, notably those between two men warring over a woman—Helen, Chryseis, Briseis—and over the possession of Hector's corpse. The tale resonates with the larger Iliadic theme of *mênis* (rage) that results from a *neikos* (quarrel) between two men, Agamemnon and Achilles, in a war over a woman, Helen, which was the result of the intrusion of Paris into the domestic space of King Menelaos of Sparta. Glaukon's account of his ancestry affirms his identity and suitability for battle and humanizes the hero Diomedes, at least for the moment. Instead of fighting one another, at Diomedes' pronouncement they exchange armor, emulating the guest-exchanges of their forebears. The inequality of the gift-exchange of gold armor for bronze, to which the poet calls attention at line 234, highlights the importance of their ancestral connection over materiality and the heroic ideal of immortal fame (Fineberg 34-37).

Conclusion

In these brief comments, I have argued that interpreting two passages from the *Iliad* with the PI Tale in mind enriches them. In the first case, resonances with PI underscore the profoundly incestuous and parricidal nature of Phoenix's compliance with his mother's request; in the second, they accentuate the nature of the actual and alleged transgressions against the Argive king. For a subordinate to sleep with the king's wife, even at her instigation—a transaction unactualized in this account—is nearly equivalent to incest, and to displace him in bed and/or in his kingdom is a form of regicide that resembles parricide (see Paul).

Phoenix's voluntary exile, his decision not to "cut down" Amyntor and be called a parricide, his act of sleeping only once with the concubine and never with his mother–all these differentiate him from a bona fide son who kills his father, commits incest with his mother, and takes over the kingdom, like Oedipus in *Od.* 11 and, less overtly, like Kronos in Hesiod's Succession Myth. Phoenix puts his past in the best light possible by emphasizing what distinguishes him from a parricidal and incestuous son. He presents his earlier acquiescence to his mother's pleas as a matter over which he had little control, even though it led to his near ruin. His compliance with his mother enacts her retaliation for the wrong committed by her husband; the only hint that Phoenix shares her view is his subsequent desire to murder the father who cursed him.

As Phoenix reprises this tale for Achilles, he presents his not yielding to the supplications of his kinsmen as a negative pathway, since it cost him dearly; Achilles, he implies, should avoid that mistake by returning to battle after he gives up his rage at the elder Agamemnon. Phoenix never denies the legitimacy of Achilles' anger at a surrogate father who would appropriate his bride-prize. The whole premise of the quarrel between Agamemnon and Achilles, the greatest warrior, is over the king's right to any woman he chooses. Nevertheless, Phoenix does offer up his autobiography as one cornerstone of his plea to the youthful Achilles not to retaliate against Agamemnon by wreaking havoc on the whole Achaean army. In using his almost-incest tale as a basis for this appeal, he accentuates his positive relation to the generous Peleus and to Achilles. He even expands the kinship passage in order to highlight the resemblances between his former self and Achilles now. Thus Phoenix has two motivations for shaping his narrative as he does: to mitigate his offenses of the past and to gain access to the heart of Achilles, so that he can persuade him to defend the Achaians in the Trojan War.

Glaukon's line of argument is less transparent. His story of Bellerophon responds to Diomedes' question at *Iliad* 6.123, "Who of mortals are you?" He offers his grandfather's tale as a way of explaining his identity. Unexpectedly, Bellerophon turns out to have been a guest-friend of Oineus, Diomedes' grandfather, and this brings about a rapprochement between the two enemy warriors, a Lykian and a king from Argos. Their rapprochement has further implications for the plot. In a sense, the gift-exchange they enact recapitulates the mending of the breach several generations earlier between Proitos, King of Argos, and Bellerophon, a breach mended within the story when the King of Lykia gave his daughter and half his kingdom to the hero and allowed him to resettle in Lykia. It also anticipates the rapprochement to come, between Achilles and Priam, in *Iliad* 24 and the truce, albeit fragile and temporary, between the Trojans and the Achaeans. That there will ultimately be a winner and a loser is perhaps anticipated by the inequality in the gift exchange: Glaukon trades gold for bronze to Diomedes.

Both passages that I have used as my examples are stories told by a character to another character. The character-narrator is like an *aoidos*, but one who draws on his own eye-witness or family-documented oral tradition—an intra-diegetic narrator in Genette's schema. The way each character-narrator shapes his story is of course geared to his pragmatic purposes, in Phoenix's case, his need to reinforce his bond with Achilles and Peleus as a basis for persuading him to yield, and in Glaukon's, the need to explain his own identity to an adversary, with unexpected and unintended results. Nevertheless, the *logic* of each story emerges when a critic analyzes its motifemes within the body of traditional narratives of the ancient Greek tradition. In that context, transformations and emphases come forth, enhanced by knowledge of the tale-type, parricide-incest, lurking beneath the surface

Frequently, in hero-tales, the relation of a suitor to his prospective royal father-in-law (*ekyros* or *pentheros*) is fraught with conflict. At stake are the king's daughter and the kingdom. The youthful hero, the mature king, and the young maiden form a triangle that reflects the same tensions we find in oedipal family tales, where the father and son contend over the body/allegiance of the mother and over who will be lord of the household and kingdom. In *ekyros* hero-tales, the elder male may try to eliminate the youth by forcing him to face one or more impossible tasks, either in his own kingdom or in a distant land. This motifeme is structurally equivalent to the double confrontation pattern, in all oedipal tales: the later conflict at *hebe* revisits the attempted infanticide at birth, itself often motivated by an oracle predicting the later confrontation. This is the case for the tale of Laius/ Oedipus/Jocasta and Hesiod's Succession Myth. When the youth in the *ekyros* tales completes his assigned tasks, often aided by a helper, the narrative may take one of several turns. The triumphant young hero may retaliate by slaying the belligerent (or recalcitrant) king, usurping his power and taking over his kingship; he may sack his city and abduct the king's daughter as a *geras*, along with the king's treasures; or he may leave the city intact, simply escaping with the princess and some of her father's wealth. Alternatively, after witnessing the completion of the impossible tasks the king may offer the youth his daughter in marriage, along with half the kingdom, a folktale ending.

The PI tale is a narrative of extremes. It operates on the principle that there can be no sharing of resources—kingdoms, females, prerogatives. There will be a winner and a loser, zero-sum. Even when a conflict occurs among the deathless gods, a great deal is at stake, as becomes especially clear in Sophocles' appropriation of the Oedipus-Epicasta story for his tragedy. The nature of the relationships in the triadic constellation of characters varies with each type of tale; yet this paper suggests that the tale-types share so many elements as to justify our notion of Father's Concubine, King's Wife, and Bride-Prize as all belonging with varying degrees of centrality, to the category of Parricide-Incest Tales.

Works Cited

Devereux, George (1973). "The Self-Blinding of Oidipous in Sophokles: *Oidipous Tyrannos*." *The Journal of Hellenic Studies* 93 (1973): 36-49.

Doležel, Lubomír. *Heterocosmica: Fiction and Possible Worlds*. Baltimore and London: The Johns Hopkins UP, 1998.

———. *Occidental Poetics: Tradition and Progress*. Lincoln and London: U of Nebraska P, 1990.

Edmunds, Lowell. *Oedipus*. New York: Routledge, 2006.

Felson, Nancy and Laura M. Slatkin. "Gender and Homeric Epic." *The Cambridge Companion to Homer*. Ed. Robert Fowler. Cambridge: Cambridge UP, 2004. 91-114.

Fineberg, Stephen. "Blind Rage and Eccentric Vision in *Iliad* 6." *Transactions of the American Philological Association* 129 (1999): 13-41.

Gaisser, Julia Haig. "Adaptation of Traditional Material in the Glaucus-Diomedes Episode." *Transactions of the American Philological Association* 100 (1969): 165-76.

Hainsworth, Bryan. *The Iliad: A Commentary*. Vol III: Books 9-12. Cambridge: Cambridge UP, 1993.
Hogan, Patrick Colm. *Cognitive Science, Literature, and the Arts: A Guide for Humanists*. New York: Routledge, 2003.
Homer. *The Iliad of Homer*. Trans. Richmond Lattimore. Chicago: U of Chicago P, 1976.
———. *The Odyssey of Homer*. Trans. Richmond Lattimore. New York: Harper Perennial, 1999.
Jouan, F. "Femmes ardentes et chastes héros chez Euripide," *Miscellanea* (1989-90): 187-208.
Hansen, William. *Ariadne's Thread*. Ithaca: Cornell UP, 2002.
Kirk, G.S. *The Iliad. A Commentary*. Vol. II: Books 5-8. Cambridge: Cambridge UP, 1990.
Paul, Robert A. *Moses and Civilizations: The Meaning Behind Freud's Myth*. New Haven: Yale UP, 1996.
Rosch, Eleanor. "Principles of Categorization." *Cognition and Categorization*. Eds. Eleanor Rosch and B.B. Lloyd. Hillsdale: Lawrence Erlbaum Associates, 1978. 27-48.
Rosner, Judith A. "The Speech of Phoenix: *Iliad* 9.434-605," *Phoenix* 30.4 (1976): 314-27.
Rubin, Gail. "The Traffic in Women: Notes on the 'Political Economy' of Sex." *Toward an Anthropology of Women*. Ed. Rayna R. Reiter. New York: Monthly Review Press, 1975. 157-210.
Scodel, Ruth. "The Wits of Glaucus." *Transactions of the American Philological Association* 122 (1992): 73-84.
West, M.L. *Hesiod: Theogony*. Oxford: Oxford UP, 1966.
Wohl, Victoria. *Intimate Commerce: Exchange, Gender, and Subjectivity in Greek Tragedy*. Austin: U of Texas P, 1998.

Narratology:
Between Dream and Scientific Intention
Or Why the Marquise no longer goes out at five

WLADIMIR KRYSINSKI
Université de Montréal

In Lieu of Preambles

> Narratology is about narrating sentences.
> Narrating sentences are about fiction.
> Fiction of literature is about facts or about imitations of human actions.

All that is well and good; however, literary texts possess more than just narrating sentences. In fact, the problem of the Marquise is polysemic, as pointed out by Paul Valéry. It is sort of the fulfillment of a narrating sentence. As we know from André Bréton's *First Surrealist Manifesto*, Valéry had "suggested anthologizing as many first sentences of novels as possible, from whose imbecility he expected a great deal." (Preface) His strong reaction to 'the Marquise went out at five' demonstrates that apart from this first sentence, there are so many other things in literary texts. Narratology simply did not succeed in elaborating a unifying analytical model.

Glorious or Postglorious Variations on Greimas

By situating the problem of narratology between dream and scientific intention, one presupposes a series of possible negative affirmations which should enlighten the epistemological situation of a science that has not yet become. The history of narratology is therefore impossible to write in terms of systematically growing knowledge. Instead it may be seen as a series of episodes and attempts at establishing a new science. Narratology may be looked at as a project which has had multiple ramifications without a satisfactory final result. Narratology has been—and still is—a series of individual undertakings inspired by obvious sources such as Russian formalism, structural linguistics, generative linguistics, but also by philosophy and mathematics, information theory and cybernetics. There are many highly instructive publications available about various matters which appeared in the critical field of narratology to constitute its fundamentals both systematically and intentionally. However, what was systematic and intentional did not continue its efforts toward establishing a new science in a systematic and intentional manner.

I would like to focus on the problem of the narrative and make observations about some of its important episodes; i.e., the semiotic theory of narrative as it developed in France, namely in the works of A. J. Greimas (*Sémantique structurale*). In fact, narrative belongs to his larger vision of meaning in which that human world defines itself as essentially the world of meaning; i.e., the world is 'human' only if it means something.

What strikes the reader in Greimassian semiotic theory is the fact that he begins with a strongly emphasized intention to develop the scientific theory of the narrative. The best manifestation of this is his *Sémantique structurale*, which dates from 1966. In this undeniably important book, Greimas achieves an important step towards a coherent formalization of the narrative. His main source is a seminal study of *The Morphology of the Folktale* by Vladimir Propp. That study from 1929 is a formalist analysis of a considerable number of Russian folktales. Greimas takes from Propp the functional understanding of actions and spheres of actions. He accomplishes an important reduction of 31 functions of acting characters in Propp's formalist analysis to six functions which will then constitute the basis of an 'actantial' formalization of the narrative. The six basic, repetitious and universally valid functions receive new names with Greimas. The six actants are the following: sender; object; receiver; helper; subject and opponent. The actantial analysis guarantees Greimas the possibility of overcoming the folkloristic parameters which inform Propp's vision and understanding of the Russian folktale. While reducing to six actants Propp's fundamental quantity of 31 functions attributed to actors involved in the folktales, Greimas establishes the relationships between the actants and the so-called "main thematic forces" such as love (sexual, familial), friendship, religious or political fanaticism, greed, avarice, hatred, curiosity, patriotism, and various fears such as that of death, pain, and losing love.

For Greimas, there is an interplay between the nature and functions of the six actants and fundamental driving forces of the world that determine the way in which people live, suffer, love, think, agonize and expire. A new important idea or conviction seems to enter his field of critical investigation. I would formulate it as follows: Literature is about passions and knowledge. We shall see the consequences of this conviction.

An intellectually honest man with a penetrating mind and an admirer of literature as aesthetic experience, Greimas understood that folktales neither are nor can be the best and complete expression or synthesis of literary creation. As a result, ten years after *Sémantique structurale*, he addressed other questions in his formal investigation. He achieved a rather spatial and cognitive analysis in a book with a strikingly modest title and subtitle, *Maupassant, La semiotique de texte, exercices pratiques* (*Maupassant, The Semiotics of the Text; Practical Exercises*). While analyzing narratively Maupassant's short story, *Two Friends* (*Deux amis*), Greimas underlines the fact that having already analyzed the structural universe of the marvelous oral tale using Propp's terms, this time he will work on a written tale. Moreover, he will work on one which turned out to be a literary genre. Striking here is the fact that Greimas recognizes that one observes a systematic decline or effacement (*dépérissement*) of the level of events in literary texts; in other words, a decline of the narrative level to the advantage of the cognitive dimension.

In his meticulous analysis of Maupassant's short story, Greimas goes further than Propp in terms of the functional description of the literary universe, be it oral or written. Greimas emphasizes such elements of literary text as systems of values (axiology), multiplicity of spatial perspectives; for instance, cognitive, topic and para-topic, strange and familiar; cognitive 'doing' such as communicative, emissive, executory, extero-ceptive, interpretative, narrative, persuasive, pragmatic, and somatic. Greimas also distinguishes between the various types of knowing present in literary texts, e.g., narrative, noological, thematic, transitive knowing, and the variable positions of the human subject facing the acquisition of knowledge. That same subject may be seen as a fluctuation of such characteristics as cognitive, figurative, idiolectal, individual, semantic, and sociolectal.

Greimas's work on Maupassant bears the subtitle *Semiotics of the Text; Practical Exercises*, which is symptomatic of a frequent phenomenon, hypertheorization. The proportion between the analyzed text and what is said about it is abusively extended in favour of theory. The reader may legitimately wonder after reading some 275 pages about a 6-page story: *What is it about? What really must be said about Maupassant's short story? What categories must be considered unavoidable and which create a constant effect of remote relationship between the original text and the theoretical vision?*

In a way, Greimas's meta-meta-meta-analysis reflects—if not creates—an exhaustion of this type of structuralism. That exhaustion conveys a feeling of boring nervousness in the reader. He or she soon realizes how difficult it would be to continue along this structuralist path and proceed to practical exercises. In the end, what is really practical in the over-theorizing discourse? Does Greimas's method announce the end of the structuralist way of approaching literary facts?

It would be difficult to be absolutely affirmative. At any rate, in order to venture out from the *selva oscura* of multiplied concepts, one should take a step back from the irrepressible insistence of theory.

Our description of Greimas's vision and analysis of a literary tale was intended to draw your attention to the fact that ten years after publishing a programmatic semiotic and narrative analysis of Propp, Greimas discovered the complexity of literary discourse. Narratology has thus the task of confronting that complexity. If we had to say what this all means in terms of understanding narratology, we would have to acknowledge that narratology remains far from reaching its own independent scientific status. Perhaps it is significant then that Greimas's last and most ambitious work was *The Semiotics of Passion: From States of Affairs to States of Feeling*, written with one of his disciples, Jacques Fontanille.

The quest for meaning is Greimas's main preoccupation. In this respect, he may or may not problematize the epistemological status of narratology. Nevertheless, as meaning for Greimas is

> meaningful only if it is the transformation of a meaning already given; the production of meaning is consequently a signifying endowment with form (mise en forme) indifferent to whatever content it may be called on to transform. Meaning in the sense of forming of meaning can thus be defined as the possibility of the transformation of meaning.[1]

One must admit that the scientific intention of narratology has had to resolve numerous epistemological problems. Among these were the functionality and nature of the narrative in terms of the cognitive. Greimas has made some important steps towards providing narratology with a solid epistemological foundation. However, by 1976 it became obvious that literary semiotics, or the object of narratology, could not be taken for granted. Lengthy further research was still required. Was it really accomplished? To some extent yes… and no.

The Marquise Does Not Move any More

If narratology and literary theory have already admitted a long time ago that literature is also about sentences, then the sentence "[T]he Marquise no longer goes out a five" may symbolize the complexity which narratology must face. Normally, according to narrative parameters and numerous French jokes, "the Marquise went out at five" has become a banal mechanism of the beginning of any narration. This entrance into the narrative *media res* as a monotonous, insane literary device was ridiculed by Paul Valéry, of course, as mentioned in our

---

[1] Greimas, 15.

introduction. In fact, Valery went further by refusing to write the sentence "[L]a Marquise sortit à cinque heures."

Indeed, that she does not go out at five o'clock underscores the distance separating narratological semiotics from a cognitive narratology and from a relevant multidimensional analysis (Lukacs, Girard). In emphasizing Greimas's importance in the development of narratology, I have sought to underline the fact that his approach to the narratological object demonstrates the dominance of the cognitive over the narrative. Yet, on the other hand, seen from Greimas's perspective, narratology evolved from the theory of the narrative toward the recognition of the multiplicity of cognitive elements which any practitioner of narratology cannot conceal. Thus narratology tended towards an all-encompassing definition of its domain. It was an intentionally posited and practically experienced field where the narration and the narrative have been caught in an interplay of dialectical forces. Society as a source and factory of the narrative exists with the human individual as an observer and critically minded tool of the different theatres of narrative stories. Furthermore, that individual has an analytically and semiotically oriented mind in search of meaning. In short, the narratological theatre goes on. The problems remain, and the cognition of literary work is still at stake.

The Banal Sentence and the Complexity of the Novel

The merits of the sentence about the Marquise going out at 5pm are quite numerous. As seen in Claude Mauriac's use of it as a title for his experimental novel (1961), whose first sentence happens to be the same "[T]he Marquise went out at five PM." The story is spatially grounded in Paris' Latin Quarter, more precisely in the Carrefour de Buci where various streets intersect. Rue Mazarine crosses rue de Buci and becomes the Rue de l'Ancienne comedie which is relatively short. It reaches boulevard Saint Germain, which is crossed by rue Grégoire de Tours. If we count all the streets converging on Carrefour de Buci, they number more or less 17. Mauriac's novel demonstrates how everyday life is something more, indeed much more, than just the narrative. In this work, the dominant sign of punctuation is the three points (ellipsis) which signify that each paragraph is a portion of life, a slice cut from the immensity of life.

The Marquise as the representative of fiction disappeared little by little.

> For centuries and centuries, this same crowd has continually passed here, through these streets, which have managed to escape Haussman's pickaxes. La foule, la foule, toujours recommencée. With the only relative interruptions of brief and partial nocturnal relief. A

crowd so much the same from one day to the other, from year to year so little changed (231).

The crowd represents the space as an ever-flowing humanity, as Mauriac describes its impact.

> The fanfares of History distract from the humble tune of the day-to-day. How could I hope to catch this murmur of ordinary life, except at some distance from the palaces. I have tried to prove nothing. I have imagined, written, completed my book without any preconceived idea save that of this theme: the reality of time both aggravated and denied by this crowd which from day to day, year to year, century to century, has unceasingly crossed the same Carrefour of my city."[...] I could not modify anything of what had taken place here and not there, in this narrow domain so exactly surveyed. I wrote down everything I uncovered word for word, returning as close to the source as possible when the information had been given me at second hand. And with very few exceptions, I discovered nothing but crimes against bodies, against hearts, against souls. Things are what they are, or rather what they appear: that is enough for the honor and the joy of writing. But if a meaning disengages itself from the accumulation of recorded facts, what can I do about it? It is not I who am pessimistic (or optimistic). It is not I who intended to prove anything, for instance, that men kill each other, and kill themselves, that they rape and betray innocence, that they are often vile. The facts say so, facts which I have mechanically recorded, like a machine geared to retain one kind of data rather than another once it has been started up in a certain way (310-1).

The novelist wants to dominate time as seen when he quotes directly from James Joyce and Paul Klee:

> ... And here, recovered at last, are the two decisive notations, recompense after the labor, illumination from which so many works are born today, and this one as well (one never does anything but rediscover, recommence, repeat). James Joyce: History is a nightmare from which I am trying to awake. Paul Klee: the temporal element must be eliminated: Yesterday and today taken as simultaneity (304).

Mauriac concludes with

> [T]he sound stilled, the fury faded, there remains—freedom. Thus the novel has in its penultimate pages gradually faded away, and disappeared, without masks or make-believe, giving way to the novelist who, if he has put himself directly into his book, has at the end purified it of its last traces of fiction by granting it a truth in which literal exactitude was preferred to literature. The Marquise did not go out at five (311).

In Mauriac's novel, the inscription of life thus dominates fiction symbolically.

In Lieu of a Conclusion

And, to beg an answer to the question: No, the Marquise can no longer go out at five. Literature is much more complicated than this sentence. The complexity of literature has rendered the task of narratology all the more complicated. This may be seen in the following example from the beginning of one of the greatest novels of the twentieth century.

> There was a depression over the Atlantic. It was traveling eastwards, towards the area of high pressure over Russia, and still showed no tendency to move northwards around it. The isothermes and isothermes were fulfilling their functions. The atmosphere temperature was in proper relation to the average annual temperature, the temperature of the coldest as well as of the hottest month, and the a-periodic monthly variation in temperature… In short, to use an expression that describes the facts pretty satisfactorily, even though it is somewhat old fashioned: it was a fine August day in the year 1913 (Musil 3).

I will stop here without saying that "it was a fine October day in the year 2007". Overall, what seems obvious to me is that despite important progress in narratology, the pluridisciplinary cognition of literary work remains a valid orientation of research.

Works Cited

Greimas, Algirdas Julien. *Du Sens*. Paris : Ed. du Seuil, 1970.

——. *Maupassant La sémiotique du texte, exercices pratiques*. Paris : Editions du Seuil, 1976.

Mauriac, Claude. *The Marquise Went out at Five*. trans. Richard Howard London: Calders and Boyars, 1966.

Musil, Robert. *The Man Without Qualities One, A Sort of Introduction The Like of It Now Happens*. Trans. Eithne Wilkins and Ernst Kaiser. London: The Picador Book, 1954.

How Kitano's Fireworks Are Made: A Structuralist Approach to Space and Time in Takeshi Kitano's *Fireworks* (1997)

ADAM GRUNZKE
University of Toronto

Takeshi Kitano's film *Hana-Bi* (*Fireworks*) is a simple tale that belongs to a genre with a long tradition in Japanese cinema. At first glance, the story of the piece seems to be nothing more than a Yakuza film—that is, a film about the Japanese mafia—in which an ex-cop called Nishi, who has borrowed money from the mob to support his dying wife and subsequently fallen into debt, decides to take matters into his own hands. He robs a bank to repay the Yakuza, but they still want more money, so he takes his wife on a road trip to avoid them. The film concludes with Nishi murdering all of the Yakuza out of vengeance, killing his wife out of mercy and love, and finally taking his own life. While the causal course of events themselves, what the Formalists referred to in narrative art as the *fabula*, do not surprise us, the way in which the film narrative is constructed, that is the plot or *sjuzhet* and composition (shot length, the ordering of the scenes, recurring images, structure, etc.), far outstrip the norm for Japanese mob pictures. In fact, *Fireworks* is a highly stylized, semantically charged piece of visual art that begs for a deep structuralist analysis.

What I intend to do is discuss several key points of a structuralist analysis of cinema: Kitano's specific use of space and time and how he treats them as signs (including a brief discussion of inter-titles), motivation of both cutting and changes of scene, and the intentional frustration of the viewer's expectations. I am interested in how all three of these contribute to the development of a conception of space, but especially how they create and direct the time-image. This will by no means be an exhaustive analysis as the film is quite pregnant with significance; however, with the help of the theorists Jan Mukřovský and Gilles Deleuze, we should be able to address some important structuralist conceptions of space and time.

Although there is no specific historical connection between the scholarship of Deleuze and Mukařovský, there are several reasons to bring them together in the course of this discussion. First of all, they both deal with the semiotics of film. More specifically, they conceive of the shot as a sign, and explain theoretically how these signs are semantically connected to form a structure (film). Even though Deleuze developed his theory in a post-structuralist world, it is clear that he still works within the same theoretical realm as Mukařovsky. Both theorists show how cutting between shots can create a conception of space and time in the viewer, so it seems only natural, then, that we bring them together in a discussion of space and time in cinema, even though they are separated by several decades, different academic lineage, and the Iron Curtain. Perhaps this unexpected marriage can help us realize the fundamental similarities between the various structuralisms.

For the sake of our discussion of structuralism, I will now run the risk of explaining the various jokes in the Takeshi Kitano's *Fireworks*, although I am loath to do so, as explaining a joke, in the end, kills it. Most films of a serious nature contain moments of lightheartedness amidst a sea of grim imagery and pain. Usually this involves comic relief, especially a single character who says and does amusing things intermittently between scenes of violence or tension. *Fireworks* also contains many upbeat moments; however, this is not due to a single character, but rather Takeshi Kitano's construction of the film—that is, Kitano includes scenes in his film that pay homage to the film styles of silent directors like Keaton and Chaplin by exposing and then exploiting artifice, frustrating filmic expectation, and playing with perspective and off-screen action. In *Fireworks*, Kitano includes thirteen such scenes, which I will hereafter refer to as "pranks".

The first principle that we observe in the film, which drives many of these pranks, is the utilization of the off-screen space to break continuity. The result of this technique is a temporary lapse in understanding of a situation, such that when a full realization of the prank is made known to the observer, it happens suddenly and makes the situation comic. In essence, this technique is dramatic irony in reverse—the characters know something that the audience doesn't, since the audience lacks a key visual or audio sign. This works contrary to Jan Mukařovský's explanation of the use of objects in cinema:

> let us assume a picture of a revolver lying on the table. It arouses the expectation that at any time a hand will appear and pick up the revolver, and this hand will emerge from the space lying outside the picture where we place its anticipated existence. (182)

In fact, in Kitano's manipulation of the off-screen space, all the vital pieces of information are located off-screen and, more importantly, the action that fully explains the events of a given situation will also occur off-screen, preventing the viewer from a complete understanding until the entire action is complete. For example, in the opening shot of the film, two punks are standing next to a car. The camera cuts to Nishi (Beat Takeshi's character) standing next to the same car, which we assume is his, with a stone-faced expression. The camera cuts to the hood of the car, which is covered with wrappers from a fast food restaurant. The fourth shot of the sequence shows Nishi with the same expression. The fifth shot is a wide-angle presentation of the entire scene. In the sixth shot Nishi reaches in his pocket, but the camera cuts before we can see what he has. The camera cuts abruptly, in what Deleuze refers to as an irrational cut or false continuity, to Nishi's view from the inside of the car, with one of the punks washing the windshield, leaving the expected fight off-screen, in the imagination of the viewer. It is almost as if thirty seconds of film, or an inter-title were missing. Mukařovský explains that continuity has become a much stronger law since the disappearance of titles:

> As long as film worked with captions, the transition between [scenes] was always possible with a simple jump, and thus it was not felt as something exceptional, even in places where there were no captions. Since captions have disappeared, the feeling of the continuity of space has become increasingly stronger (187).

Kitano recognizes this fact, so he begins to play with continuity. The lack of continuity between the fight scene and the scene that follows is quite jarring. Whereas in silent cinema, there would have been some inter-title explaining what happened, the audience of this film is simply left wondering. Throughout the exchange between Nishi and the punks, there is no dialogue. We do not know that the car is Nishi's until the final shot of the sequence. There is no expectation of an intervention by an object or person from the off-screen space as Mukařovský discussed. Rather, the off-screen space is completely unknowable; thus, the viewer is forced to make assumptions concerning the situation, because his knowledge is limited or, as Deleuze puts it "perception and actions [cease] to be linked together, and spaces are now neither co-ordinated nor filled"(40). This limited knowledge is due to the fact that there is no dialogue, nor are there any inter-titles. In essence, Kitano, the director (not the character), is playing a joke on the viewer. What makes the scene comedic is the fact that our understanding is limited due to the breaks in continuity, and then our ignorance is revealed suddenly. It is not the situation that is particularly amusing, but rather the presentation of the situation.

Deleuze's concept of the time-image (image-temps) is especially useful here. As he explains, in typical realist cinema we are presented with a series of movement-images (image-mouvement), events presented in such a way that the viewer constructs an *indirect* image of time. In short, time is subject to movement. What happens in Kitano's film is that the series of movement-images is disrupted, or more precisely, they become subject to the *direct* time-image. As Deleuze says in

The Time-Image, "it is no longer time that depends on movement; it is aberrant movement that depends on time"(41). Also, "the time of the event comes to an end before the event does...the whole event is as it were in the time where nothing happens"(100). This "time where nothing happens" corresponds to the ellipsis (the actual brawl) in the punk scene in *Fireworks*.

It might help to conceive of the time-image in terms of a calculus of film. In calculus, the derivative constitutes the rate of change of a given function of X in relation to Y. In film we might think of the time-image as a derivative of the filmic function, that is, the progression of shots in a sequence. In a continuous function, the derivate is an aggregate of rates, constantly looking backward to define the present. We must not take for granted the mathematical terminology here: the function is continuous, but so is film; that is, they are both subject to continuity. The time-image is a rate-of-change as well, looking both at the immediate past and the present. The director constructs a filmic function through the continuous accumulation of discreet time-images (rates-of-change of time). Kitano finds a way to manipulate this rate of change by making the normally continuous filmic function discontinuous; he breaks apart our concept of the moment, the present-of-the-past and the actual present. In the example with the punks, we have the present of the immediate past (Kitano reaching in his pocket for something), but the actual present (the fight) is removed by an abrupt cut. Deleuze remarks, "the camera instead of marking out a fictional or real present, constantly reattaches the character to the before and after which constitute a direct time-image" (*Time-Image*, 152). This is precisely what the first prank accomplishes in *Fireworks*.

The way Kitano develops the next type of prank is through the unexpected conclusion of a long set-up. For example, in the second prank scene in the film, Nishi looks down, and the camera cuts to a baseball rolling toward feet (presumably his feet). The camera then cuts to two young men with baseball gloves, whose gestures tell us that the ball is theirs. The camera cuts to Nishi, who signals to them that he will throw the ball to them. The camera cuts to one of the boys squatting like a catcher to receive the ball, then to Nishi winding up to pitch. The action is resolved not when the ball is thrown to the boy, but rather when Nishi in an act of mean-spiritedness throws the ball in the opposite direction. The camera cuts to the boys looking at the direction the ball went, then again to Nishi, who laughs slightly. Once again, the comedy arises as a result of a breach in the laws of cinema. We expect that situations that are set up will be resolved in a certain way. When they aren't, the situation is potentially comedic. By showing the audience discreet moments and movements in a seemingly logical sequence, he leads us down the primrose path. In fact, the audience's conception of the filmic space is completely false, which enables the director to shatter our illusory sense of continuity. When the baseball is thrown in the opposite direction than the one we expected, we realize the error of our assumptions. Another example of this occurs when Nishi and his wife are at the beach watching a young girl trying to fly a kite. The first shot of the sequence is of Nishi and his wife looking off-screen, and then the camera cuts to a girl with a kite, then back to Nishi and his wife. Then we have a close-up of the girl, smiling and holding a kite. In the next shot, we see Nishi holding the kite and giving the girl non-verbal cues indicating what she should do to get the kite in the air (e.g. run into the wind). The camera cuts to the girl taking off running with the kite, then to the kite string tightening. The camera cuts abruptly to Nishi, holding the two wings of a broken kite, then cuts to the girl running into the wind with a pathetic kite flopping lifelessly on the ground. We expect that Nishi will help the young girl get the kite in the air, and all of a sudden those expectations are destroyed, leaving us with an unexpected and pathetically amusing shot of a girl with a broken kite. Let us keep in mind what Mukařovský says:

> When there is a change from one shot to another, whether it occurs smoothly or abruptly, the focusing of the objective or the placement of the entire camera in space is, obviously, always changed. And this spacial shift is reflected in the viewer's conciousness through a peculiar feeling which has already been described many times as the illusory displacement of the viewer himself. (182)

Once again, the movement-image is subject to the time-image. This "peculiar feeling" is the result of a rift between the continuity of the film (logic sequence of space-images and movement-images) and the viewer's typical mode of perception. This can either be a product of a direct presentation of the time-image, as in my first example with Nishi and the punks or with Nishi and the kite, or in a peculiar ordering of the diegetic space, which we will see in the following example.

The most complex of Kitano's pranks plays with the audience's expectation of dramatic irony. In one scene Nishi's wife is sitting in the front seat of a car, and Nishi is sitting in the back. They are playing a simple game in which Nishi's wife picks a card from a deck, and Nishi tries to guess which card it is. The first shot of this two-shot sequence is of the outside of the car, and we hear a voice-over of Nishi listing the names of cards. The camera cuts to a view from the back seat, such that Nishi's wife takes up the right half of the frame, and the rear-view mirror is visible in the left side of the frame. Each time Nishi's wife picks a card, she lifts it, and its reflection is visible to Nishi, who guesses correctly every time. This might be considered dramatic irony, since Nishi's wife's facial expression is that of astonishment; however, at the conclusion of the prank, Nishi's wife (who in fact has known that Nishi has been cheating from the start), places a chocolate bar over the back of the card. This time, Nishi answers not with a card name, but the brand name of the chocolate. Jan Mukařovský points out that "film space...operates as a semantic factor only through a change in shot" (184). In the context of this prank, a partial understanding of the situation is achieved through Kitano's cut from Nishi's wife's view to Nishi's view. The unfolding of the scene through various cuts creates a virtual, seemingly more holistic space-image. However, once again we encounter an elliptical situation (discontinuity in the filmic function), where vital information is not present in the sequence. In fact, this prank plays with dramatic irony, as we expect that we know more about the situation than Nishi's wife, since the shot is set up in such a way that we see part of the on-screen space that is not visible to her. There were parts of the scene that we were not privy to (i.e. the mental state of Nishi's wife and the set-up of the prank). Throughout Kitano's film, the audience is presented with a situation that has not been fully explained by the semantic context. This, when executed well (as Kitano does), deautomatizes the viewer's perception as well as actualizes established devices.

Kitano manipulates both the space-image and the time-image to provide a stylistic alternative to a derivative genre in Japan (something akin to the "buddy cop" movies or the World War II epic in Hollywood). In fact, most of the main action that would be shown in explicit detail is not shown overtly in the film. Fights may be shown, but through shadows on the floor or creative cutting to delay the understanding of who won. Similarly, the penultimate shot of the film is a prime example of creative use of off-screen space. When the shot opens, it is a wide-angle shot of Nishi and his wife sitting on a log at the beach. The camera pulls back, revealing more of the surf and drawing the attention away from the couple. Then it pans to the left, leaving the two in an off-screen space. The music theme that has been playing through the entire scene comes to its conclusion, and the final sounds we hear are two gunshots—presumably Nishi shooting his wife out of love and mercy, then himself to be with her. Deleuze deals with the importance of out-of-field sounds in *The Time-Image*.

In short, sound, in all its forms comes to fill the out-of-field of the visual image, and realizes itself all the more in this sense as component of that image: at the level of the voice, it is what is called voice-off, whose source is not seen (*Time-Image* 235).

We do not ever see this action unfold, but we do hear the action unfold; just like the very first prank, in which we must assume that the car is Nishi's, so too at the end must we make an assumption, for we cannot be sure that those two sounds were Nishi killing his wife and himself. The entire film works in such a way as to question the art of cinema, with all of its laws of continuity and construction, for its dominant role style. The action unfolds in an interesting way because of the breach of the director-viewer contract. Kitano forces us to make assumptions, watch unwittingly as the action unfolds, and ultimately remain one step behind, due to his tinkering with the artifice of genre films. This remaining one step behind is the foundation of the conception of the time-image, which "simultaneously makes the present pass and preserves the past in itself. There are, therefore, already two possible time-images, one grounded in the past, the other in the present" (*Time-Image* 98).

Besides cutting or montage, unusual or discordant framing is another way that Kitano bends the space-image. One such scene could have been included in the discussion of the pranks, but its usefulness seems more apparent here. When Nishi and his wife are visiting a Shinto shrine, they stop the car to take a picture of themselves in front of a pagoda. The first shot of the sequence is of Nishi fiddling with a camera and his wife standing next to him in front of the pagoda, and then Nishi walks off-screen. The camera cuts to Nishi setting up the camera across the street to take a picture of them, and then he runs back in the direction of his shot, presumably to get in the frame with his wife. The camera cuts again, such that we can see Nishi's camera, and the scene that the camera is about to shoot. Nishi and his wife wait for about seven seconds, then a car comes by, and we hear the click of the camera that Nishi has set up just as the car passes in front of the camera. What is fascinating about the last shot of the sequence is the way in which the structure of the film is mirrored by the artifice of the film; that is to say, what Nishi wants to capture on film within the diegetic world is almost the same as what Kitano captures in the making of the film. The car that moves in front of Nishi's camera at the critical moment also cuts in front of Takeshi Kitano's camera (albeit in a contrived situation) at the critical moment.

Kitano in this scene is underscoring the subjective perceptions of all involved: the director, the characters, the viewers, and the camera itself. Deleuze says that "evolution of the cinema, the conquest of its own essence or novelty, was to take place through montage, the mobile camera and the emancipation of the view point, which became separate from projection" (*Movement-Image* 3). In the case of this scene, we are given the perspective of a non-existent character framing the shot. That is to say, Kitano gives up the "emancipation" of the camera and instead chooses to limit his framing to a single view point, specifically the view point of Nishi's framing. The illusory world of shots and montage is temporarily suspended, and through the limited view of space (framing), we recognize Kitano's *Fireworks* for what it truly is: a mechanical manipulation of perceptive phenomena—movement-images, space-images, and time-images.

In closing, allow me to bring the discussion to the topic at hand, Structuralism(s) Today. What I have aimed to do is provide evidence that the theories of Mukařovský and Deleuze, whether they be twenty or sixty years old still have the potential to deal with works of contemporary art. Here I have tried to outline the various ways in which Deleuze's image theories can be applied to a specific film. We have seen how Kitano's elliptical narratives are a prime example of a direct time-image, that is, time emancipated from the movement-image. Thus, "film ceases to be images in a chain...an uninterrupted chain of images each one a slave of the next...It is the method of BETWEEN, between two images, which does away with the cinema of One" (*Time-Image* 180). When Kitano jumps ahead thirty seconds, removing a pivotal moment in the sequence, we become aware of the time-image. Similarly, when we are presented a scene piecemeal, Kitano is able to create a virtual, fictional (and sometimes even false) conception of space in the conciousness of the viewer, and as Mukařovský points out, "this is the space provided by the technique of the shot.? When Kitano pulls the rug from under the feet of the viewer, he underscores the artifice inherent in cinema. Space and time themselves become signs. Structuralism can help us make sense of how these signs relate to one another and, more imporantly, it can explain the joke, the effect that such a field of signs can create on the viewer. Ultimately what Deleuze and Mukařiovsk˘ help us do is shatter the illusory world of cinema set up by space-images and movement-images.

Works cited

Deleuze, Gilles. *Cinema I: The Movement-Image*. U of Minnesota P, 1986.

———. *Cinema II: The Time-Image*. Minneapolis: U of Minnesota P, 1989.

Deleuze, Gilles. *The Time-Image*. University of Minnesota Press, Minneapolis. 2007.

Mukařovský, Jan. "A Note on the Aesthetics of Film." *Structure, Sign, and Function*. Tran. and ed. John Burbank and Peter Steiner. New Haven and London:1977. 178-190.

Between Theatre and Ritual in Švankmajer's *Faust*

Elisa Segnini
University of Toronto

One of the most challenging themes in the Prague school theatrical discourse is the nature of the sign and its interpretation. Scholars like Jindřich Honzl, Karel Brušák and Petr Bogatyrev have written widely on the topic, and have argued that a symbolic understanding of the sign, rather than its direct identification with reality, is what differentiates theatre from the form it originally came from, the religious ritual. My intention here is not only to introduce the views of these scholars on the nature of the sign, but also to illustrate how these theories can be used to read a work of art. Svankmejer's *Lekce Faust*, a 1994 Czech filmic production, works very well as an example of how art is capable of playing with the liminal space between ritual and theatre. In this work, play and magic alternate, run parallel, and are mistaken one for each other. As a thread throughout this game, Švankmajer makes use of two important themes: the contrast between the actor and the puppet and the theatrical function of the imaginary space.

This version of *Faust*, in which a very pale Petr Čepek is impersonating the main character, is usually described as a "very free adaptation" of Goethe, Marlow and Grabbe. The plot is built around the old legend of the man that sells his soul to the devil, yet in Svankmejer's version, Faust is not a hero: he simply happens to be a passer-by who, intrigued by a map drawn on a leaflet, finds himself in a bizarre puppet theatre and is gradually caught in a theatrical performance which involves opera singers, giant puppets and strange clay creatures that refuse to perform within the assigned theatrical stage and often wander off into the streets of Prague.

From the very beginning, the spectator understands that he is watching a film in which the urban landscape is only one of the action's settings and in which the message will circulate in different semiotic spaces: the white credits open against an ordinary Prague's street, busy with trams, cars and pedestrians, but this image is intermittently interrupted by frame shots of engravings representing the devil and medieval bestiaries, while Gounod's *Damnation of Faust* is playing in the background. Throughout the film, music always originates from the action of one of the characters - the stage director switching on the tape recorder, the puppeteer creating sound effects, one of the characters singing. The opening and the closing of the film are the only occasions in which the music does not appear rationally motivated or where it does not, in other words, originate from the action of one of the characters. This opening is far from having the function of a mere soundtrack: rather than emphasizing the emotional quality of what is shown on the screen, it hints at a completely different dimension. The busy street belongs to a prosaic and monotonous routine, while the pompous cantata echoes powerful, irrational forces.

The music disappears with the beginning of the action. Two figures, later identified as Cornelius and Valdes, are handing out leaflets to the people who are passing by. The camera follows each of the potential receivers - and finally focuses on Faust, who grabs the leaflet and takes his time to look at it. The use of the camera already suggests a fundamental hint for understanding the film: Faust is not chosen according to his qualities, he only happens to be the one who picks up the leaflet, but his role could have been performed by any of the other passers by. At the beginning, the spectator still has a chance to glimpse at Faust's mail, at his apartment, at his eating habits - he knows that he has friends who visited Italy, that he likes to eat bread with cheese, that he is probably living as a bachelor – yet this attempt to gather information and to construct an identity for the main character is soon frustrated by the taking up of a theatrical role that wipes out the few details one knew about him as individual. From the moment in which the protagonist enters the legendary Faust house in Prague, every thing he does is manipulated and determined – he speaks the words of a script, wears the clothes prepared for him, eats the food ordered by others and moves according to an already planned track.

> It is not difficult to read Faust's adventures as an allegory of the process of mechanization to which the ordinary man is subjected in our everyday life. "A testimony to Švankmajer's theme of manipulation," writes Peter Hames, "Petr Čepek's rueful and crumpled exterior is that of a 20th century Faust, caught in an ill-defined mental, political and economic trap, manipulated still in a post Stalinist world" (42). The same Švankmajer, in the diary kept during the filming, does not hesitate to comment on the impossible struggle for freedom in a determined world:
>
> Am I religious? Definitely not in the form put forward by the Church. But I do believe that man is, in a certain way, determined. I am convinced that we are still manipulated: By the stars, by our genes, by our repressed feelings, by society, its education, advertising – repression of all kinds. ("Excerpts" xiii)

Yet Faust's protagonist, with his unquestionable acting, can also be seen to represent the ideal actor, in Craig's words the *Übermarionette*, able to efface his materiality to the point where there exists no tension between his subjectivity and the text. This reading is further complicated by the fact that, if the protagonist of the film is performing the role of Faust, Petr Čepek is playing a character who is in turn performing a role – a detail that is not negligible, since movement between different semiotic levels constitutes an essential dynamic in the work. Seen in this light, it is not a coincidence that the notes taken by Švankmajer during the shooting constantly refer to what he ironically calls "Mephisto's work," accidents, illnesses and misfortunes that took place during the shooting:

> *2 September*
> While shooting Čepek's feet running, the cameramen tripped [..] fell and broke his front tooth, grazed himself all down his face and hands, and hurt his knee. Camera destroyed.
>
> *August*
> Finished shooting in the studio at Knoviz. [..] Svatopluk Malý told me he found out that the Yugoslav who bought the house at Nerudova 27 had been shot. In other words, the man for whom we had to give up the studio there. The studio in which [...] we made a substantial part of Faust. [..] Anyway, he was shot, the people in the house told Svat'a. He was walking down the road with his wife, when suddenly a strange man came up to him in broad daylight, shot him and disappeared. The police haven't found anything yet. Another victim of Mephisto?
>
> *1 November*
> Čepek is getting worse and worse. He can't sleep at night for the pain.
>
> *3 November*
> The whole time I was afraid that Čepek would be taken into hospital at any moment, and we wouldn't get it done. In the car on the way home from Barrandov, Čepek asked me why it was that Mephisto had planted himself in his stomach and left me alone. I replied, joking, that he was Faust and not I, that I was only narrating it. ("Excerpts" vii-xiv)

Besides testifying to bad luck and a certain tendency to superstition, these notes introduce a thematic unity between the empirical reality and the subject treated in fiction. Not only the gray Prague that functions as a film setting, but also the "real" city where the author is shooting is here being read and interpreted through codes provided by a fictional work. These notes suggest that no semiotic level is hermetic to the others: the spectator must read the film as a frame in a frame, or better, as a series of consecutives frames: the magical world of puppets, of signs that free themselves of their semiotic context and become real;

the everyday Prague that functions as fictional setting and the empirical reality that is, in its turn, interpreted through codes suggested by the fictional world that it has created. The game that Švankmajer is playing is not far from the dynamic that Lotman describes in his well-known essay "The Text within the Text":

> The play with meaning that arises in the text, the slippage between the various kinds of structural regularities, endows the text with greater semantic potential than have texts codified by means of a single, separate language. [. . .] Including the pedestal or the frame in the text intensifies the ludic moment because the conventionality of these elements also keep them excluded, distinct from what is inherent in the basic text. When the figures of a baroque sculpture climb on the pedestal or descend from it or when figures in a painting leap down from the frame, the effect is to emphasize rather than to obscure the fact that one element belongs to material reality while the other belongs to artistic reality. (378)

In *Faust*, the crossing of semiotic levels (for example, the puppets walking off stage into Prague's busy streets) underlines the fictional status of the props: they appear funny and ridiculous, performing a bizarre role in the "wrong" context. Yet, at a certain time, the relation changes: the puppets are no longer restrained in their roles, act off-script, become magic symbols rather than props. The public's reception, in this case, changes radically: the wooden creatures stop being entertaining and begin to evoke terror.

In the prelude of Goethe's *Faust*, God and Mephisto make a bet about Faust's destiny and on whether he will or will not fall into the devil's temptations, predetermining the tragedy that follows. Švankmajer goes even further: his Faust moves through different semiotic spaces, but he never acts of his own will, and remains trapped in a performance. As Švankmajer explains in one of his diary entries, he is not a hero nor a rebellious titan, but simply an actor:

> What makes it different from Goethe's or Marlow's? In Goethe and in Grabbe, Faust is a rebellious titan. A romantic view of the omnipotent of knowledge. In Grabbe, Mephisto even regrets at one point that Faust is only a man: "there is something truly good like in you."[..] In my version Faust is not even an exceptional person (he is manipulated into the role of Faust, and other Fausts coming along; indeed, the role of Faust is offered to anyone who takes a leaflet). Nor is it revolt (or, if it is, then revolt kneeling down). Faust is "led" for the whole of his journey, both metaphorically and literally. [..] The Faust in my film is not, therefore, a romantic rebel Titan; even less is he a criminal. He is a "chance" person who has let himself be manipulated into a tragic position (role) which he plays to the bitter end. ("Excerpts" xii)

There are numerous hints in the film that Faust is performing. The actors are few and play several roles - the toilet lady is also the witch with the black cat at the window, the man with the ash is also the man who carries around a human leg, Cornelius and Valdes are leaflet distributors, waiters, musicians, clients of the pub, audience of the opera and helpers in its production. In his dialogues with Mephisto, Faust always appears to be reading or remembering the script—sometimes he even sticks out his tongue looking at himself in the mirror, or stumbles and hesitates having forgotten the lines. Not only the music, but most signs of magic are the result of orchestration: Valdes and Cornelius stand under Faust's window with white, matt eyes, but are shown taking off contact lenses as soon as Faust draws the curtain. Wine miraculously springs from a table in a *Biergarten*, but the waiter (again, Cornelius) turns a tap off as soon as Faust takes his leave. After a scene in which the puppets are killed by drowning, the theatre is flooded with water, but a tap is found open in the bathroom. Magic is always apparent, it is no more than an orchestrated trick, and yet most details of its orchestration are kept carefully hidden from the main actor—a trick easily performed by the camera, which turns away from Faust's perspective to point out at details that he is not allowed to see. If performing means having semiotic awareness of one's role, can we still say that Faust is performing? This question becomes essential in Faust.

It is clear that Faust's words are not his own, that he is simply reading a script. Yet he is denied the opportunity to understand the cyclical nature of his rehearsal. As he enters the house indicated by the leaflet, he is hit by a man who is running toward the exit - but he never has the time to realize that this terrified man is nothing but a senior Faust and that he, himself, will run away in the same way by the conclusion.

Faust is playing, but he is not aware that the text he is given does not constitute the whole script and that Prague, with its *Biergarten*, pubs and busy streets, is also part of the theatrical set. It might happen that, in theatre, both spectator and actor perceive the performance as real and occasionally suspend their disbelief. This mechanism is though unintentional and must remain sporadic since, to put it into Bogatyrev's words, "perception of the theatre as real life through the whole performance must inevitably lead to results violating the theatre" ("Forms" 52). If the perception of the theatre as real life stops to be occasional and unintentional and becomes stable, semiotic awareness is lost and the theatre becomes ritual.

In the article "Ritual and Theatre," Honzl argues that these two activities have two fundamental similarities: that they are both actions, and both signifying actions (136). The main difference is that, according to Honzl, "religious interpretation does not separate a symbol and its meaning but abstracts from a symbolic representation certain parts that are identified with reality (making them a vehicle or real meaning or divine power, or an event which has or will happen). It represses the other parts of the symbol below the threshold of attention or even consciousness" (15).

The protagonist of *Faust* changes, throughout the film, his perspective from purely theatrical to ritualistic: gradually, the symbols used in the theatre are not interpreted as signs but read as part of reality. This process is further underlined by the fact that the text in the text is, in the case of *Faust*, a puppet theatre, and that puppets are mere representation of the human being: their voice is the only sign of reality on stage, and even the voice is counterfeited.

It is at this point useful to take a look at Zich's famous analysis of the puppet theatre and at Bogatyerev's argument against it. According to Zich, the spectator of the puppet theatre perceives the puppets either as lifeless props or as living people. In the first case, they are treated as "lifeless material", their speech and movements are not taken seriously and have an overall comical effect ("We consider them puppets, but they want to consider them people, and they certainly make us merry!") (Zich qtd. in Bogatyrev "Contribution" 58). In the second case, the puppets are perceived as living beings, and appear thus as a deviation:

> Consciousness of the actual lifelessness of the puppets then recedes and surfaces only as sense of something inexplicable, as mystery evoking our wonder. In this case the puppets affect us mysteriously. If they had real human size and if their facial expression were as perfect as possible, this manner of conceiving them would produce terror in us [. . .]. One can find examples of such animated matter in legends and in literature: the commander's statue (in Don Juan) or Golem. Everyone will concede that these creatures of fantasy make a much more ghastly impression on us than living corpses do, for here is something completely unnatural- life in a lifeless, inorganic substance- while with the corpse it is merely a matter of life in a substance that was once alive. I think that even our puppets would cause us to feel uneasy if they were as large as people, but the reduction in their dimensions completely precludes this and renders them merely mysterious. (Zich qtd. in Bogatyrev "Contribution" 58)

Bogatyrev contests Zich's view, pointing out that his mistake consists in the fact that he does not consider the puppet theatre as a distinct system of signs, but that he always juxtaposes it to an actor's performance: "If we regarded the puppet theatre- just like every other theatre and ultimately like every art—only as a system of signs, not even a puppet would strike us as ridiculous, though its movements do not fully conform to the movements of living people" ("Contribution" 61). While the actor, besides being a sign, is also the only organic reality on stage, puppets are in fact, Bogatyrev argues, merely signs of a sign. To take the performance seriously requires therefore higher semiotic training- a training that is mastered by children and by the public familiar with the puppet theatre, who are able to watch it without constantly comparing it to a real actor's performance. Yet in *Faust* the puppets, which are much taller than human beings, are not only constantly presented next to the figure of the actor but also appropriate human gestures: they run off in the streets, wear real people clothes, drive cars and devour cakes with whipped cream. While the initial juxtaposition to human beings makes them appear ridiculous, the appropriation of gestures that exceeds the puppet's repertoire slowly renders them uncanny. At the beginning of the film, Faust finds the wooden creatures ridiculous and entertaining. He shakes his head amused glimpsing at a puppet on the toilet, laughs at the clown's confused performance, climbs up on the scene to give the Wagner puppet a pat in the back. Yet, when he meets the lifeless Wagner backstage, he hesitates and then kicks it, as if requiring a proof that the wooden legs will jumble: a gesture that implies a doubt on whether the puppet *really* is only a wooden prop. Gradually, Faust's perception changes, until he runs away in terror at devil puppet's sight in the last scene.

The dichotomy between the puppet and the human being, between man and his lifeless representation is one of the most important leitmotifs of the film and it is closely linked to the concept of semiotic awareness: Faust's theatrical performance becomes ritual when the representation of the human being (the statue, or the puppet) stops being perceived as sign and acquires magical faculties. The introduction of this motif goes back to the very beginning of the film where Faust, while collecting his mail, is distracted by a rhythmic thump that comes from the stairs. He looks up and sees a woman carrying a child who, on his turn, is dragging a doll by its leg, letting the head noisily bump against the steps. When the woman heads off in the streets, the door closes on the doll's porcelain head, which gets smashed in the impact. The reason why the doll's scene is so disturbing to us viewers depends mainly on the contrast between the child and the doll, which is virtually a lifeless double of the human being – we are in fact given a close up of the child's face just before the doll's head gets trapped in the door.

This scene, although not relevant in terms of plot, is essential to introducing the leitmotif of the statue, of the lifeless representation that later becomes the motif of the statue on stage. The statue is a key element in Grabbe's *Don Juan und Faust* and, as Roman Jakobson suggests, is also one of the most famous cases of aesthetic paradoxes: being made of timeless inorganic material, it suggest eternity and duration and yet, at the same time, represents an ephemeral stage of life. Analyzing the recurrence of the theme of the statue in literature, Jakobson mentions the creative potential of the contrast between the organic animate and its lifeless representation:

> A statue—in contrast to a painting—so approximates its model in its three dimensionality that the inorganic world is nearly canceled out of its themes: a sculptural still life would not suitably provide the distinctive antinomy between the representation and the represented object that every artistic sign includes or cancels. Only the opposition of the dead, immovable matter from which a statue is shaped and the mobile, animated being which a statue represents provides a sufficient distance. (352)

According to Jakobson, even though a statue is the most faithful representation of a human being, its natural state is a state of rest, the contrary of the essence of human life: "whereas human life is a vigorous manifestation of cosmic activity, and rest is the only negation of this life, only a deviation, only an anomaly, for a statue, on the contrary, rest is the natural, unmarked state, and the motion of a statue is the deviation of a norm" (362). The motion of a statue is thus clearly a perversion, a deviation which can easily become terrifying.

These paradoxes play an essential role in the film, and are especially central to the scene in which Faust assists to the artificial creation of life in a medieval kitchen hidden behind the theatre. Here an embryo begins to grow at supersonic speed in the viscous liquid of an alembic, changing rapidly into the shape of a fully formed new born baby and finally resting still like a beautiful clay doll. Faust shatters the alembic, lifts carefully up the doll and puts it on a table. He then draws from his pocket a creased bit of paper and writes on it the symbols of the "life-giving Shem ha-m'forash" (Švankmajer *Faust* 13). With a knife, he forces the mouth of the clay doll to open and inserts in it a piece of paper. Until this moment, the clay baby had been nothing but a beautiful doll, and the spectator had perceived the opening of the mouth as a displeasing, but not as a terrifying gesture. Yet as soon as the doll receives the piece of paper in its mouth, it also receives the illusion of life and any violence toward it is perceived much more violently. The clay baby opens his eyes, sits, blinks and claps hands. While its body remains the same, its head suddenly begins to grow- first into the head of an older child, then into the head of a young adult and finally into a double of Faust's face. In this last stage, the homunculus incarnates the essential definition of a statue: the representation of a human being in three-dimensional form, in inorganic, durable material. The fact that the clay doll is moving effaces the only difference between the subject and its representation, creating an almost identical double. The clay face begins then to grow old at supersonic speed, to decay, and it finally turns into a Skelton that chatters his teeth with the same stylized gesture of the devil puppet. Faust squeezes the unsuccessful homunculus into a heap of clay that continues to move in agony until the piece of paper is torn and the clay becomes, once again, lifeless inorganic material.

The mimicry of death in a statue, that is by definition made of inorganic material and that will thus never be subjected to deterioration, appears terrifying and perverse; in a sense, Faust's clay doll is the opposite of Goethe's homunculus, who is made of fire, has no matter and must live inside his phial to be protected from the world. While Goethe's homunculus is at the desperate search of matter, the little clay monster created by Faust IS pure matter: the *shem* can be read as a symbolic interruption of semiotic awareness, the moment in which the lifeless material (the clay creature, or the puppet) stops to exercise a symbolic value and is perceived by the public as real.

Wooden, clay and porcelain figures dominate the scene in *Faust*. Yet the line between animate and inanimate is in this film as ambiguous as the border between theatre and ritual. When Faust is dressed up and led to perform on stage, a puppet head is lowered on his head and wooden hands are added. When he, however, cuts his wooden wrist in order to sign the devil's contract, real blood emerges. And when he later tries to take off his costume, he is able to get rid of the puppet mask, but not of pulling the wire out of his head. Once backstage, he angrily kicks the devil puppet—while at the same time, on stage, tiny devils puppets are engaged in a battle with minuscule porcelain angels, who are quickly smashed and broken to pieces with a move that the spectator, despite the fact that the creatures are only wooden props, perceives as an extremely violent act.

After performing, these creatures jump down the stage and retreat into a magical space, either in a forest or in a sunlit alley. This introduces another essential element that this film shares with theatrical performance: the notion of imaginary action space. Karel Brušák argues that, in theatre, the imaginary action space constitute an invisible extension of the dramatic space that is concretized in the mind of the spectator:

> It is argued that the strict delineation of the stage has preconditioned the spectator to presume its continuation beyond its limits. If a scene represents a forest, the spectator automatically imagines the forest continuing at the sides of the stage or behind, if a room, he imagines further rooms, and so on. The relationship of the outer to the dramatic space proper can remain dormant but they can enter into active relationship when the action from the imaginary space invades the stage, when it overflows from the latter to the former or when it is completely relegated to beyond the boundaries of the stage. (148)

In *Faust*, this imaginary action space is not only indicated, but realized through surreal *tableaux* that, though their visual quality, differ from the usual shooting and are closer to the subconscious. This imaginary stage is divided into angelic (sunlit alley) and demonic spaces (forest), which are not only the point of escape of wooden ad clay characters but also the place where they are created by an invisible puppeteer. The process of assemblage is unsuspected by the character and only revealed to the spectator: it is, in Brušák words, not only an invisible part of the structure, but also "the time space continuum from which the play emerges and in which continues, if there are intervals between the acts and into which it finally retires" (159). Surreal images, closer to a visual tableau than to a filmic shot, materialize the imaginary action space replacing the narrative element of the theatrical performance: if in a play, the clown would simply mention where he is running while quickly disappearing off stage, in *Faust*, we are visually presented with a materialization of this space. There is even a case in which the imaginary space becomes the setting of a play in the play, the narration of Faust's adventures in Portugal. Here the imaginary space, or sun lit avenue, is for the first time presented as a garden in which "real" people walk, and in which the public assembles to watch the puppet show. When the clown makes his exit from the stage, he hides behind the park's bushes, in front of a luxuriously table laid with "real" food. Confusing the spectator, he stuffs his wooden mouth with whipped cream—creating the same effect between comical and grotesque that the spectator had experienced glimpsing at the puppet sitting on the toilet. The spectator faces a doubt for the first time: is the sun lit avenue a part of Prague? Is this boring and everyday city, where people walk in gray raincoats looking at the floor, also part of the imaginary action space?

The answer is not simple. Brušák argues that there is a complete parallelism between magic rites and dramatic structures, that the main constituents, which are "the stage, the scene, the action space, the imaginary action space and the spectators", are common to both, even if the structures differ semiologically and functionally. According to Brušák, the action space and the imaginary action space are the main sources of energy that generate tension within the structure, and the only difference is that in the magic rite, the amount of energy in each of them is rigidly fixed, while in the dramatic structure it fluctuates between them (160).

Keeping in mind Brušak' and Honzl's reflections, we are left with two readings of Švankmaier's film: if we consider the Devil a simple puppet, Faust's journey will be read as an extension of the imaginary space and the conjuring ceremony will be nothing but a theatrical performance. If we, on the other hand, consider the Devil puppet a vehicle of Evil force, Faust will no longer be seen as performing but as participating in the ritual. Yet the spectator should not feel pressured to choose between either of the interpretations: on the contrary, what the film argues for is the acceptance of the ambiguity that any of these readings would carry.

The recognition of a space of ambiguity in the ritualistic- symbolic discourse is interpreted by Honzl as a sign of freedom. In his essay, he points out that an identification of certain symbols has often been imposed by the main ideologies of a society, thus depriving the population of a different, more personal interpretation. As an example he mentions how, through history, Catholicism has imposed a literal reading of the Eucharistic ceremony, considering heretic anybody who dared to read the host as symbol and not as the actual body of Christ. The refusal to identify a symbol with reality can thus, according to Honzl, be interpreted as a sign of individual rebellion with respect to the reading imposed by a leading ideology.

Faust never succeeds in this rebellion. It is not difficult to read Faust's adventures as an allegory of the process of mechanization to which the ordinary man is subjected in our everyday reality. Faust is a passive character throughout his whole journey: he never succeeds in an individual reading of reality, his terror in the last scenes clearly shows his inability to separate a sign from its symbolic meaning. His personality is completely annihilated by the theatrical orchestration of his world- by the end of the film, he has become a puppet, while the puppets have been transformed into religious symbols with magical power. Playing with the ambiguity of theatre and ritual, the film suggests not only that man is constantly determined throughout his daily life, but that this manipulation is perceived as the most natural of realities. "We have to rebel to manipulation," writes Švankmajer in his Faust journal, "by creation, magic, revolt. This rebellion is the way to freedom. Freedom as such does not exist; all that exists is freeing. This freeing, however, does not relieve us of our tragic fate, it only makes it more logical. And it makes life fuller and more fun, and above all more meaningful" ("Excerpts xii).

An analysis of the film suggests that *Faust* is not about theatre nor about ritual, but about the ambiguity and the merging of these two activities as they are performed in our daily life.

Works Cited

Bogatyrev, Peter. "A Contribution to the Study of Theatrical Signs." Steiner 55-64.

——. "Forms and Functions of Folk Theatre." *Semiotics of Art: Prague School Contributions.* Eds. Ladislav Matejka and Irwing R. Titunik. Cambridge and

London: The MIT Press, 1976. 51-56.

Brusak, Karel. "Imaginary Action Space in Drama." *Drama und Theatre. Theorie-Methode – Geschichte*. Eds. Herta and Hedwig Král Schmid. München: Otto Sagner, 1991. 144-62.

Hames, Peter. "The Film Experiment:" *Dark Alchemy: The Films of Jan Švankmajer*. Trowbridge: Flick Books, 1995.

Honzl, Jindřich "Ritual and Theatre." Steiner 134-173.

Jakobson, Roman. "The Statue in Puškin's Poetic Mythology." *Language in Literature*. Eds. Krystyna Pomorska and Stephen Rudy. Cambridge: Harvard UP,1987. 318-167.

Lotman, Yury. "The Text within the Text." *PMLA* 109.3 (May 1994): 377-384.

Steiner, Peter, ed. *The Prague School: Selected Writings, 1929-1946*. Austin: U of Texas P, 1982.

Švankmajer, Jan. *'Faust,' The Script. Including a Preface by the Author and Excerpts from his Diary Kept during Filming*. Trowbridge: Flick Books,1996.

———. *Lekce Faust*, Anathol Videorecording: 1994.

Naturschik or Film Figure?
On Russian Formalists' Views of Film and Theatre Acting:
Structural and Semiotic Reformulations

Yana Meerzon
University of Ottawa

The 1927 collection *Poetika Kino*, the cornerstone of the Russian Formalists' studies of film and its language, aimed to devise a methodological apparatus to study film as an independent media originating at the crossroads of literature, theatre, and fine arts. The book not only "objected to the reduction of the object of [...] study to factors of the author's biography, socio-historical determinants, or philosophical ideas", it now set to find out and agree on those "structural factors which were transforming 'moving photographic images' into an independent art from" (Eagle 2). The collection proposed to identify and study major cinematic paradigms: the film's distinct language, its idiosyncratic ways of storytelling, the uniqueness of cinematic space, time, and film acting. Nonetheless, in its attempts to differentiate film from other arts (theater, photography, sculpture and book illustration), the collection demonstrated a number of theoretical flaws. Although the book recognized the interconnections between theater and film, for example, it presented a theatre play as archaic, static, and verbally overwhelming instance of Aristotelian linearity, dominated by the continuity of cause and effect relationships. In their assessment of differences between the novel poetics of film and the old fashion aesthetics of theatre, Russian Formalists relied upon the 19th century melodrama and naturalism curiously ignoring the most evident connections between the newly established art form and theatre practice of the time. Thus, theorizing *montage* as an example of *a cinematic metaphor* —the core of film's dramaturgy, style and composition—the volume took no notice of Vsevolod Meyerhold's concurrent experiments in theater (his invention of *montage of attractions*, the point of departure for Sergey Eisenstein's theory of montage in film) and were not ready to foresee Brecht's experiments with fragmented dramaturgy, foreground mise-en-scene or estranged acting.[1] Thus defining film aesthetics, the

---

[1] In their remarks, Formalists overlooked the dynamics of *montage as metaphor*

collection simply denied other visual arts, theater in particular, the dynamism and the power of symbolic expression. The subsequent cinema and theatre studies of Prague Linguistic Circle and Tartu Semiotic School brought the ideas of dynamism and metaphor back to theatre studies, putting the analysis of drama and performance into larger, structural and semiotic context. Specifically, Mukařovský's studies of acting in film and Veltruský's concept of *stage figure* modified the Russian Formalists' views of the stage-audience dynamics.

This article analyzes Russian Formalists' ideas on the interrelationships between film and theatre presented in *Poetika Kino* and examines the semiotic interdependency between film and theatre aesthetics as it emerges in the works of Mukařovský, Veltruský and Lotman. It argues that in the late 1920s due to the ideological changes in the country and to the film techniques' modifications (i.e. introduction of sound in film) Russian Formalists began to experience the major shift in their analytical methods. *Poetika Kino* presented a methodological transition from purely formalist to structural, semiotic and even sociological approaches.[2] Specifically, in the theory of film acting, Eikhenbaum, Piotrovsky and Kazanski foresaw its further semiotic developments as interdependency of *stage* and *film figures* proposed by Prague theoreticians.

***

In his opening article, "Problems of Cinema Stylistics", Eikhenbaum summarizes the Russian Formalists' views on the relationships between film and theatre as rivalry and competition, in which the young (film) takes over the old (theatre).[3] Eikhenbaum writes,

> cinema can be defined as a 'photogenic' art which makes use of the language of motions (facial expressions, gestures, poses, etc.). On this ground it has come into competition with theatre—and has been victorious. A significant role in this victory was played by the following circumstance: the film viewer has the possibility of seeing details

---

used in Brecht's anti-Aristotelian drama. Based on the fragmented plot structure, epic drama escapes the linearity of Aristotelian cause/effect relationships, linear development of the conflict. It similarly to film relies upon the employment of flashbacks and flash-forwards, dream-inserts and various meta-theatrical devices.

[2] Not only introduction of sound to silent film but also commercialization and politicization of the industry significantly alternated its expressive language: thus no analysis of the pure artistic forms taken out of their historical, cultural and social contexts was able to present reader with a coherent critical narrative of audio-visual arts of the time and their evolution.

[3] Curiously enough, most of the authors contributing to *Poetika Kino* (except Adrian Piotrovsky) came to study film as fully developed scholars of literature and poetry.

(facial expressions, objects, etc.), of being transported from place to place with a facility which matches the imagination, of seeing before him people and objects at various distances, from various camera angles, with various lighting , etc. The dynamics of cinema unfolding on the screen defeated the theatre, moving it to the position of some sort of 'tender relic'. (1981:65)

Formalists embraced the linguistic simplicity of the new media, seeing in the silence of film the potential for the expressivity of its spectacle, free from the dominance of text. In their eagerness to differentiate film from theatre, to define film's language anew, Formalists render theatre as a "syncretic art" defined by the "immobility of the proscenium and the concomitant invariability of [spectators'] point of view and distances" (Eikhenbaum 1981:65). Moreover, as Formalists argue, in its experiments with the elements of spectacle, theatre badly mimics film and loses to the latter in the dynamics of the visual expressivity. As Eikhenbaum continues,

> The visual effects of a theatrical presentation (mime, gestures, set decoration, objects) inevitably run into the problem of the *distance* between the immobile stage and the viewer. The play of visual details is almost impossible in the theatre; likewise, mimicry and gesture are fettered in their development and the actor who possesses great gifts of mimicry cannot express them in the theatre. The immobility of the stage also leads to the fact that the actor plays against a set which remains in a single fixed position: this restrains the dramatists and introduces into the verbal dynamics of theatrical art something which is alien, superfluous, static. The object in theater plays a completely passive role, witnessing or spying on the actor in a superfluous manner and boring the viewer by its presence. The subdivision of theatrical space (by lighting effects), the use of revolving stage, etc., do not change the essence and are only perceived as a sad imitation of cinematography. That which constitutes the very essence and nature of cinema looks vulgar, heavy like vain attempts at witticisms made by a person who is not witty. (1981:65)

In their opposition to theatre studies of the time, Russian Formalists choose to disregard the discoveries of symbolist, futurist and expressionist drama and performance, which influenced film's aesthetics. Moreover, even in such retrospective books as Viktor Shklovsky's biography of Sergei Eisenstein (published in 1976), Formalists (in the voice of Shklovsky) still argued that even if the 1920s Russian theatre practice contained any elements of experimentation, it was under the radical influence of film. Typically to Formalists' thinking, Shklovsky emphasizes the dominance of language in a theatrical event and juxtaposes the verbality of theatre to the silence of film. In his opinion, theatre resembles a book with "moving pictures": it is a set of moving tableaux unfolding in the audience's real time and in the space of a theatre stage.

In reality, the rivalry between film theory and theatre practice produced startling results. The 1920s films of Sergei Eisenstein, Dziga Vertov, and Lev Kuleshov changed the status of Russian cinematography, making it a unique form of art. Eisenstein, a theatre student of Meyerhold, brought the ideas of his mentor into film. Eisenstein used Meyerhold's experiments with simultaneous stage (in order to make his spectacle more dynamic, Meyerhold broke a single theatre space into several sections indicating different fictional locales; he made action move from one locale to another in nonlinear fashion that pointed at the same time at the fictional time passing); and his ideas on *montage of attractions* as his major cinematic principles. Using his theatrical experience, Eisenstein not only created his particular cinematic language but also generated the optimal principles of cinematic narration and cinematic text.[4] Eisenstein's theory of montage, as Shklovsky writes, was not "a technique of changing one close-up with another; of camera's moves: it was the method of creating literary, theatrical or cinematic, or any other system of speech, with its own semantics" (1976:73). Remarkably, reflecting upon his experience as a theatre-maker,[5] Eisenstein describes how his experiments with theatre aesthetics gave him an opportunity to play with the audience's reception, predetermined in theatre by the illusory nature of performance and in film by the supposedly anti-illusory, direct, presentation of objects and events on screen. Eisenstein directed Alexander Ostrovsky's play *Enough Simplicity in Every Sage* at the Proletcult Theatre, Moscow, in March of 1923.[6] There every action that was to take place in the imaginary action space (beyond the horizons of the audience's gaze), and everything that the spectators were to imagine, was staged directly in front of their eyes, in the centre of the auditorium.[7]

---

[4] Eisenstein also took notice of the theoretical foundlings of the formal school of theatre studies, specifically the works of Aleksey Gvozdev and Adrian Piotrovsky, who researched the fragmentary nature of commedia dell'arte and the simultaneous staging in Medieval and Ukrainian puppet theatre.

[5] The article was first published by *Sovyetskoe Kino*, November-December 1934, and later translated by Paya Haskelson under the title "Through Theatre to Cinema" and published in *Theatre Arts Monthly*, New York, September 1936. Here it is quoted from its reprint, published in Eisenstein, Sergey. *Film Form. Essays in Film Theory*, Ed. Leyda Jay. New York: Harcourt Brace Jovanovich. 1977. pp. 3-18.

[6] His dramaturge and co-director was Sergei Tret'yakov, who introduced the expressionistic style and its dramatic techniques to Russian theatre.

[7] Since film derives from photography, the medium based on reality recording as it presents itself to the machine, to the camera, it acquires to Eisenstein the

"While the other scenes influenced the audience through intonation, gestures, and mimicry, our scene [the fighting at the ring—YM] employed realistic, even textual means—real fighting, bodies crashing to the ring floor, panting, the shine of sweat on torsos, and finally, the unforgettable smacking of gloves against taut skin and strained muscles" (Eisenstein 7). This process was directed to expose and explore "an actual-materialistic element in theatre" (Eisenstein 7), to search for more immediate stage/audience relationships, more direct forms of spectators' manipulation. Staging *The Sage*, Eisenstein included a short (120metres) comic film under the title *The Glumov's Diary*, which served as one of the play's *attractions:* it translated theatrical aesthetics into the language of another media and introduced the potential of filmic utterance on stage. Here Eisenstein not only revealed a singular directorial device but also exposed theatricality as such, the intermedial potential of a theatre performance.[8]

Formalists, however, proposed to cure theatrical archaism not through the experiments with theatrical space and time, but by bringing *actor* to the foreplay of a theatrical event. As Eikhenbaum insisted, theatre "should proceed along another road", it has to secure "the transformation of the proscenium into an arena for the exclusive activity of the actor by means of destruction of theatrical space as a defined place of action—i.e. by returning to the principles of Shakespearean theatre" (1981:66); and so, theatre "must realize itself anew—no longer as a syncretic form, but as an individuated art in which the word and the body of the actor should be freed from other elements" (1981:65).

---

power of direct juxtaposition between the real world of the filmgoers and the screen world of the characters and fictional events presented (Eisenstein 3).

[8] In his study "Between Literature and Visual Arts", Jan Mukařovský examines the intermedial potentialities of visual and verbal arts, taking as his point of departure Lessing's statement on the natural delimitation of the arts "according to the nature of [their] material" (Mukařovský 1977:207). As Mukařovský suggests, for Lessing it is the material that encourages the artist and at the same time dictates her creative choices, whereas the history of art (especially its today's practice) demonstrates that every art form "strives to overstep its boundaries by assimilating itself to another art" (Mukařovský 207). Therefore, any theatrical performance (even if it is based on improvisation or set in theatre as a round or as a site-specific event with the audience's interactive involvement) still offers the intermedial possibilities. Theatre, by the nature of its material is already intermedial and interdisciplinary: in its expressivity it mixes various creative materials from linguistic codes to light, color, sound, human body, rhythm and energy (to name a few). Thus, as a multilingual text, a theatre performance that openly embraces and draws upon other art forms (film or painting, for instance) manifests its meta-intermedial potential as well as genre's flexibility.

Adrian Piotrovsky, a contributor to *Poetika Kino* and a scholar of the Classical theatre, saw the actor's presence and his personal time coinciding with the time of the spectators during a play as the advantage and at the same time the "intrinsic limitation" to theatre (1981:132). As he wrote, theatre is conditioned by "the presence of living actors, 'living on stage', moving only towards the "future"; it is also conditioned by the keen feeling of temporal reality which the theatre itself inevitably generates" (1981:132). The combination of the actors' energy and the spectators' involvement in the act of making a theatrical event provides the dynamism of a theatrical communication. Stage in theatre presents a "battlefield of human passions and drives which have been artificially isolated from the material worlds and from nature. [...] The human being is the basic and most important material of the drama and the foundation of the dramatic action" (Piotrovsky 1981:134). In this respect, theatre remains form of art stronger, and more powerful than cinema. In cinema, as Piotrovsky acknowledges, "this priority of the human being is by no means so evident and unquestionable. *Photogeny* puts the human being on the same perceptual plane with the object or nature. The isolated "drama of human beings" and their "human drives" are not characteristic for cinema: such "drama" is not intrinsic for cinema's nature and impoverishes its expressive potential" (Piotrovsky 1981:134). Overall, cinema remains the technological art of mise-en-scene and montage that in Formalists' opinion needs to find and define anew the laws of dramatic composition (film's scenario) and its expressive powers (cinematography, lighting and sound effects).

Although most of the contributors to *Poetika Kino* acknowledge the privileged position of a human being on screen, Boris Kazanski, the author of "The Nature of Cinema", comes closest to the semiotic reformulation of the actor's presence in film, later developed by the Prague Linguistic Circle's scholars, specifically Mukařovský and Veltruský, who proposed to render a theatrical acting sign as a tripartite structure in comparison to a cinematic acting sign as a dual phenomena. Kazanski points out the materiality of theatrical signs, including objects and people on stage, in contrast to the pure semiotic quality of cinematic signs. Tracing film's direct dependency of the art of photography, Kazanski states that since photography "cannot tolerate any falseness", film, the photography's next of kin, "demands only nature as its filmed object" (2001:74; 1981:114), and thus can reproduce only shadows of objects and people not these objects or people themselves.

Moreover, Kazanski recognizes the discrepancy between stage and film people in their dependency to the previously existed dramatic text, as the major point of differentiation between stage and film figures. As Kazanski writes, "The stage actor is presented with the following difficult task: the image created by him is dictated by a drama (usually known beforehand) and therefore controlled by the viewer; the image must withstand comparison with the image already formed in the imagination of the viewer. In film, this dualism of the drama and the stage image is absent, since the scenario, as a rule, remains unknown to the public. Thus, the performer in cinema is free from any control on the part of the viewer and from the dangers of competing with the viewer's imagination" (1981:112). Film actor, therefore, is equal to a *model* standing in front of a painter, and film acting is only *a type of modeling* found in fine arts. Although Kazanski's terminology is far from semiotic discourse, his idea on discrepancy between stage and film figures is valuable: he does not elaborate enough on the structural and aesthetic mechanisms participating in actor's constructing film images, but brings into the discussion the concept of the audience's controlling function and the role of spectators actively but differently participating in constructing theatrical and cinematic artifacts. As Kazanski states, even if we accept the perfect craft of Hollywood stars such as Chaplin or Keaton, we cannot forget the fact that we see on screen first of all a human being—Charlie Chaplin, and only then his film image—Chaplin in the role of a beggar. This way, Kazanski declares, film actor always "serves as 'nature' for reproduction", and "to that extent he exists for the viewer only in the sense of 'a natural type', 'a model'. The fact that he is an actor has no significance in principle. He might simply be the sort of type that he is representing. That he possesses expressive abilities is also in the final analysis only the artist's good fortune, like an attractive face or a well-built body. To call the performer of a 'role' in a film an actor is just an incorrect as calling a film 'theatre.' If cinema is a shadow painting, i.e. a graphic art, then the actor reproduced as a representation on the screen must in principle be only a model" (Kazanski 1981:113). In 1990, in his analysis of cinematic *celebrity* phenomenon, Michael Quinn operated with the ideas of resemblance and correlation between the nature/model of cinematic representation and the representation itself. As Quinn argues, celebrity represents the public persona of an actor playing a role. "Celebrity in its usual variety, though, is not composed of acting technique but of personal information. [...] In the context of this public identity there then comes to exist a link between performer and audience, quite apart from the dramatic character" (Quinn, 1990:156). In fact, the dominance of the actor's subjectivity over his/her stage figure that is typical for theatre is dismissed in film: film audience "expects the actor to execute the code precisely, erasing his inventive impulses while focusing his subjectivity in gestures that conform expertly to coded expectations" (Quinn 1995:76).

    Historically, it was the Prague Linguistic Circle, which focused on the development of semiotic theory of theatrical and film acting. Founded in 1926 PLK extended the study of poetics onto the study of aesthetics and looked at the work of art as a semiotic construct, a sign, and a socio-cultural fact. The circle proposed to study theatrical performance as a combination of anthropological and aesthetic signs, which makes constant communication between the stage and the audience possible. They acknowledged the dynamics of a theatrical sign, which simultaneously represents a thing, a phenomenon of material reality, and its semantic signification, an ideological phenomenon.

Acting, a dialectic phenomenon consisting of the actor's activity and the product of its activity, became the central issue for Prague theorists, when Veltruský stated that the stage action consists of the juxtaposition of human beings and their actions, and when he acknowledged that in theatre performance, text is only one of the expressive tools available.[9] According to Mukařovský, *an acting sign*, like any other artistic sign, is *an autonomous sign*: simultaneously "an artifact functioning as perceivable signifier", an aesthetic object or signification "registered in the collective consciousness", and "a relationship to a thing signified" in the "total context of social phenomena" (Mukařovský 1977:9). Thereby, an acting sign is a vehicle generating an aesthetic object as a dynamic image in the minds of perceiving audience. In the tripartite structure of an acting sign (actor—stage figure—dramatic character), *actor* signifies the actor's physical appearance and identity, *stage figure* signifies the viewer's image of the actor's onstage creativity, and *dramatic character* signifies a construction both on the part of the actor and the spectator.[10] In his article "An Attempt at a Structural

---

[9] In "Semiotics of the Folk Theatre" (1938), Bogatyrev describes the central subject of theatre, the actor, as "a sign of sign", standing for both a living human being and a system of signs. In theatre, unlike in film, actor acquires the double function of the originator of action and its product, since he/she functions both as the material and as the subject of a production (Bogatyrev 1976:48).

[10] Otakar Zich formulated the concept of the stage figure as the actor's physical representation of dramatis persona in *Estetika dramatického umûnî/ Aesthetics of Dramatic Art* (1931). In Zich's understanding, the stage figure is one of the constant elements of the performance text: it represents the actor's activity on stage; it is also opposite to the dramatic character, a product of the spectator's activity. "The distinction between Stage Figure and Dramatic Character consequently makes possible the expression: the figure is what the actor makes, the character what the audience sees and hears. The special fact allows the one to be observed from the wings, the other from the auditorium. Psychologically speaking: the figure is the product of the actor, the character the product of the observers. [...] The stage figure is the formation of the physiological kind, the dramatic character a formation of the psychological kind." (Zich 1931:56 in Quinn 1989: 76) If Zich treats the stage figure mostly as a product of the actor's activity, Mukařiovsk˘ believes that it is more feasible to treat it as both the actor's stage activity itself and the product of this activity, i.e. as a sign.

Analysis of an Acting Phenomenon" (1931), Mukařovský responded to Shklovsky's earlier study of acting in film, to his view on film acting as cine-hieroglyph and cine-language, the actor's putting a mask of his character on.[11] Mukařovský analyzes Chaplin's acting, using the term "dramatic figure", which he views as a structure within a bigger artistic system—a performance or film. Mukařovský's *dramatic figure* is more flexible then Shklovsky's *mask*, it signifies the objective or ideal stage image of a dramatic character (e.g. the ideal Hamlet) that is unattainable, because every performer brings to the stage his own psycho-physiological individuality. This individuality each time concretizes the ideal image. As Mukařovský writes, stage figure appears in theatre "in multiple relations, for example, the actor and the stage space, the actor and the dramatic text, the actor and the other actors" (1978:172). As he notes, this actor/dramatic text connection is of a dialectical nature, since it is the text that introduces and predetermines what the actor depicts in stage figure, but it is the actor who chooses how she does that. Stage figure, therefore, expresses the dialectics of performativity as simultaneously a process (imitation) and a result (representation).

Veltruský, unlike Mukařovský, understands acting as the only unique art embedded in the structure of a theatrical performance. It consists mostly of other, "borrowed" arts: it is rather synthesis than unity. According to Veltruský, the dramatis persona (he calls it *dramatic*

---

[11] Shklovsky defines Chaplin's acting as a cine-language using the categories of gesture, movement, rhythm, and facial expressions as its primary elements: "The cine-people and cine-action we see on screen are perceived as long as they are comprehended. Cinema very much resembles Chinese painting. Chinese painting is situated between the drawing and the word. People moving on the screen are a kind of hieroglyph. [...] These are not cine-images but cine-words, cine-concepts. Montage is the syntax and etymology of the cine-language" (Shklovsky 1985:30-35). The cornerstone of Chaplin's cine-language is clowning. His film figure resembles Harlequin from Commedia dell'Arte: Chaplin's fool functions in melodramatic situations and those of the adventure novel used in film either for the development of the story line or for its interruption. Chaplin creates a tragicomic character that embraces opposites. Stylistically, it is built on the dual relationships between melodrama and slapstick; psychologically it represents the heroism of a little man, who is always pitiful and laughable. "Chaplin never says anything in his films and there are no explanatory remarks between the scenes. [...] Chaplin does not speak, he moves. He operates with cinematic material rather than translating himself from the theatrical language to that of the screen. The humour of Chaplin's movement is [...] in its mechanization. Chaplin's acting consists of a number of passages, each one ending in a period—a pose". (Shklovsky 1985:21) But Chaplin's character is always the creation of a mask of the Other. Chaplin's persona is indeed recognizable under such a mask, but the mask is as important as the persona itself.

character), the point of departure for an actor constructing a stage figure, is a component of a literary text that in performance becomes only one of the elements comprising the complex structure of a theatrical utterance. In his article "Man and Object in Theatre" (1940), Veltruský defines his stage figure as a complicated structure of both linguistic and extra-linguistic signs, a system of systems that enters another structure of signs—the performance. Secondly, an acting sign involves not only the actor's activity but also that of the spectators. Veltruský, in "Contribution to the Semiotics of Acting" (1976), considers the processes of constructing the stage figure and perceiving the dramatic character to be the result of actor-spectator communication and creative activity, the consequence of which is the construction of the audience's image, "the primary addressee of the 'acting event'" (1976:588). Therefore, the image is substituted by the sign, which conveys a code and is converted into meaning by the receiver's consciousness.

As Jakobson maintains, the aesthetics of film is different from that of theatre, since the language of the former is composed exclusively of signs. If in theatre objects function both as things and as signs, on screen "it is precisely things (visual and auditory), transformed into signs that are the specific material of cinematic art. [...] Film works with manifold fragments of objects, which differ in magnitude, and also with fragments of time and space likewise varied. It changes their proportions and juxtaposes them in terms of continuity, or similarity and contrast; that takes the path of *metonymy* and *metaphor*" (Jakobson 1976:146). Unlike theatre, film is a technical construct, "merely patterns of light and dark on a screen" (Bordwell 24). Cinema assumes a conventional verisimilitude or correspondence between peoples' behaviors in life and on screen. As Lotman states, "the screen image of a human being approximates life and consciously aims towards eliminating theatricality and artificiality. And at the same time it is—more so than on stage or in fine arts—maximally semiotic, filled with secondary connotations. [...] An actor in film functions as a dual entity: as the creator of a particular role and as a cine-myth. The meaning of a cinematic image consists of the interrelationship (identity, conflict, struggle, and shift) of these two different semantic structures" (1998:356-360).

Film figure, therefore, is a construction both on the part of an actor and on the part of a spectator, which signifies the viewer's image of the actor's creativity on screen. Film figure represents "a system of components aesthetically deautomatized and organized into a complex hierarchy, which is unified by the prevalence of one component over the others" (Mukařovský 1978:170). Similar to the stage figure, a film figure acquires a number of sub-structures meant to express the character's emotions. All of them carry the dynamics of a character "by the interference [...] of two types of gestures: gesture-signs and gesture-expressions" (Mukařovský 1978:174). In addition, film figure is in its functions equivalent to cinematic lighting, sound, time, and space. In fact, it constitutes the film's mise-en-scène as any other object does (furniture, make-up, costumes and props), the significance of which is to express the artistic will of a narrator/film director staging the event for the camera. As an aesthetic object, film figure corresponds to character, which is an agent of cause and effect in a continuous narration. It is a collection of traits that involve "attitudes, skills, preferences, psychological drives, details of dress and appearance" (Bordwell 86) determining the structure of a film figure and the audience's reception of the film narrative. The nature of cinema explains its method of constructing a film figure not only with actor's means of characterization but also with those of a director, who controls "what appears in the film frame" (Bordwell 119). This way, as Lotman argues, film figure "enters the art of cinema as a world full of complex cultural signs. On one end is the symbolism of the human body present in different cultures [...]; on the other end is the actor's work as a means of communicating with the audience and as a certain semiotic construct" (1998:324). The creation of a film figure is objectified, therefore, by cinematic mise-en-scene, actor's everyday behavior; and her craft embracing a mixture of documentary and artistic representation.

***

As this paper demonstrates, *Poetika Kino*, a pioneering but controversial collection, remains today not only an engaging historical artifact (an example of silent film theory), but also is beneficial for theatre and cinema studies. It introduces the semiotic interdependency between film and theatre aesthetics, specifically acting theory, the subject of Prague and Tartu's cinema studies.

Works cited

Bogatyrev, Peter. "Semiotics in the Folk Theatre." Matejka and Titunik 33-50.
Bordwell, David and Kristin Thompson. *Film Art*. New York: Knopf, 1986
Carroll, Noel. Philosophical Problems of Classical Film Theory. Princeton: Princeton UP, 1988.
Eagle, Herbert. *Russian Formalist Film Theory*. Ann Arbor: U of Michigan P, 1981.
Eikhenbaum, Boris. "Problemy Kinolstilistiki." Kopylova 13-39. ("Problems of Cinema Stylistics." Eagle 55-81.)
Eisenstein, Sergei. *Film Form: Essays in Film Theory*. Trans. and ed. Leyda, Jay. New York: Harcourt Brace Jovanovich, 1977.
Jakobson, Roman. "Is the Cinema in Decline?". Matejka and Titunik 145-152.
———. "Linguistics and Poetics." *Language and Literature*. Cambridge: Harvard UP, 1987: 62-95.
———. "The Metaphoric and Metonymic Poles." *Fundamentals of Language*. Paris: Mouton. 1971: 90-96.

Galan, František. *Historic Structures: The Prague School Project, 1928-1946.* Austin: U of Texas P, 1985.

Gurevich, Stella. *Leningradskoe kinovedenie. Zubovskiy Osobnyak. 1925-1926.* St. Petersburg: RIII. 1998.

Ivanov. V.V. "O strukture znakov kino." *Readings in Soviet Semiotics.* Eds. Ladislav Matejka, Serge Shishkoff, Mark Suino, and I.R. Titunik. Ann Arbor: U of Michigan P, 1977. 314-320.

Kazanskij, Boris. "Priroda Kino." Kopylova 60-90. ("The Nature of Cinema." Eagle 101-131.

Kopylova, Roza Dmitrievna, ed. *Poetika Kino and Perechityvaya Poetiku kino.* St. Petersburg: REEE 2001.

Leyda, Jay. *Kino: A History of the Russian and Soviet Film.* London: Allen & Unwin, 1973

Lotman, Yuri. *Analyz poeticheskogo texta.* Leningrad: Prosveschenie, 1972.

———. "Semiotika kino i problemy kinoestetiki". *Ob iskusstve.* St. Petersburg: Iskusstvo - SPB, 1998

Matejka, Ladislav and Irwing R. Titunik, eds. *Semiotics of Art: Prague School Contributions.* Cambridge and London: The MIT Press, 1976.

Mukařovský, Jan. *Aesthetic Function, Norm and Value as Social Facts.* Trans. Mark E. Suino. Ann Arbor: U of Michigan, 1970.

———. "Between Literature and Visual arts." *The Word and Verbal Art.* Trans. and ed. John Burbank and Peter Steiner. New Haven and London: Yale UP, 1977. 205-235.

———. *Structure, Sign, and Function.* Trans. and ed. John Burbank and Peter Steiner. New Haven and London: Yale UP, 1978.

Piotrovskij, Adrian. "K teorii kinozhanrov." Kopylova 93-110. ("Towards a Theory of Cine-Genres" Eagle 131-147).

Shklovsky, Viktor. *Eisenstein.* Moscow: Iskusstvo, 1976.

———. *O teorii prozy.* Moscow: Federatsiia, 1929.

———. *Za 60 let. Raboty o Kino,* Moscow: Iskusstvo, 1985

Quinn, Michael. "Celebrity and the Semiotics of Acting." *New Theatre Quarterly* 22 (1990): 154-162.

———. "The Prague School Concept of the Stage Figure." *The Semiotic Bridge: Trends from California.* Eds. Irmengard Rauch and Gerald F. Carr. Berlin: Mouton de Gruyter, 1989. 75-85.

———. *The Semiotic Stage: Prague School Theater Theory.* New York: Peter Lang, 1995.

Rozik, Eli. "Theatrical Experience as Metaphor." *Semiotica* 149.1/4 (2004): 277-296.

Tynianov, Yuri. "Literaturnyi fakt." *Poetika, Istoriya Literatury, Kino.* Moscow: Nauka, 1977. 255-270.

Veltruský, Jiří. "Contribution to the Semiotics of Acting." *Sound, Sign and Meaning.* Ed. Ladislav Mateika. Ann Arbor: U of Michigan P, 1976. 553-605.

———. "Puppetry and Acting." *Semiotica* 47.1/4 (1983): 69-122.

———. "Man and Object in Theatre." The Prague School Selected Writings, 1929-1946. Ed. Peter Steiner. Austin: U of Texas P, 1990. 83-92.

Yampol'skii, Mikhail. ""Smyslovaya Vesch'" v Kinoteorii OPOYAZA". Tynianovskii Sbornik. Vol. 3. Riga: Zinatne, 1988. 109-120.

Golems and Robots in the Theatre and Cinema: Intermediality, Hybridity and the Prague School[*]

Veronika Ambros
University of Toronto

> *Now shall I tell of things that change, new being out of old: since you, O Gods, created mutable arts and gifts ....*
>
> Ovid

> *In the age of electronic memory, of film and reproducibility, theatre performance appeals to living memory, which is not a museum but metamorphosis.*
>
> (Barba, *The Paper Canoe*, 96)

Many contemporary scholars (Couchot, Müller, Helbig, Paech) agree that the expansion of intermediality and hybridity in modern art, especially in the performing arts, calls for a revision of the traditional division of sciences. This conclusion is not necessarily new. Scholars and artists (as early as Lessing, Kleist and Coleridge) have expressed this opinion before. The current discourse on intermediality is indebted both to these predecessors and to the work by several members of the Prague School including Jan Mukařovský, who devoted a number of studies to various aspects of the interrelation between literature and the visual arts; Roman Jakobson, who examined the statue in Pushkin's work; Jiří Veltruský, who analyzed the object and man on stage, and Petr Bogatyrev, who investigated folklore and theatre. French theorist Edmond Couchot[1], for instance, evokes Mukařovský's notions of intentionality and actualization when he says that:

---

[*] I wish to thank Joanne Mackay-Bennett, Ruth Rosenblood and Dr. Elisabeth Fitzpatrick for their help and suggestions.

[1] Edmond Couchot, "Media Art: Hybridization and Autonomy." This paper was presented at the REFRESH! conference, First International Conference on the Media Arts, Sciences and Technologies held at the Banff Center sept 29-oct 4 2005 and cosponsored by the Banff New Media Institute, the Database of Virtual Art and Leonardo/ISAST. 5n

The enhancement of the level of hybridization draws several consequences. The most important concerns the relations between an author, a work and its audience. The work is no longer a fixed object; it may be modified, under certain conditions, by the spectator. It is nothing else than a set of potentialities and only exists and has meaning in so far as the spectator actualizes it. In such a way the addressee of the work becomes in turn its co-author.

Couchot conceptualizes the mobility of intermedial works, as did Mukařovský. in his earlier observation that:

> The recipient puts a certain intentionality into the work of art, which is evoked by the structure of the work. All the components of the work invite his attention. The unifying semantic gesture with which he approaches the work strives to encompass them in all its unity.[2]

The term *semantic gesture*, as the unifying force of a work of art, departs from the formalists' notion of the *dominant* as formulated by Roman Jakobson. Richard Murphy, a British theorist of the avant-garde, however, uses this concept in order to describe postmodernism. In his view, "any definition of postmodernism must inevitably depend upon a prior understanding of ... earlier phenomena. Postmodernism might be then thought of as a change of 'dominant'[3] within modernism..."Murphy, who contests Peter Bürger's theory of the avant- garde and argues for an inclusion of expressionism, seems to follow an approach close to Felix Vodička's concept of concretization, that is, "the reflection of a work in the consciousness of those for whom it is an esthetic object."[4]

It is my intention to trace the "change of dominant" as well as to examine several aspects of intermediality and hybridity, developed during the last century, by investigating the concretization of golems and robots in theatre and cinema.[5] Using Lubomír Doležel's notion of

---

[2] Jan Mukařovský **Structure, Sign, and Function**: 89-128, a lecture at PLK in 1943, published 1966.

[3] Richard Murphy *Theorizing the Avant-Garde* Cambridge, Cambridge UP, 1999, p.2 Murphy, who expands the previous understanding of the avant-garde (Bürger) by including expressionism, applies Bakhtin's theory of heteroglossia to suggest the hybridity in Kafka (136).

[4] Felix Vodička,. "The Concretization of the Literary Work. Problems of the Reception of Neruda's Work"in Steiner, Peter. *The Prague School. Selected Writings, 1929 - 1946*. Transl. By John Burbank, Olga Hasty et al. Austin: University of Austin Press, 1982: 103-33. (110) Struktura – 283-321, 1998.

[5] My investigation follows the suggestion of the German scholar Jürgen Müller to open up the traditional poetics and media theories (Müller 32), cf. Jürgen Müller Intermedialität als poetologisches und Medientheoretisches Konzept" Jőrg Helbig(ed.) *Intermedialität*. Berlin, Erich Schmidt Verlsg, 1998, 31-40.

hybrid fictional worlds, in which "the natural and supernatural, animated and unanimated merge" as my point of departure, I will explore different types of hybridity and intermediality in theory and arts. My examination will follow the example of the Prague School by applying the *zig zag* method, one that moves back and forth "between universal categories and concrete descriptions." (Doležel, 2000, 82)

The golems and robots of my title refer to hybrid characters, images, and fictional worlds, which belong to the repository of contemporary highbrow and popular culture especially cinema (from the horror movies of the expressionistic era and today to Amos Gitai's highly experimental Golem trilogy). They predate aspects of contemporary theatre practice listed by Christopher Innes: "the performance of Robert Wilson, Robert Lepage and Josef Svoboda corresponds to Craig's principles of abstract movement, simplification and the physical precision in acting embodied by Craig's Über-marionette." According to Christopher Innes "Svoboda's (actually Radok's)) 'Laterna Magika' is even closer [to Craig, VA] in its blending of dance and mime with video images through mirrors."[6]

The fact that Innes mentions Svoboda, a set designer, alongside two directors, shows the increased attention that space and scenography have received over the years. It is important to remember that as early as 1931 Otakar Zich, in his *Esthetics of dramatic art*, considered dramatic art, meaning performance, "a pictorial art [art of images]."[7] In Jindřich Honzl's, avant-garde performance in 1930s "the scenery became an actor" (Honzl, 84), as it did in the *Laterna Magika* of theatre and film director Alfred Radok in 1958 where Svoboda's set designs explored intricate intermedial techniques introduced earlier in the cinematic and theatrical practice of Eisenstein, Meyerhol'd, Piscator, E.F.Burian and Honzl to name just a few.

Golems and Robots as Hybrids?

> *Narrative allegory is distinguished from mythology as reality from symbol; it is, in short, the proper intermedium between person and personification.*
> (Coleridge) [8]

---

[6] Christopher Innes "Gordon Craig in the multi-media postmodern world: from the Art of the Theatre to Ex Machina" http://www.moderndrama.ca/crc/resources/essays/craig_lepage_wales.php. The *Magic lantern*, was the brain-child of director Alfred Radok, and set designer Josef Svoboda.

[7] Zich, 211 quoted in Honzl English transl. has "art of images" Matejka Titunik, 74

[8] Coleridge in: T.M. Raysor ed. *Coleridge's Miscellaneous Criticism*, , Folcroft PA, 1936, 33.

> *In the field of art, hybridization is the crossing between heterogeneous technical, semiotic and aesthetic elements.*
>
> (Jürgen Müller, 31n)

Since the turn of the twentieth century, Prague has had the reputation of a "magic city."[9] Theatre and cinema have contributed substantially to this label, as they share the penchant of art of that period for "hybrid fictional worlds" (Doležel). Although Doležel bases his concept on Kafka's and Čapek's fiction, it can be applied to the Golems and Robots on stage and screen, albeit in a modified form.

Golems and Robots[10] share an ancestry of androids rooted in mythology, tales, and fiction that are actualized by a predilection for mysticism and fascination with science and technology. Those discussed here, however, inhabit hybrid worlds in theatre and cinema. Although some researchers (Zich, Nelson) list them under the rubric of puppets, golems and robots have a provenance that is ontologically different since their existence is motivated by a definite purpose. The Golem's task is to protect a group of people, a robot's *raison d'être* is to liberate mankind from drudgery. Both are the results of past and future human aptitude, and intention, and, unlike Gregor Samsa of Franz Kafka's *Die Verwandlung* [*Metamorphosis*], are no chance products of inexplicable transformation.

Long before they entered the film and theatre lexicons, Golems were "born" from an amalgam of different legends and stories, an embodiment that has been rendered visible[11] by many artists. Theoretically, however, they belong to the dichotomy of man and object on stage, theorized by several scholars of the Prague School, most prominently by Veltruský (1964:83-91), but also by Mukařovský (1978) and Honzl (1976a, 1976b). These theorists all speak about the potential interchangeability between man and object so typical of modern theatre, where on the one hand: The action may fall to the "zero level," the figure then is converted into a part of the *set* (Veltruský, 86), and on the other "the scenery becomes an actor" (Honzl, 84).

Hybridity of object and man also applies to the Golem presented by Paul Wegener, in *Golem, how he came into the World*,[12] which he directed in 1920. His Golem is a lifeless statue and an animated creature,

---

[9] Cf. the title of a book on Prague by the Italian literary scholar Angelo Ripellino. Ripellino, Angelo Maria. *Magic Prague*. David Newton Marinelli <trans.>Berkeley: Universityof California Press, 1994.

[10] For Karel Čapek the Robot is the „Golem made flesh by mass production" (Prager Tagblatt, 1935:6, in Karel Čapek R.U.R.,1966).

[11] Cf. Czech painter Mikolas Aleš included this picture when he illustrated volume of old legends by A. Jirasek.

[12] The third and only preserved film of his Golem trilogy.

conjured up by the revered Rabbi Loew, the "Jewish Faust"[13] who, in the Jewish Ghetto in 17th century Prague,[14] entered into a pact with God to produce an assistant to protect his flock. Hence, the creation of the man of clay[15] is *motivated* by the danger the Rabbi perceives his flock to be in, and enabled by his alleged knowledge of the magic art and his "bizarre"[16] supernatural power. Wegener's Golem is a hybrid creature with human facial expressions and features and the movements of an animated statue. In contrast to Gregor Samsa, however, his transformation is *intentional* and *presented* on screen.

In comparison, the robots of Karel Čapek's groundbreaking play, *RUR* (1920), were produced from a biological substance, that is not like the mechanical machines of our contemporary understanding, but rather as creatures who closely imitate human beings but who do not have certain 'redundant' features, such as reproductive organs, and, initially, emotions. This deficiency explains the fact that the robots lack facial expressions and appear to be wearing masks. Such a feature according to Veltruský, neutralizes the semiotic qualities of the face, dehumanizing it in the process.[17] An opposite effect is achieved in Wegener's *Golem* by the fact that Wegener, who was one of the leading actors of Max Reinhardt's theatre, the vanguard of expressionist staging, plays the Golem.[18] Unlike the robots, his facial expressions make him more human while at the same time his appearance and movements signify a statue-like creature endowed with emotions.

Čapek's robots are distinguishable from their human counterparts by the redundancy of their speech. Nonetheless, for an outsider (a

---

[13] "Die Golemsage in der deutschen Literatur" Prager Presse, Jg. 14, Nr. 335, v. 7.12.1934, S.4.

[14] Architect Hans Poelzig created the sets, a reproduction of the medieval Jewish ghetto of Prague. He designed them specifically to be filmed, presenting highly expressionist imagery. The cinematography of Karl Freund, in collaboration with Poelzig and Wegener, is cited as one of the most outstanding examples of German Expressionism.

[15] In Amos Gitai's film *Birth of a Gol*em, 1989 the image of an androgynous woman (Annie Lennnox) evokes the man of clay.

[16] Doležel uses this term to "refer to the entities in the hybrid world that violate physical possibility" (*Heterocosmica*, 188).

[17] Veltruský, J. „ Dramatic Text as as a Component of Theatre" .,in Matejka, Ladislav and Irwin R. Titunik (Eds.), *Semiotics of Art*. Cambridge: MIT P..:107.

[18] In the late nineteenth century the golem legend was included in Alois Jirasek's Book of old Czech legends. Gustav Meyrink's 1915 novel *Der Golem* alludes to the tales of the golem created by Judah Low ben Bezalel. Of the three films by Paul Wegener focusing on Golem only *The Golem: How He Came Into the World* (also released as *The Golem*, 1920, USA 1921) is still available.

human being such as the character Helena), the robots appear indistinguishable from the human inhabitants of the island of the utopian prologue. In addition, and in contrast to the Golem, who is a unique servant and whose statuesque quality is foregrounded, the robots' uniformity and similarity with *Masses Man* (*Masse Mensch*) (even before Ernst Toller's eponymous play of 1923) defamiliarizes the human beings.[19] Toward the end, however, when they acquire human emotions, they share with the last surviving man

> one unified fictional space, of the physically possible and physically impossible fictional entities (persons, events). Physically impossible events cannot be interpreted as miraculous interventions from the supernatural domain... all phenomena and events of the hybrid world,... are generated within this world, spontaneously and haphazardly (*Heterocosmica*, 187n).

INTERMEDIALITY

> A medial product becomes an intermedial one, when it transposes the multi medial parallels of quotations and elements into a conceptual whole whose (aesthetic) refractions and distortions open new dimensions of experience and perception.[20]

> Shakespeare is a multimedia author *ante litteram*, because for us he has created an instrument capable of revealing human properties, to play in the same way as other instruments, sadly, tragically, or with great joy. And thanks to this instrument, you can express the entire story of humanity.[21]

In Wegener's *Golem*, an episode in which film within film is used, there is an allusion to the interrelationship between theatre and film. It occurs in the scene when the emperor encourages Rabbi Loew to show him and his court one of his magic tricks. This request motivates an insertion of a film sequence that depicts the Jewish patriarchs. As a result, the court audience, as well as the spectators of the film, are confronted with another historical level and another fictional world. Yet, while this episode additionally foregrounds the hybridity between

---

[19] Jan Mukařovský " K umělecké situaci dnešního českého divadla", In: Jan Mukařovský *Studie I*, Brno, Host, 415-427

[20] [Ein mediales Produkt wird dann inter-medial, wenn es das multi-mediale Nebeneinander medialer Zitate und Elemente in ein konzeptioneleles Miteinader überführt dessen (ästhetische) Brechungen und Verwerfungen neue Dimensionen des Erlebens und Erfahrens eröffnen]. Jürgen Müller Intermedialität als poetologisches und Medientheoretisches Konzept" Jörg Helbig (ed.) *Intermedialität*. Berlin, Erich Schmidt Verlag, 1998, 31-40.

[21] http://www.thescenographer.com/dettaglio.asp?ID=4

stage and film of the depicted fictional world, it is presented as a product of "supernatural intervention," as a confrontation of two different domains, that for a brief moment fuse into one realm.

Friedrich Kiesler achieved a similar effect when he staged *RUR* in 1923 in Berlin, by turning Čapek's drama into a remarkable intermedial event using loudspeakers and the fair-ground technology of the so-called *tanagra*[22], distorting both the appearance and speech of the characters by presenting miniature images of the actors in a mechanized fictional world.

As Kiesler describes his show:

> This *R.U.R.* play was my occasion to use for the first time in a theatre a motion picture [a small cinema projection was also incorporated in the set] instead of a painted backdrop, and also television[23] in the sense that I had a big, square panel window in the middle of the stage drop which could be opened by remote control. When the director of the human factory in the play pushed a button at his desk, the panel opened and the audience saw two human beings ....a foot-and-a-half tall, casually moving and talking, heard through a hidden loudspeaker. It was quite an illusion, because a minute later you saw the same actors appear on stage full size. There was, inevitably, a burst of applause at this moment....I mention it because these new devices to present the interplay of reality and illusion brought many artists to the theatre.[24]

---

[22] Tanagra Theatres existed in many European cities in the years 1910-1920 (Viefhaus-Mildenberger, 1961:27-30). The name comes from the figures excavated at Tanagra in the 1890s whose name became synonymous with perfect living miniatures, particularly female. The sideshow illusion consisted of a miniature stage where living actors appeared as real but tiny figures, through an arrangement of plain and concave mirrors. Its development as a sideshow attraction came about as a by-product of research into optical instruments which could better sustain the perception of depth (von Rohr, 1920). The use of concave mirrors has a long history in magic but for the Tanagra the stronger light of electricity was essential. Patricia Pringle "Seeing Impossible Bodies: Fascination as a Spatial Experience" *Scan Journal* vol 1 number 2 june 2004.

[23] "It was only television in the sense of suggesting control over remote spaces. No screen is involved in a Tanagra, the images are viewed in a concave mirror". Patricia Pringle "Seeing Impossible Bodies: Fascination as a Spatial Experience", In: Scan Journal vol 1 number 2 June 2004, http://scan.net.au/scan/journal/print.php?journal_id=34&j_id=2#_edn2.

[24] Kiesler, F., interview, Progressive Architecture, XLII, July 1961, p. 109 cf. Scan Journal, vol 1 number 2 June 2004 opt. cit Patricia Pringle "Seeing Impossible Bodies: Fascination as a Spatial Experience" Scan Journal vol 1 number 2 June 2004, http://scan.net.au/scan/journal/print.php?journal_id=34&j_id=2

Kiesler's use of modern technology confirms Honzl's claim, "that not only can a person be an actor but so can a wooden puppet or a machine." (Honzl, 1984, 75) Kiesler turned his stage into an actor by merging elements of reality and illusion into a unique hybrid fictional world. The spectacular set design, however, turned Čapek's fictional world upside down, since Kiesler radically changed the notion of the space. Not only was the three-dimensional space confronted with the two dimensionality of the film, but

> ... Kiesler's 'electromechanical' set was a huge montage, compiled from the most diverse apparatuses and machine parts (megaphone, seismograph, tanagra device, iris diagram, light bulb) . . . ."[25] Despite the message of the play, Kiesler reveled in the possibilities of machines to expedite social change through communication, innovation, and increased knowledge.[26]

Certainly one of the models of contemporary theatrical practice, including the acclaimed *Magic Lantern*, this montage technique also shifted the spatial distribution of the play. The stage directions called for two sets of rooms divided along gender lines, alluding to the core opposition between reason and intuition. Kiesler's staging defamiliarized the familiar settings (office, sitting room), which as in a cubist painting, appeared fragmented in similar way to the dialogue, which was segmented by dashes in order to "indicate a pause in conversation, a hesitation in excited or shy speech" as mentioned by Mukařovský. Consequently, the biological quality of the robots was lost. They were comparable to Craig's Übermarionette. No longer almost human, they became closer to the man of clay and therefore more like the animated statue, or mechanical robot, that appeared in Fritz Lang's *Metropolis* and with which we are familiar now.

Puppets, Statues, Machines: Prague School and Beyond

> Structuralism ... is not an "invention" of an individual but a necessary stage in the history of modern science. ... the individuality of each scholar recedes into the background in favour of collaboration... ... an impulse for change in art, even if it comes from the sphere of

---

[25] Barbara Lesák, "Visionary of the European Theater," in Lisa Phillips, *Frederick Kiesler*, New York : Whitney Museum of American Art, in association with W.W. Norton, 1989, 40.

[26] It may not come as a surprise then , that Kiesler was invited immediately after the opening night, to organize an international scenography exhibit in Vienna in 1924.

social action, can be instrumental only to the degree and in the direction necessitated by the previous stage in the development of art. (Mukařovský, "Structuralism," 70)

The Prague School project is not a historical monument, but a guide for the future" (Doležel "Epistemology," 23)

Otakar Zich, the Czech founder of the semiotics of theatre, discusses two perceptions of puppets. In his view if we stress their inanimate material, they appear to be comical, even grotesque (Zich, 318) whereas if we perceive them as living creatures, their inanimate nature retreats into the background and the puppets make a mysterious impression. He claims that were they presented as life-sized puppets, they would evoke fear in us. Zich considers such fantasy creations even more frightening than animated corpses because the latter display life in previously living matter whereas life is unnatural in golems for instance life itself is unnatural. This quality, used by Wegener and his successors, encouraged the association of horror with the golem. Amos Gitai, on the other hand, who used a human body for his reflection on Golems, did not achieve a horror effect, but defamiliarization.

Although Zich's distinction is very useful for the discussed opposition between golems and robots, he does not distinguish between puppets as creations with a definite purpose and animated statues or automatons on screen and stage.[27] He suggests, instead, the affinity between statue and the stage figure,[28] which resounds in Mukařovský's description of the modern actor as a union between the plastic art and human movements:

> The immobility of a statue and the mobility of a live person is a constant antinomy of the poles between which the dramatic figure oscillates on stage. And when Craig posited his famous requirement of the actor—' as Übermarionette '... he ... drew attention to this hidden but always present antinomy of the art of acting. What is usually called a 'pose' is clearly a sculptural effect. ... the transition between

---

[27] Neither does Victoria Nelson in her more recent study on puppets. Her highly acclaimed book *The Secret Life of Puppets* Cambridge, Ma, Harvard, 2001 discusses the topic across the literary genres without distinguishing puppets on stage and screen, statues and toys.

[28] "As much as marble is not a sculpture, but only formed marble, so ...the 'figure' is [character] only the 'formed actor', with one difference: the actor, *ie,* the same actor who is being formed [shaped] does the forming [shaping]. (transl. mine VA) Jako není sochou mramor, nýbrž až zformovaný mramor, tak je, ... postavou až *zformovaný* herec, s tím rozdílem ovšem, že tuto formaci provádí herec sám, týž herec, jenž je formován (41) Zich's original term is *herecká postava* (45)

> the immobility of a solid mask and the make-up of a modern actor is quite continuous... (Mukařovský, 1978 b: 206)

Hence, the fundamental hybridity inherent in actor's performance in general, is foregrounded when using golems and robots.

Yuri Lotman suggests yet another dichotomy namely, of dolls and puppets, inherent in both meanings of the Russian word *kukla*. He differentiates between an adult audience of *recipients* of an artistic text versus a children's audience of *participants* in the game/play. The first case is connected with the reception of information, while in the second case information is produced in the process. In the first example, the focus is on the author while in the second, the text serves only as an impulse to the addressee for the game, which produces meaning. The puppet is associated with a statue that has to be perceived, while the doll has to be moved. Like Mukařovský, Lotman notes that a moving, wind-up doll elicits two responses: as an inanimate object, the puppet is closer to a human being, while as a "human being", its' *uslovnost'*, its "artificiality", comes to the fore.

> On stage it is perceived in relationship to the live actor, as the representation of representation, that is, sign of sign. This poetics of doubling lays bare the artificiality and the language of art. That is why the puppet on stage can be easily ironic and parodic and on the other hand, it shows the ... tendency to experiment. Puppet theatre lays bare theatricality.[29]

Analogous to Formalist notions of literariness, theatricality and poeticity, Lotman coins the term *kukolnost'* [puppetness], which in live theatre consists of two components the face—mask, and *preryvistost*, the fragmentation of movements [or language, VA]. Together they enable the actor to express inner conflict and can have not only comical effects but also truly tragic ones. Again Lotman's example is an animated statue.

Like Lotman's puppets and dolls, the hybrid quality of Golems and robots lays bare the device on stage and screen, revealing a world that, to use Doležel's observation, oscillates between the "two Bohemian versions of the hybrid world—Kafka's stories and Čapek's tales ... Kafka's hybrid world [a]s a space of existential anxiety and permanent threat, Čapek 's space of exciting child-like adventure." This duality reveals the function of the hybridity of golems and robots as a sub-category of either animated statues or biologically-produced androids. They might evoke an existential anxiety especially when they are part of a fictional world where the hybridity is not motivated or they can induce the recipient to participate in the game.

---

[29]Lotman, ...648n).

Hence, the play *Golem*, written and performed by the Czech comedians Voskovec and Werich, defamiliarizes the horror figure and lays bare the toy. In contrast, in the *Birth of a Golem* the Israeli director Amos Gitai, experiments with the hybrid nature of the character by featuring vocal artist Annie Lennox as a female golem, who is ironically, like Wegener's character, silent. Using images and movements, Gitai creates a cinematic collage that *desautomatizes* our view of Golem not only with respect to gender.

Similarly, Jan Švankmajer's (1994) *Lesson Faust*, as well as Otomar Krejča's stage version of Goethe's *Faust* (1997) mentioned above show an actualization of the Faust legend by using intermediality and creating hybrid fictional worlds. *Lesson Faust* conjures up a hybrid fictional world reminiscent of Kafka's "space of existential anxiety and permanent threat" because of the intrusion of the supernatural into the quotidian world of contemporary Prague. Krejča's *Faust*, on the other hand, relies less on characters or acting than on intermediality: mirrors, projections, and light circling the stage and evoke divine intervention thus replacing the God of the prologue. The intermedial spectacle foregrounds the fictional world as a location of an expressionistic introspection.[30]

The intermediality in Švankmajer's *Faust* achieves a different dominant. It actualizes the world of fairs and folklore where people are transformed into puppets and dolls, a golem is evoked in the shape of a child that turns into a monster, and objects of everyday life, defamiliarized beyond recognition, are transformed into hostile traps. They inhabit an uncanny, hybrid world where rhyme and reason are missing. The use of intermediality helps to foreground different types of hybrids, to shape their dominant. Both works are close to what Hans-Thies Lehman calls postdramatic theatre, where the "rupture between being and meaning has a shock-like effect"[31] Hence the expressionistic creatures and surreal objects clad in a post-modern garb haunt us even

---

[30] As Jarka Burian remarks: "Although constitutionally averse to much of what is considered postmodernism, Josef Svoboda anticipated many of its practices and helped develop specific theatrical forms and devices that became staples of so called postmodern performance. A distilled synthesis of some of those very forms and devices is evident in his work on Goethe's Faust in Prague's National Theatre, which premiered in 1997... I refer to his radical alterations of stage space by means of projected and reflected images integrated with kinetic stage elements. The result in Faust is perhaps paradoxical: in a production whose overall aim and spirit is not post modern, Svoboda's scenography can be seen as a complex, sophisticated variant of postmodern staging."

[31] Lehmann, *Postdramatic Theater*: Abingdon, [England] ; New York : Routledge, 2006 : 146.

today, and not just in "magic Prague". "In Bohemia," Doležel has remarked in reference to Čapek and Kafka, "the borderline between fairytale and nightmare is fuzzy" (L. Doležel, 1992: 27). His comment has lost none of its validity—particularly when the borderline becomes even fuzzier with the recognition, as Couchot and Mukařovský maintain that we are the co-creators of these hybrid worlds.

Works Cited

Barba, Eugenio. *The Paper Canoe: A Guide to Theatre Anthropology*. London and New York: Routledge, 1995.
Burian, Jarka. "Josef Svoboda's Scenography for the National Theatre's Production of Goethe's Faust : Postmodern or Merely Contemporary?". *Culture to Culture* 6 (1997). Online version: http://www.scenography-international.com/journal/issue6/faust.pdf
Čapek, Karel. R.U.R. Praha, Československý spisovatel, 1966.
Coleridge, Samuel Taylor. *Coleridge's Miscellaneous Criticism*. Thomas Middleton Raysor. Folcroft, PA: Folcroft, 1969.
Couchot, Edmond (2005) "Media Art: Hybridization and Autonomy". Paper presented at the REFRESH! Conference, First International Conference on the Media Arts, Sciences and Technologies. Banff Center. Sept 29-oct 4 2005. Database of Virtual Art and Leonardo/ISAST. 5n.
Doležel, Lubomír. *Heterocosmica: Fiction and Possible Worlds*. Baltimore and London: The Johns Hopkins UP, 1998.
———. *Occidental Poetics*. Lincoln and London: U of Nebraska P, 1990.
———. "Possible Worlds of Fiction and History." *New Literary History* 29.4: (Autumn 1998): 785- 809.
———. "Epistemology of the Prague School" Eds. Vladimír Macura and Herta Schmid. *Jan Mukařovský and the Prague School*. Potsdam, Universität Potsdam, 1999. 14-25.
Gitai, Amos. *Birth of a Golem*. France, 1989.
Honzl, Jindřich. "Dynamics of Sign in the Theater." Matejka and Titunik 75-94.
———. "The Hierarchy of Dramatic Devices." Matejka and Titunik 118-27.
Innes, Christopher. "Gordon Craig in the multi-media postmodern world: from the Art of the Theatre to Ex Machina" Canada Research Chair in Performance & Culture. Online version: http://www.moderndrama.ca/crc/resources/essays/craig_lepage_wales.php
Kiesler, F. *Progressive Architecture* XLII (July 1961): 109.
Lehmann, Hans-Thies. *Postdramatisches Theater*. Frankfurt am Main: Verlag der Autoren, 1999.
———. *Postdramatic Theater*. Abingdon and New York: Routledge, 2006.
Leppin, Paul. "Die Golemsage in der deutschen Literatur". *Prager Presse Jg.* 14, Nr. 335, v. 7.12., S.4, 1934.
Lesák, Barbara. "Visionary of the European Theater." *Frederick Kiesler*. Ed. Lisa Phillips. New York : Whitney Museum of American Art, 1989.
Lotman, Yuri. "Kukly v sisteme kul'tury" in Y. Lotman. *Ob iskusstve*. St. Peterburg: Iskusstvo, 1998. 645-650.

Matejka, Ladislav and Irwing R. Titunik, eds. *Semiotics of Art: Prague School Contributions*. Cambridge and London: The MIT Press, 1976.

Müller, Jürgen. "Intermedialität als poetologisches und Medientheoretisches Konzept". Intermedialität. Ed. J_rg Helbig. Berlin: Erich Schmidt Verlag, 1998. 31-40.

Mukařovský, Jan. "Intentionality and Unintentionality in Art." *Structure, Sign and Function*. Eds. John Burbank and Peter Steiner. New Haven: Yale UP: 89-128.

——. *Studie z estetiky*. Praha: Odeon, 1966.

——. "On the Current State of the Theory of Theater." *Structure* 201-219.

——. " Structuralism in Esthetics and in Literary Studies." *Steiner* 65-82.

Murphy Richard. *Theorizing the Avant-Garde*. Cambridge: Cambridge UP, 1999.

Nelson Victoria. *The Secret Life of Puppets*. Cambridge: Harvard UP, 2001.

Otwell, Andrew. "View Magazine's Marcel Duchamp Special Issue, March 1945." *Andrew Otwell Website*. Online version: www.heyotwell.com/work/arthistory/thesis/chapter4.html

Pringle, Patricia (2004) "Seeing Impossible Bodies: Fascination as a Spatial Experience" *Scan Journal* 1.2 (June 2004). Online version: http://scan.net.au/scan/journal/print.php?journal_id=34&j_id=2#_edn2

Ripellino, Angelo Mario. *Magic Prague*. Trans. David Newton Marinelli. Ed. M. H. Heim. Berkeley: U of California P, 1994.

Steiner, Peter, ed. *The Prague School: Selected Writings, 1929-1946*. Austin: U of Texas P, 1982.

Veltruský, Jiří. "Dramatic Text as a Component of Theater." Matejka and Titunik 94-117.

——. "Man and Object in the Theater." *A Prague School Reader on Esthetics, Literary Structure, and Style*. Ed. Paul L. Garvin. Georgetown: Georgetown UP, 1964. 83-91.

Vodička, Felix. "The Concretization of the Literary Work. Problems of the Reception of Neruda's Work." *Steiner* 103-33.

Zich, Otakar. *Estetika dramatického umění*. Praha: Panorama, 1986.

Anthropomorphic City Horizon: Structuralist's Foregrounding in Antony Gormley's Sculptures

SILVIJA JESTROVIĆ
University of Warwick

This paper will take Prague Structuralist concept of foregrounding (*aktualizace*) out of its habitual context of linguistic and literary studies to use it as a means of exploring the relationship between artistic object and its environment. Czech Structuralists (Mukařovský and Havránek) introduced the notion of *aktualizace* in their theories of poetic and practical language. *Aktualizace* (foregrounding), the Czech version of making the familiar strange, is based on the principles of subverting the receiver's expectations by violating the automatised aesthetic canon, and/or the norm of the standard utterance. The notion of *aktualizace* also includes the process of making something topical. Thus it works both on the spatial and temporal axes of the artistic process, highlighting the relationship between artistic object and its context. Although the notion of *aktualizace* has been conceived within the linguistic discourse, the Structuralists' interest in performance and other artistic fields enables a multidisciplinary study of signs, suggesting that the transfer of concepts from one medium to the other can be a fruitful adventure.

The paper will focus on a recent project *Event Horizon* by one of the leading British sculptors Antony Gormley. Gormley is best known for his public sculptures that engage with the relationship between human body and its environment. He won the prestigious Turner Prize in 1994 for *Field for the British Isles*—a work of 35,000 miniature terracotta figurines that change configuration with every new display site, yet they always give the sense of an infinite army of miniscule bodies. The project *Event Horizon* is an installation of 31 iron sculptures cast of the artist's body and displayed on the rooftops of central London significantly changing the familiar urban landscape. *Event Horizon* was commissioned by Hayward gallery and it coincided with Gormley's exhibit *Blind Light*, thus complementing the experience of the gallery show as it too explored the intersection between body and space. The gallery exhibit comprised of different kinds of abstract and often disorienting architectural spaces, while the visitors, journeying though the gallery, served as their temporary inhabitants. Outside the gallery, Gormley's sculptures of men in the image of their author stood atop buildings including National Theatre, Hayward gallery, and along walkways of South Bank and Waterloo Bridge. They formed a broad circle around the gallery as if monitoring the activities surrounding the exhibit. Anthony Vidler, writing on the relationship between the two exhibits—*Blind Light* and *Event Horizon*—observes that "by implication this establishes the exhibition in a double circle, the first within the walls of the Hayward, the second deeply embedded in the city itself" (Vidler). Our interest is in the outer circle—the *Event Horizon*—that does not only establish self-referential links to the gallery exhibition, but branches out to make the vistas of London anthropomorphic, superimposing life-size human bodies upon the city architecture.

In this paper I will use Gormley's project to foreground two points: 1) Some concepts of Prague Structuralism could still be very useful even when analysing an aesthetic phenomenon where Structuralism is not enough to explain all its implications. Moreover, contemporary public art projects, such as the *Event Horizon*—that blur the line between artistic media and between art and everyday life—do not only partially embody some of the Structuralist concepts, but infuse them with new dimensions and possibilities. 2) The analysis of a project such as the *Event Horizon* is impossible without "reading" the city; in order to do so, it is not enough to treat the city as text, but to view it as a performance text—a perpetual mise en scene.

Before I get to my analysis of Gormley's iron-cast men in London through the lance of a Prague Structuralist concept, I would like to give some further explanations for this somewhat odd coupling between the work of a contemporary British sculptor, whose early philosophical influences reach back to Indian mysticism and an interdisciplinary movement, whose approach has been strongly rooted in logos. Theorist of the urban, Henri Lefebvre attacked structuralism arguing that the world should not be perceived as "text", but as "texture," and that to understand the environment as a codified system of meaning is to favour the eye over other senses. Nevertheless, Gormley's sculptures in their interplay with the city's architecture create a set of relationships and juxtapositions that call for an attempt to, as Foucault puts it describing Structuralism, "set them in opposition or link them together, so as to create a sort of shape" (348).

The reason I have been attracted to this particular case study is that it both invites reading and points to its limits. In his explication of the project's title, Gormley writes:

> The title comes form cosmological physics and it refers to the boundaries of the observable universe.[...] One of the implication of Event

Horizon is that people will have to entertain an uncertainty about the work's dimensions: the spread and number of bodies. Beyond the figures that you can actually see, how many more are there that you can't see? ("Antony Gormley / Blind Light")

Like Lefebvre, Gormley too suggests, that there are dimensions beyond the textual, hence that his project could only be partially "read." Nevertheless, he still makes references and encodes dichotomies that not only enable structural relations, but invite us to read what the eye is able to reach and perhaps even relate our reading—by way of imagination, logic or association—to what is absent from the view.

Gormley's iron-cast men are ambivalent figures—they bring an anthropomorphic element to the city vistas, but they are at the same time invading the urban landscape, like an army of iron-made soldiers. They establish a variety of "intertextual" links—from Renaissance sculptures of the saint protectors that adorned the rooftops of public and private buildings to the humanized angels standing on the edges of Berlin rooftops in Wim Wenders' iconic film *Wings of Desire*. The sculptures exhibit a dichotomy between the vulnerability of the bare body standing on the edge of a tall building and its iron cast material— a makeup far more resilient than that of humans. Gormley's angles of cast-iron,[1] whose bodies are above pain, sparkle an array of metaphors and references to city dwelling, security, and surveillance. And by the same token, they place the city and its familiar tourist vistas into a context of a topical discourse, especially prompted after the July 7 bombings.

If Gormley's sculptures indeed stand for angels, they are to some extent akin to Walter Benjamin's *angelus novus*—the mechanical angel with enigmatic eyes inspired by a drawing of Paul Klee that, as Theodor Adorno observes, "forces the viewer to ask whether it proclaims complete disaster or the rescue hidden within it." (92) Gormley's iron-cast men/angels replicate this duality, standing on London rooftops as *guards* and as *guardians*.

Between Body and Object: from theatre to everyday life

Gormley's project deals with the relationship between body (whether static or mobile) and architecture, and it toys with binary oppositions of stasis/mobility and body/object if only too blur the lines between

---

[1] This is not the first time the notion of angel has been linked to Gormley's sculpture. Most overt example is his, arguably, most famous piece called *The Angel of the North*—a large steel sculpture (20m high and 54 m wide), a composite of man, angel and totem, placed on an abandoned mining site overlooking a highway near Newcastle.

them. The project utilises some of the basic principles of Structuralist foregrounding in making the static and familiar urban horizon unpredictable and performative and in involving the viewer in a more active way. I will argue that Gormley's iron cast men are *sculptures that perform* and that they are based on a foregrounding strategy best described by Prague Structuralist Jiri Veltruský as a dialectical antinomy between man and object that he finds central to theatrical performance.

In the article "Man and Object in Theatre," Veltruský wrote that in theatre a lifeless object can be perceived as a performing subject, and a live human being may appear as an element completely without will:

> The function of each component in the individual situation (and in drama as a whole) is the result of the constant tension between activity and passivity in terms of the action, which manifests itself in a constant flow back and forth between the individual components, people and things. It is therefore impossible to draw a line between subject and object, since each component is potentially either. (90)

Veltruský starts with the premise that the relationship between the animated and the lifeless in reality is a stable one, whereas theatre has the potential to destabilise this relationship, creating a "dialectic antinomy" between the human body and the object on stage. Gormley's project explores the changeable dynamics between passivity and activity and between mobility and stasis outside the framework of theatre and through the interplay between art and everyday life. This dynamic relationship is established through Gormley's unpredictable placing of his iron-cast men—on the edges of buildings, as if they could jump or flip over at any given moment and turn stasis into mobility, or in a narrow pathway of Waterloo bridge so that passers-by have to manoeuvre their way around the sculpture and interact with it, sometimes touching it accidentally, other times hugging it to pose for a photo.

An article about Gormely's *Event Horizon* published in the Guardian begins by noting the public's confusion over animated and lifeless:

A. Gormley "Event Horizon", London, photo S. Jestrović.

> In 1992, the German sculptor Stephen Balkenhol placed a life-sized, carved wooden figure on a pontoon floating on the Thames, as part of an exhibition at the Hayward Gallery. For weeks people kept calling the emergency services about a distraught man they'd seen, about to throw himself in the river.
> This week the phones have been ringing again, on account of the life-size casts of Antony Gormley that have been appearing on rooftops on both sides of the river, as well as on the Waterloo bridge itself. There's a naked man on the roof. Come quick. Blimey, there is another. It must be some sort of epidemic. (Searl)

Whether the figures are perceived as passive or animated is in direct correlation with what is going on in their surrounding. In return, the presence of the figures in unexpected places alters the movement and perception in the given environment.

Event Horizon extends the filed of application of Veltruský's concept taking it outside the framework of theatre, but it also suggests that the dialectic antinomy between man and object might be experienced differently and require different analytical strategies. For Veltruský man and object could trade places in theatre, while their relationship in everyday life remains more or less stable. Gormley's project shows that even in everyday life the boundaries between animated and lifeless could be flexible and transitory. Although in theatre it is possible to move from an acting subject to a thing "completely without will," as Veltruský has pointed out, I would argue that this unstable man/object relationship still needs a temporary stability in order to take place. In theatre the dialectic antinomy between human being and object is rehearsed, repeated according to a prescribed scenario with every new performance, and it is of a certain duration, which makes the transformations from man to object and vice versa perceptible. In projects like Gormely's *Event Horizon*, which exercise the transitional dynamic between animated and lifeless in everyday life, transformations from being to object and vice versa are random, unrehearsed, and in constant flux. Gormely's work, however, explores the dialectic antinomy between body and object on a variety of levels, both illustrating Veltruský's essay and broadening its field of application.

Genesis of the Iron Man

Gormley's artistic process itself is the case in point, since the artist uses his own body to make casts for his sculptures. In order to do that he needs to lay for a couple of hours completely motionless in the cast, to mummify his own body in plaster, to become a sculpture himself before he could make one for display. Although the *Event Horizon* sculptures were made of cast-iron, they still in a way carry some of their authors' "DNA," adding a new twist to the dialectics between animated and lifeless. The sculpture becomes a *metabody* both self-referential and generic, doubling its maker, while deliberately submerging the artist's subjectivity. I overheard a passer-by who, looking at Gormely's iron-cast double on Waterloo bridge, asserted "It's Adam, for sure." The author's body has become standardised when transformed into another matter.

In other words, once Gormley's bo-dy gives shape to the iron sculpture its individual characteristics diminish and he becomes a kind of *everyman*. This generic body turns into an empty vessel, which is possible to fill with different and even conflicting meanings. His *life-ness*[2] becomes complicated and conflicted. On the one hand, the sculpture is an object, not just modelled on the artist's body, but literally cast of it. On the other hand, the live body of the artist "freezes" and deadens once captured in the iron cast. Hence, the duality between *life-ness* and *life-less-ness* is injected into the statues through the very process of their making. This ambiguity is the one element that can never fully leave neither the iron-

A. Gormley "Event Horizon", London, photo S. Jestrović.

---

[2] I have coined the term *life-ness* to better describe the phenomenon of the body/object dynamic. Obviously, it is the opposite of lifeless, but it does not necessarily mean alive, rather it describes something that appears (for a moment or for a longer starch of time) as alive. Whether the object is literary (i.e. physiologically) alive in the moment of reception is irrelevant. The term *life-ness* is also different from *liveness*—a neologism explored by Philip Auslender to deal with the relationship between presence and mediation in performance. *Life-ness* is less about presence and mediation, but rather it describes the relationship between stasis and motion as they impact the perception of an object/body.

cast body nor indeed the pulsating flash and blood one—it is the uncanny double detected by Freud, which follows its owner like a shadow until the very end.

A. Gormley "Event Horizon", London, photo S. Jestrović.

Proofs of Life/ Signs of Deadening

One sunny afternoon I was sitting on the lawn in front of the National Theatre in London looking at one of Gormley's sculpture atop of the building that appeared lonely being the only anthropomorphic shape on the "horizon." Then theatregoers, wanting to catch a bit of sun and fresh air during the intermission, started to fill the buildings long balconies. Suddenly, the building seemed adorned with bodies and the only one among them made of cast-iron became indistinct. From the distance it was impossible to spot movements and motions of the people, which made it seem as if Gormley's man, atop the building of the National Theatre, has multiplied. The audience became part of the project, and from where I was positioned they could as well be made of the cast iron. The presence of the sculpture in this unlikely place has played tricks on perception turning life bodies into inanimate objects and vice versa.

    Moreover, the transitions between being and object took place over a stretch of time long enough for this dynamics to be perceived in a similar way as in theatre. Nevertheless, in theatre the relationship between being and object is manipulated by changing the hierarchy of theatrical devices and their relations to the dominant component of the work. In everyday life though the dynamic between *life-ness* and *life-less-ness* depends on perception(s) of motion and speed. In a way the relativity theory, is its only pre-existing script.

A. Gormley "Event Horizon", London, photo S. Jestrović.

Veltruský identifies the *lifeless* as being "completely without will"; its opposite—the animate—would, thus, be something that shows a certain *will*. This echoes Schopenhauer's definition of dramatic character as that which has *will*. I would like to add to this yet another well-known axiom of drama and theatre—*doing, action*. The animated could be defined as that which posses a certain *will*, while *doing/action* is a manifestation and an expression of that *will* in a given time and space. In other words, *doing/action* certifies the existence of *will*—it is a proof of *life* (or of *life-ness*) of the object. In everyday life, *life-ness* unfolds as motion—be it verbal or physical—in space.

In a photo I took on my city-tour of Gormley's work, one of his iron-cast man stands on the pavement in front of a gigantic poster of a woman. When juxtaposed to a two-dimensional oversized image—the three-dimensional iron cast sculpture of human proportions gave a sense of *life-ness*. It appeared as if Gormley's iron-cast man has stopped for a moment to view the poster. It was only when I developed the photo that I realized additional components participating in the man/object dynamic as I took notice of yet another three-dimensional figure in the corner of the photo—a man walking fast towards the sculpture. I was taking a photo of a relatively stable "street scene" set by the artist, but my camera captured a moment when the given scene has been reinforced by an unpredictable, yet common element of the city's everyday life. Viewing the triad my camera has captured, it becomes clear that only the poster remains stable in its two-dimensional oversized lifelessness, but the standing iron-cast man and the human body in motion looked as if they could trade places any given moment. The stillness of the statue was in a way broken by the body in motion approaching it. In other words, it seems as if the man could have stopped to take the place of the statue and as if the statue could have left the site of the curvaceous beauty painted on the poster and walked away. The dialectics between animated and lifeless in everyday life is often realised as a domain of imaginative possibilities.

The last element of this "street scene" is the one that could not be in the photo—the photographer herself. In order to take the photo of Gormely's sculpture, I had to, for a very brief moment, assume the same position as the statue. I was standing in front of the poster, my body positioned under the same angle as the statue's, looking at the iron-man, who was "looking" at the poster. I was standing in between the stillness of the statue and the motion of the man who was approaching it. My presence mediated and altered the passivity/activity dynamics of the two other figures. However, full mediation and analysis could only take place *post festum* and with the photo of the "street scene" at hand. This is partly because in everyday life mutual transformations between stillness and motion, life-ness and lifelessness often take place at such a speed that they could only be perceived once captured and slowed down by the camera. The other reason why the photographer saw less than her camera was because she was not a distant observer as it might have seemed at the first glance, but a participant in the transformation—a player in the dialectic antinomy between body and object.

City as "total body": from text to mise-en-scene

What has been after all foregrounded in this relationship between body and object in Gormley's project? And how does the notion of foregrounding enable the readability of all these disparate elements —objects, buildings, bodies—that Gormley's project brings together? In *Event Horizon*, viewing the art-work is inseparable from navigating the city. The project foregrounds the city in two ways: 1) as a body and 2) as a performance text. In his note to another project called *Allotment*, Gormley writes "body is our first habitation, the building our second" ("Anthony Gromley/Blind Light") stressing that there is an organic connection between body (whether made of flesh and blood or of cast-iron) and architecture. Indeed, he suggests that architecture is a body. *Event Horizon* foregrounds the idea of the city as organism, that I will call here the "total body." This "total body" encompasses a complex network that includes millions of live bodies constantly moving through the city, around and below Gormley's iron-cast men, (that make the second set of bodies in this constellation), and the architectural bodies. The body does not only see, it feels, it hears, it smells. The body is, thus, broader than its textual embodiments.

Yet, that body of the metropolis has constantly been shaped and reshaped thorough inscriptions—in a heteroglosa (to echo Bachktin) of historical, social, architectural, personal and other narratives. Roland Barthes in his essay "Semiology of Urban Design" writes:

> The city is a discourse and this discourse is truly a language: the city speaks to its inhabitants, we speak our city, the city where we are, simply by living in it, by wandering through it. Still the problem is to bring an expression like 'the language of the city' out of the purely metaphorical stage. (168)

The problem Barthes points to might be in thinking of the city in literally terms. Barthes writes that city is a poem "which unfolds the signifier and it is this unfolding that ultimately the semiology of the city should try to grasp and make sing" (172). Nevertheless, when he lists the means by which the city becomes a discourse he talks about "speaking", "living," and "wandering"—he describes the language of the city in verbs, not in nouns. The language of the city is not constituted through narrative means, but through *action* and it is in the first place physical. The "language of the city" is the language of performance, thus performance vocabulary might be better suited than that of literature to describe it. The city is not so much a discourse, as it is a mise-en-scene. I do not use the term mise-en-scene here as a metaphor, but as a descriptor of the city's theatricality and performativity. *Event Horizon* foregrounds the city as a performance text and by doing so makes it susceptible to semiotic decoding. And so we are back to reading, but a reading of a different kind, where the script is open and where the process of inscribing and decoding is interchangeable and in flux. This open "script" might require some parallel readings, with Veltruský and Mukařovský in the one hand and Freud and Lefebvre in the other.

Reading without the Dominant

The issue is not whether cities should be read or not, and whether bodies, objects, and events should be decoded, both synchronically and diachronically, through structural relationships to their environment. What is at stake is to understand the ever-changing backgrounds, the competing norms, and contesting values. According to Mukařovský an artwork is dominated by the aesthetic function, and it does not exclude the presence of other functions. The Structuralist concept of defamiliarization is viewed within the framework of an aesthetic system and through the relation of this system to other structures (ideological, social, political, and so on). The notion of making the familiar strange is not seen simply as the result of a certain aesthetic treatment of a material, but as depending on the hierarchy of the components and their relation to the dominant component within an artistic structure. Roman Jakobson defines the notion of the dominant element "as a focusing component of a work of art: which rules, determines, and transforms the remaining components. The dominant guarantees the integrity of the structure" (82). But what happens with structuralist concept in the world without a dominant or in the context of competing and contesting dominants?

In *Event Horizons* the art-work is not only the set of anthropomorphic sculptures, but the performance that takes place in the interplay between the city and the body/object dichotomy. The borders where the artistic object ends and extra-artistic realty begins are allusive. This performance-text does not have one dominant component, the focus shifts all the time, all the components of this mise-en-scene have been mutually transforming one another, and the structure is amorphous. Nevertheless, I would argue that all is not lost to Baudrillardian simulacrum since signs and referents have not entirely lost their connections. In *Event Horizon* the city is foregrounded as a performance text within which the signifieds are transient. Barthes remarks that the signifieds are "mythical creatures, extremely imprecise and at a certain point they always become the signifiers of *something else*" (169).

In *Event Horizon* binaries are allusive, but they still are; foregournding takes place against a multifaceted and ever changing background, but estrangement of the familiar and familiarization of the strange still affects perceptions (no matter how diverse they might be); and with the figure of a naked iron-cast male turned with his back to the St. Paul's Cathedral and the Big Ben, a worn-out tourist vista becomes fresh and topical again, embodying Structuralist *aktualizace* in a new and unforeseen way.

Works Cited

Adorno, Theodor. "Commitment." *Notes To Literature*. Vol. 2. Ed. R. Tidemann. Trans. S. Weber. New York: Columbia UP, 1976. 72-8.
"Antony Gormley." 20 Aug. 2008. <http://www.antonygormley.com/>.
"Antony Gormley / Blind Light." Hyward Gallery. 20 Aug. 2008. <http://www.southbankcentre.co.uk/gormley/light.html>.
Barthes, Roland. "Semiology of the Urban." Leach 166-172.
Foucault, Michel. "Of Other Spaces: Utopias and Heterotopias." Leach 350-6.
Garvin, Paul, ed. *A Prague School Reader on Esthetics, Literary Structure and Style*. Washington: Georgetown UP, 1964.
Havránek, Bohuslav. "The Functional Differentiation of the Standard Language." Garvin 3-16.
Jakobson, Roman. "The Dominant," *Readings in Russian Poetics*. Eds. L. Matejka and K. Pomorska. Ann Arbor: U of Michigan P, 1978. 82-7.
Leach, Neil, ed. *Rethinking Architecture: a Reader in Cultural Theory*. London and New York: Routledge, 1997.

Mukařovský, Jan. "Standard Language and Poetic Language." Garvin 17-30.
Searl, Andrew. "Antony's Army," *Guardian*. 15 May. 2007 <http://arts.guardian.co.uk/art/visualart/story/0,,2079824,00.html>.
Veltruský, Jiří. "Man and Object in the Theatre." Garvin 83-91.
Vidler, Anthony. "Uncanny Sculpture." 20 Aug. 2008. <http://www.antonygormley.com/>.

(Impossible) Representation in García Lorca's *The Public*

Andrés Pérez-Simón
University of Toronto

1. On Actor and Character: A Theoretical Incursion.

Jan Mukařovský's "Art as Semiotic Fact" (1934) is generally considered to be one of the foundational texts in twentieth century semiotics. Instead of adopting Saussure's idea of twofold sign (signifier/signified), Mukařovský proposed a three-part model consisting of artifact, aesthetic object, and a relationship to the things signified. The first element, the artifact, constitutes the "sensory symbol" (88); the second one, the aesthetic object, is the meaning in collective consciousness; and the third one, the relation to the thing signified, refers "to the total context of social phenomena" (88) such as science, philosophy, or religion. The way in which Mukařovský emphasized the materiality of the sign, by defining the artifact as the first of its three aspects, is particularly significant. As Michael Quinn observed, Prague scholars "placed special emphasis on the idea that the material make-up of the sign often has significant properties of its own, in addition to any explicitly coded significance" (20). It is precisely the materiality of the sign that I intend to explore in the present essay. Two key concepts developed by Prague School members will be revisited: on a general level, Mukařovský's distinction between artistic *intentionality* and *unintentionality*; in the specific field of theatrical studies, Jiří Veltruský's notion of *stage figure*. I will also incorporate a third idea that indirectly relates to Prague School: the concept of *ostension*, originally developed in the 1960s by the Czech semiotician Ivo Osolsobě, and later expanded by Thomas Sebeok and Emil Volek. The main assumption underlying this essay is that the Saussurean dichotomy needs to be superseded by more complex models when dealing with the intricacies of the relationship existent between actor and dramatic character. This is because the actor's body is far from constituting a neutral signifier, or artifact. There is no doubt this anthropological factor becomes central when it comes at describing the ethic/aesthetic tensions in modern and contemporary drama.

Despite the numerous subversions in modern/postmodern drama, an anthropomorphic response to the representational fact is inevitable. As it is well known, the transitional period from symbolism to avant-garde witnessed multiple attacks against the mediating figure of the actor (see Sidnell), from the allegoric modes in symbolist and expressionist theatre to the postmodern reification of the characters, from the idea of *Über-Marionette* to the return of the Greek masks. In *The Death of the Character* (1996), Elinor Fuchs details the efforts of symbolist playwrights to produce a "de-individualization in favor of the Idea. The chief obstacle to achieving this ideal, they realized, was character as represented by the living actor" (29). Mallarmé's ideal *Hamlet* epitomizes this retreat from realistic aesthetics. In Fuch's words: "*Hamlet*, one of Hegel's chief examples of a tragedy of character, has here moved into a realm of abstraction that borders on allegory, with all characters functioning as symbols, aspects, or projections of an "imaginary and somewhat abstract" hero" (31). Yet, despite this radical defiance of the human figure, spectators will still judge stage action according to mimetic criteria. This is because, in contrast to music or painting, theatre cannot achieve a total independence from figurative depiction and, I dare to say, from an ethical evaluation.

In his First Letter to the Intimate Theatre, August Strindberg described acting in terms of a total identification of actor and character. In his words: "I assume that the artist gets into a trance, forgets himself, and finally becomes the person he is to play. It reminds me of sleepwalking [. . .]. If he is disturbed in this state or awakened to full consciousness, he becomes confused and lost" (23). Acting can be understood as a state of trance, as in this case, but it can also serve to deliberately expose the distance between actor and character –Brecht is a paradigmatic example. Be it illusionistic acting or not, the substitution of signifier/signified for actor/character seems to be a noncontroversial move. Apparently, there is nothing wrong in describing the actor's task according to a dichotomy familiar to every student of Semiotics 100. Keir Elam, who prefers the term "sign-vehicle" to "signifier," confirms this general assumption when he asks "where better to look for direct similitude between sign-vehicle and signified than in the actor-character relationship?" (20). Nonetheless, this equation is not free from certain inaccuracies. Otakar Zich, the great predecessor of Prague School, was the first scholar who reported the pitfalls of a rough application of Saussure's binary model. In his *Aesthetics of Art* (1931), Zich developed a three-part model by adding an intermediary concept: the stage figure (*herecká postava*, literally "figure of the actor"). The stage figure becomes *signans*, while the dramatic character functions as *signatum*. As Zich explains:

> the figure is what the actor makes, the character what the audience

sees and hears [. . .] the figure is the product of the actor, the character the product of the observers [. . .] the stage figure is a formation of the physiological kind, the dramatic character a formation of the psychological kind. (Zich qtd. in Quinn 77)

To date, Zich's contribution has not caught the attention of theatre semioticians, with a few exceptions.[1] This oblivion is not surprising if we consider that Zich's trichotomy was not even popular among Prague scholars. In his retrospective essay "The Prague School Theory of Theatre," Veltruský observed that "Most of the theoreticians belonging to the Prague Linguistic Circle were reluctant to adopt this concept of the stage figure as distinct from both the actor and the character" (232). Veltruský himself was the only writer who developed the concept of stage figure after the death of Zich in 1934.

In the 1940s, Veltruský expanded Zich's ideas by incorporating some of Mukařovský's main contributions in the field of semiotics of art. The concept of artistic intentionality, as redefined by Mukařovský, proved to be particularly fertile when applied to theatre. In proposing a phenomenological description of intentionality, Mukařovský was able to liberate semiotics from the weight burden of authorial intention. Against the distorting presence of psychological/biographical elements, Mukařovský claimed the central role of the perceiver in organizing the dominant forces inside the artistic work. He defined intentionality as

> the force which binds together the individual parts and components of a work into the unity that gives the work its meaning. As soon as the perceiver adopts an attitude toward a certain object, which is usual during the perception of a work of art, he immediately makes an effort to find in the organization of the work traces of an arrangement that will permit the work to be conceived as a semantic whole. ("Intentionality" 96)

Mukařovský noted that the perceiver's initiative "provides the possibility that different perceivers (or rather different groups of perceivers) will invest the same work with a different intentionality, sometimes considerably divergent from that which its originator gave it" (98). With Mukařovský's contribution in mind, Veltruský pointed out that the stage figure inevitably contains traces of the actor's physi-

---

[1] See particularly Quinn's study *The Semiotic Stage* (reference listed below). On the specific topic of stage figure, see also his contributions: "Svejk's Stage Figure: Illustration, Design, and the Representation of the Character." *Modern Drama* 31.3 (1988): 330-339; "The Prague School Concept of the Stage Figure." *The Semiotic Bridge*. Eds. Irmengard Rauch and Gerald F. Carr. New York: Mouton de Gruyter, 1989. 75-85.

cality, even if that is not the intended purpose ("Contribution" 578-579). The corporeality of the human being motivates that an indefinite number of physical traits become semiotized the moment after the actor steps onto the stage. And, despite the effort of the directors, it is impossible to totally control the fluctuation between non-motivated signs—pertaining to the actor—and those consciously integrated in the stage figure. Edward Gordon Craig epitomized the concerns of avant-garde creators when he declared that acting "is not an art. It is therefore incorrect to speak of the actor as an artist [. . .]. In the modern theatre, owing to the use of the bodies of men and women *as their material*, all which is presented there is of an accidental nature" (56). Gordon Craig's solution was the transformation of the actor into a *Über-Marionette*; and if several symbolist and modernist playwrights simply returned to puppetry it was because the puppet "can be shaped in such a way as to be composed only of those signs that are intended, that is to say relevant for the theatrical structure concerned. In other words, the puppets can be, and often are, pure signs like text, a picture or a statue" (Veltruský, "Puppets" 109).

Mukařovský related the opposition intentionality/unintentionality to the dichotomy sign/thing. Even though the recipient perceives the sign as an artistic artifact, its 'natural,' unmediated condition is present to a smaller or greater degree. According to Mukařovský, "the perceiver constantly fluctuates between a feeling of intentionality and one of unintentionality; in other words, for him the work is simultaneously a sign (a self-referential sign lacking an unequivocal relation to reality) and a *thing*" ("Intentionality" 106). A paradigmatic example of this oscillation between sign and thing is Kurt Schwitters's *Revolving* (1919). This canvas contains circles and diagonal rods made of wood, metal, cord, wire, and leather, with the result that "Objects are literally nailed onto the picture, reinforcing its "thinglike" status as a relief painting that hangs on the wall" (Reed 336). In the particular case of theatre, the spectators' response varies depending on how they resolve the tension between sign and thing –or sign and reality. I will explore the ideological implications of these diverging reactions in my forthcoming analysis of Lorca's *The Public*. But, first, I will review the last of the three concepts announced above: the idea of (theatrical) ostension.

Umberto Eco conceives ostension as "a particular mode of sign production [. . .]. Ostension is one of the various ways of signifying, consisting in de-realizing a given object in order to make it stand for an entire class" (103). In this view, the ostended object functions as a sample, a token standing for a class of objects. Eco follows the traditional idea of "ostensive definition" as understood in twentieth-century logic—see, for instance, Wittgenstein's *Philosophical Investigations*—one that consists in pointing out the object that serves as example. But it is also possible to recall an idea of ostension that partially differs from this one. In the late 1960s, the Czech semiotician Ivo Osolsobě proposed a revised idea of ostension that was later expanded by Thomas Sebeok and Emil Volek. In Volek's words,

> ostension, in common language, also refers to "the action of showing, exhibiting, displaying." Not "pointing to" but "showing" something or itself to somebody, even in the sense of willful "ostentation," or "showing off" [...] Osolsobě, drawing on theatrical experience and cybernetic modeling, develops rather this side of ostension, understanding it as the act of displaying some reality significantly, presenting it for attention, scrutiny, and interpretation. ("Habitat" 193)

In *Metaestructuralismo* (1985), Volek connected the concept of ostension to Mukařovský's duality thing/sign. As Volek explains (239), it is by means of ostension that the sign establishes a dialogue with its own materiality, a dialogue that is also one with the communicative potential inherent to things. As a consequence of this, the material condition of the sign does not remain neutral with respect to the meaning the sign conveys. If the sign is necessarily inscribed in material things, Volek argues, then "its material substratum exceeds both the ideal differences on which the sign relies (such as phonemes) and its representational dimension. This *excess* is also potentially semiotic, and it can even expand throughout the whole semiotic dimension of the sign" (238-239, my translation). And, even though Veltruský never mentions ostension, I believe his words on the "overwhelming reality" ("Dramatic" 115) of the human body can be applied to the ostensive potential of the actor: "Most of the elements of which stage figures and action are made up are a priori expressive. Even off the stage, the face, the voice, the delivery and bodily behavior are expressive, whether they are intended to be so or not" ("Contribution" 578).

2. An Impossible Theatre: Lorca's *The Public*.

Lorca finished the first version of *The Public* in 1930, and later he revised the manuscript at least two more times. In 1936, a few days before he was killed, Lorca announced that "right now I'm putting the final touches, and the play looks wonderful" (qtd. in Martínez Nadal 23).[2] Yet this final version got lost after the Spanish War exploded, with the result that the 1930 draft is the only manuscript known to date. Lorca handed this first version to his friend Rafael Martínez Nadal

---

[2] All the translations from Lorca's original sources are mine. Excerpts from *The Public* have been taken from Carlos Bauer's English version (see works cited).

before he left Madrid for his hometown of Granada. It was in Granada where Lorca was arrested and executed by Francoist troops on August 18, 1936. Martínez Nadal recovered the manuscript of *The Public* in 1958, but it was not until 1976 that he obtained permission from Lorca's state to publish the play. In part due to this unfortunate textual history, *The Public* has received scarce attention in comparison to Lorca's plays of the rural trilogy—*Blood Wedding*, *Yerma*, and *The House of Bernarda Alba*. In the 1980s, almost half a century after the Lorca's death, international scholars began to acknowledge the centrality of this play in relation to Lorca's project of radical theatre.[3] As a consequence of this critical shift, *The Public* ceased to be considered a peripheral work of the Lorquian canon. Lorca himself explained the importance he attributed to *The Public* in a 1936 interview: "I have written theatre according to a well-defined trajectory. My early plays are irrepresentable [. . .]. My real ambition resides in these impossible plays. Yet I had to offer other works in order to exhibit my personality and gain respect from others" ("Al habla" 1811).

Lorca denounced the mediocrity of Spain's commercial theatres, replete with naturalistic dramas and inoffensive comedies whose main function was providing "women at marrying age" ("Una interesante" 1717) with a pretext to meet their future husbands. Lorca attempted to develop a style of acting radically different from that of contemporary Spanish companies, but he could hardly achieve his purpose. In 1933, for instance, Lorca had to rehearse *Blood Wedding* with comedy actors. Many of the spectators that attended the premiere took it lightheartedly, clearly conditioned by the comic roles the actors had enacted in the past (Dougherty and Vilches de Frutos 243). This anecdote evidences the obstacles Lorca faced in his attempt to redefine the staging practices of his time. Carlos Bauer perfectly summarizes Lorca's situation:

> Lorca realized that a multilevel drama of this type required experimental staging, staging that would make a complete break with all theatrical convention, that would constantly try the limits of technical possibility. In *The Public*, we have characters continually pulling off one costume, one "disguise," to reveal yet another, we have a male character who passes behind a folding screen and comes out a woman, a wall opening up into a tomb, a capital turning into a screen, gloves raining down, and snow falling. (xiv)

---

[3] See: Chicharro, Antonio and Antonio Sánchez Trigueros, eds. *La verdad de las máscaras: Teatro y vanguardia en Federico García Lorca*. Granada: Alhulia, 2005; Harretche, María Estela. *Federico García Lorca: Análisis de una revolución teatral*. Madrid: Gredos, 2000; Huélamo Kosma, Julio. *El teatro imposible de García Lorca: Estudio sobre* El Público. Granada: Universidad de Granada, 1996. Hispanistica XX, Centre d'études et de recherches hispaniques du XXème siècle, Université de Bourgogne, 1999.

Besides this challenge to theatrical conventions, when Lorca called *The Public* an irrepresentable play he was aware of a second, and much stronger, type of resistance: the censorship of an audience who will not accept overt references to homosexuality. In an interview in Argentina, in 1933, Lorca mentioned the manuscript of *The Public* and explained that "I don't intend to stage the play in Buenos Aires, nor in any other place, for I believe there is not a company willing to perform it neither a public that could tolerate it without indignation" ("Llegó" 1731). When the journalist asked him about the reason of this impossibility, Lorca replied: "Because it [*The Public*] is the mirror of the audience [. . .]. And because everyone's drama can be really painful, and generally it is far from honorable, spectators would immediately jump out of their seats, full of indignation, and they would prevent the performance to continue" ("Llegó" 1731).

In the opening act of *The Public*, the Director discusses with his actors the way they should perform *Romeo and Juliet*. He is criticized for submitting himself to the expectations of the bourgeois audience, who expects the theatre "in the open air." At first, the Director proclaims that "My theatre will be in the open air" (3), but later he changes his mind and decides it is time to unveil the theatre "beneath the sand." Lorca's theatre "beneath the sand" aims at a collective ceremony that encompasses actors and audience, a ceremony of self-recognition that attempts to expose sexual taboos such as homosexuality or incest. The presence of *Romeo and Juliet* does not occur by accident, since the insertion of intertextual references to Shakespeare constituted a constant practice throughout Lorca's whole career. Andrew A. Anderson registers "more or less explicit references" (189) to *Hamlet*, *Othello*, *Macbeth*, *Richard III*, *The Taming of the Shrew*, *Troilus and Cressida*, and *Much Ado About Nothing*. Besides these works, Anderson stresses the central role of *A Midsummer Night's Dream* and *Romeo and Juliet* in Lorca's *Play without a Title* and *The Public*, respectively. In these last two plays, Lorca rejects the transparent model of a play within a play by adopting a more oblique relationship to the Shakespearean texts. Shakespeare's plays are verbally invoked rather than actually presented on stage: *Play without a Title* contains an off-stage rehearsal of *A Midsummer Night's Dream*; in *The Public*, the scandalous *Romeo and Juliet* is also performed in an absent, unseen space, and the only information about it comes from the diverging testimonies of different witnesses.

I will study the way in which Lorca foregrounds homosexuality and how, at the same time, he challenges contemporary ideas on the act of impersonating a character. Lorca conceives *The Public* as a metatheatrical incursion that ends up revealing the ideological implications underlying the public performance of a love scene. Homosexual behavior, latent throughout the whole play, becomes explicit when the

Director and Man 1 acknowledge their love in the third act. But, paradoxically, it is through the representation of a heterosexual love scene that Lorca questions the moral rules determining the process of theatrical production and reception. Accordingly to the concepts revisited in the first section of the present essay, it can be said that Lorca challenges traditional ideas on sexual identity by laying bare the artificiality of a necessary identification among actor, stage figure, and character.

As indicated above, Lorca conceives *The Public* as a metacritical exercise on the act of performing a play in front of an audience. The Director advocates for a theatre 'beneath the sand' that will break away from commercial practices, yet he still fears the rejection of the spectators. He is also afraid of recognizing the homosexual desire he feels for one of the actors. But, what happens when the real theatre, the theatre "beneath the sand," is finally unveiled? According to the reports by those who attended the show, the audience violently reacted against the staging of the sepulcher scene of *Romeo and Juliet* (Act V, iii). Since Lorca places this performance in an absent space, we can only rely on dialogues such as this one:

BOY 1. The audience wants the poet to be dragged off by his hair.
LADY 1. But, why? It was a delightful drama, and the revolution doesn't have any right to profane tombs.
LADY 2. Their voices were so alive, and their appearances, too. What need was there for us to lick the skeletons?
BOY 1. She's right. The act in the tomb was prodigiously developed. But I discovered the deception when I saw Juliet's feet. They were so tiny.
LADY 2. And delightful! You'd never ever want to find fault with them.
BOY 1. Yes, but they were too small to be the feet of a man. They were too perfect and too feminine. They were a man's feet, feet invented by a man.
LADY 2. How ghastly! (35)

After the spectators discover the "deception," they run onto the stage and kill the actors. They also attempt to execute the Director, for they cannot accept that a love scene could actually happen between two men. But, is there something "actually" taking place on stage? Applying Mukařovský's terminology, it can be argued that the audience interprets the love scene to be part of an unintentional reality, a "natural" event. The two other concepts I previously summarized—stage figure and ostension—can also help understand the riots narrated in *The Public*. Lorca's own poetics becomes visible in the dialogue among four anonymous students, a typical expressionist device:

STUDENT 4. The rioting started when they saw that Romeo and Juliet really loved each other.
[. . .]

STUDENT 1. There's everyone's big mistake and for that reason the theater's in the throes of death. The audience shouldn't try to penetrate the silk and cardboard that the poet erects in his bedroom. Rome could be a bird and Juliet could be a stone. Romeo could be a grain of salt and Juliet could be a map. What difference does it make to the audience?
[. . .]
STUDENT 2. It's a question of forms, of masks. A cat could be a frog and the winter moon could very well be a bundle of firewood covered with terrified maggots. The audience is to fall asleep upon the words and they must not see through the column to the sheep bleating and the clouds traveling across the sky.
[. . .]
STUDENT 2. In final analysis, do Romeo and Juliet necessarily have to be a man and a woman for the tomb scene to come off in a heart-rending and lifelike way?
STUDENT 1. It isn't necessary, and that was what the stage director brilliantly intended to demonstrate.
STUDENT 4 [*irritated*]. It's not necessary? Then let the machines stop... and then go throw grains of wheat upon a field of steel. (35-36)

This discussion illustrates two conflicting opinions on the creation of the dramatic character. Students 1 and 2 believe that the stage figure, and not the actor, is the key element in the construction of the character ("Romeo could be a bird and Juliet could be a stone [. . .]. What difference does it make to the audience?"). If everything becomes semiotized on stage, then there is no point in fighting over the materials that are used—for they will be automatically transformed into a sign, be it an icon, index, or symbol. Nonetheless, the ostensive condition of the human body impedes the total transformation of the actor into a pure sign. This is why student 4, who perceives an excess of meaning that could be potentially disturbing, defends the strict identification of actor, stage figure, and character.

Even though student 4 approves the censorship of *Romeo and Juliet*, he condemns the "detestable" reaction of the audience. Student 1 uses the same adjective but with a different idea of theatre in mind:

STUDENT 4. The audience's attitude was detestable.
STUDENT 1. Detestable. A spectator should never be part of the drama. When people go to the aquarium they don't murder the sea snakes or the water rats or the fish covered with leprosy, rather they run their eyes over the glass and learn.
STUDENT 4. Romeo was a man thirty years old and Juliet a boy of fifteen. The audience's censure was effective.
STUDENT 2. The stage director brilliantly prevented the bulk of the spectators from becoming aware of that, but the horses and the revolution have destroyed his plans. (38)

Student 4 agrees with the audience in that it is scandalous that a man could love a fifteen year old boy, no matter if the scene constitutes a fictional act or not. What is paradoxical is the fact that, when Shakespeare's play was originally represented in the Elizabethan England, a boy impersonated Juliet because actresses were not permitted on stage. In consequence, *The Public*, an "irrepresentable" play containing a play impossible to perform, exposes the constant presence of ideology in the evolution of theatrical conventions. Lorca's play confirms the impossibility of establishing a radical distinction between the ethic and the aesthetic implications of the work of art. Lorca, who lamented that "theatergoers refuse to let somebody else make them reflect on moral issues" ("Los artistas" 1767), lays bare the ideological/aesthetic tensions determining the collective reception of a play.

Mukařovský's opening words in a lecture delivered in 1941 can be applied not only to Lorca's *The Public*, but to the works of other contemporary authors such as Pirandello and Brecht: "One of the important problems which the contemporary theater has been trying to solve in various ways is how to establish active contact between the spectator and the stage" ("On the Current" 201). It is my perception that this issue remains unresolved today, despite multiple advances in the field of theatre studies. By bringing into play the concepts of stage figure, artistic (un)intentionality, and ostension, I have attempted to uncover the ideological values that can be attached to the human body. The presence of the anthropological element impedes the uncritical import of linguistic terminology (signifier/signified) into the field of semiotics of theatre. As Veltruský notes:

> The idea that the sign has simply two facets, the *signans* and the *signatum*, does not quite apply to acting. In a specific work of acting, it is often hard and sometimes utterly impossible to determine what belongs to the stage figure and what to the character. The borderline between the two is blurred, a great many features are part of the *signans* in some respect and of the *signatum* in some other [. . .]. It does not follow that the distinction between *signans* and *signatum* is any less important in the theater than in the other semiotic systems. What does follow is that the two terms are not simply two facets of the sign, like the two sides of a coin, but two poles of a dialectical antinomy, the internal antinomy of the sign. ("The Prague School" 233)

The acknowledgment of the non-neutral condition of the actor's body is far from constituting an anecdotic aspect. This assumption opens up a discussion that not only involves semiotics of theatre, for, as Veltruský notes, "if this is true of the sign created by acting, it must be true of any sign whatever. Or else the very term of sign would be metaphorical, and semiotics a fiction" ("The Prague School" 233).

Works Cited

Anderson, Andrew A. "Some Shakespearian Reminiscences in García Lorca's Drama." *Comparative Literature Studies* 22.2 (1985): 187-210.
Bauer, Carlos. Introduction. *The Public and Play Without Title: Two Posthumous Plays.* By Federico García Lorca. Trans. Carlos Bauer. New York: New Directions, 1983. xi-xx.
Dougherty, Dru and María Teresa Vilches de Frutos. "Federico García Lorca como director de escena." *El teatro en España: entre la tradición y la vanguardia, 1918-1939.* Eds. Dru Dougherty and María Teresa Vilches de Frutos. Madrid: CSIC-FGL-Tabacalera, 1992. 241-252.
Eco, Umberto. *The Limits of Interpretation.* Bloomington and Indianapolis: Indiana UP, 1990.
Elam, Keir. *The Semiotics of Theatre and Drama.* Rev. ed. New York: Routledge, 2002.
Fuchs, Elinor. *The Death of the Character,* Bloomington and Indianapolis: Indiana UP, 1996.
García Lorca, Federico. *Obras completas.* Ed. Arturo del Hoyo. Madrid: Aguilar, 1971.
___. "Al habla con Federico García Lorca." *Obras* 1808-1813.
___. "Charla amable con Federico García Lorca." *Obras* 1722-1725.
___. "Llegó anoche Federico García Lorca." *Obras* 1728-1733.
___. "Los artistas en el ambiente de nuestro tiempo." *Obras* 1762-1767.
___. "Una interesante iniciativa." *Obras* 1717-1720.
___. *The Public and Play Without Title: Two Posthumous Plays.* Trans. Carlos Bauer. New York: New Directions, 1983.
Gordon Craig, Edward. "The Actor and the Über-Marionette." *On the Art of the Theatre.* London: Heinemann, 1968. 54-94.
Martínez Nadal, Rafael. Introducción. *El público y Comedia sin título.* By Federico García Lorca. Eds. Rafael Martínez Nadal and M. Laffranque. Barcelona: Seix Barral, 1978. 13-29.
Mukařovský, Jan. *Structure, Sign, and Function.* Eds. and trans. John Burbank and Peter Steiner. New Haven: Yale UP, 1978.
___. "Art as a Semiotic Fact." *Structure* 82-88.
___. "On the Current State of the Theory of Theater." *Structure* 201-219.
___. "Intentionality and Unintentionality in Art." *Structure* 89-128.
Quinn, Michael L. *The Semiotic Stage: Prague School Theater Theory.* New York: Peter Lang, 1995.
Reed, Peter. "Objects, Walls, Screens." *ModernStarts: People, Places, Things.* Eds. John Elderfield et al. New York: The Museum of Modern Art, 1999. 332-339.
Sidnell, Michael J. "Aesthetic Prejudice and Modern Drama." *Modern Drama* 44.1 (2001): 16-30.
Strindberg, August. "Memorandums to the Members of the Intimate Theater from the Director." *Open Letters to the Intimate Theater.* Ed. and trans. Walter Johnson. Seattle: U of Washington P, 1967. 15-53.
Veltruský, Jiří. "Contribution to the Semiotics of Acting." *Sound, Sign and Meaning: Quinquagenary of the Prague Linguistic Circle.* Ed. Ladislav Matějka. Ann Arbor: U of Michigan, 1976. 553-606.
___. "Dramatic Text as a Component of Theater." *Semiotics of Art: Prague School*

Contributions. Eds. Ladislav Matejka and Irwin R. Titunik. Cambridge and London: M.I.T. Press, 1976. 94-117.

———. "Puppets for Adults: The Théâtre du Manitout." *SubStance* 6.18/19 (1977): 105-111.

———. "The Prague School Theory of Theater." *Poetics Today* 2.3 (1981): 225-235.

Volek, Emil. "Habitats of language/language inhabited: From ostension and *umwelt* to the possible worlds of communication and culture." *Dynamic Structure: Language as an Open System*. Eds. Johannes Fehr and Petr Kouba. Prague: Litteraria Pragensia, 2007. 186-219.

———. *Metaestructuralismo: Poética moderna, semiótica narrativa y filosofía de las ciencias sociales*. Madrid: Fundamentos, 1985.

Afterword

Dear friends and colleagues:

I am grateful for being asked to say a few words in conclusion of this conference. It gives me the opportunity to express my thanks to those who made this conference possible, to Veronika Ambros, Tomáš Kubíček and Roland Le Huenen, its organizers, to all who presented papers and participated in discussions, to those who formed with us a temporary, but very involved collective and, last but not least, to all the sponsors, especially the Centre for Comparative Literature (with particular thanks once again to its director Roland Le Huenen and to its executive secretary Aphrodite Gardner) and the Department of Slavic Languages and Literatures. What is remarkable about this conference is the participation of many young scholars, especially the doctoral candidates in comparative literature and in Slavic literatures. They are a proof that the situation in the field of literary study is changing. They engaged positively with ideas which only a few years ago were not only sharply criticized, but scorned.

We discussed four episodes in the history of 20th-century structuralism. This is only a selection of formalist and structuralist trends in Europe; we are aware of prominent groups of Polish and Italian scholars who would have deserved more than a brief mention at this conference. Our group of four includes three trends that took place in Slavic countries—Russian formalism, Prague School structuralism and Moscow-Tartu school of semiotics—and one, French structuralism, in what is generally called the Western culture. But all structuralisms have one basic idea in common: they saw literature as art, as a member of a group of cultural activities, which includes music, painting, sculpture, dance and other arts. While not denying many secondary social functions of literature, they insisted that its primary function is aesthetic. This view has taken them on a collision course with all trends and individuals who see literature primarily as an expression or tool of various ideologies.

Unfortunately, the political conditions in the Slavic home countries of structuralism brought to unrestricted power dogmatic ideologies, first in the former Soviet Union, later in the former Czechoslovakia. We have discussed what the theoretical heritage of Slavic structuralisms is, but we have not noticed how they died. In fact, none of them died a natural death of ideas—by which I mean exhaustion or replacement by better ideas—but they all died unnatural death, they were killed. Russian formalism was the first to go this way to its grave. Shortly after the October revolution, prominent Marxist ideologues, particularly Trotsky, criticized the Formalists and after the establishment of Stalin's totalitarian regime they were prohibited to publish, to teach and generally to express their ideas. Some of them took refuge in emigration, others in fictional writing, some accepted the verdict. Prague structuralism was a part of the interwar avant-garde culture of the country and was killed with it when the Germans occupied the Czech lands. Prague School structuralism came to new life after the war, only to be liquidated by another totalitarian regime. In Bohemia we can particularly witness a prolonged conflict between structuralism and totalitarian regimes. When the totalitarian regime weakened and then was liquidated during the Prague spring, a third generation of Czech structuralists became active. They entered the public scene with great élan and in the internationalist spirit of the Prague school established contacts with French, Polish and Italian structuralists of the time. As if in revenge, the new oppression after the Soviet invasion was particularly severe, driving many members of the third generation into exile and chasing those who stayed from their jobs and from public life. Being designated a structuralist meant to be treated as an "enemy of the people". Only those who repented (or performed the so-called self-criticism) were spared. The Moscow-Tartu school came into existence in the Soviet Union during a brief period of "thaw" after the 20th congress of the ruling party. But its existence was terminated when a new ideological totalitarianism prevailed. Again, we see a massive exodus of scholars from the country and an acceptance of the verdict by others.

Do these historical experiences suggest that the clash between structuralism and totalitarian ideology is inevitable? I think they do. We have to recognize that all ideologies have a tendency to monopolize the cultural field. Structuralism as a theoretical and "scientific" activity is in the way of this monopolization; it has to be removed before an ideology can take unrestricted control over a culture.

We have gathered here to study structuralism and to find out what makes its heritage still interesting and stimulating; we did not gather for a wake, nor for launching another episode of structuralism. This conference continues a tradition at the University of Toronto which should not be forgotten. In the 1970s and 1980s this university was the seat of very lively activities of the Toronto Semiotic Circle which for several years sponsored the International Summer School of Structural and Semiotic Studies. Then as now we were aware that we cannot return to structuralism but that we have to imitate it in resisting monopolizing ideologies. Genuine theoretical thinking and genuine scholarly research is possible only in conditions of free speech, free writing, and a free exchange of ideas. This is, in my opinion, the main message that we receive from the historical experience of structuralism.

Lubomír Doležel
Toronto, 2007